Routledge Revivals

George Orwell

First Published in 1985, the aim of this book is to define an aspect of Orwell's literary identity which underlies and informs the sociopolitical content of his novels, and which may account for his being 'more widely read' than perhaps any other serious writer in the twentieth century.

It is the author's contention that the thematic source of the Orwell novel is the problem of authentic existence, and that Orwell's particular sociopolitical concerns were expressions of this problem. In chapter one selections of Orwell's autobiographical writings are assessed, for in these the existential conflict between authentic and inauthentic modes of existence is traceable from childhood onwards. Orwell, it is argued, developed an inauthentic self -for- other in response to authoritarian oppressions, and he consequently pursued a double life characterized by the contradictions of 'doublethink'. Chapter two is an account of existential authenticity and provides both the terms and perspectives subsequently applied in the separate chapters in which each of Orwell's five novels are analyzed. In every case, J. P. Sartre's 'bad faith', Martin Heidegger's 'mine' and 'they' and Martin Buber's 'I', 'Thou' and 'It', are seen to be crucial explanatory notions within the Orwell novel. In his conclusion, therefore, Dr Carter redefines Orwell as an existential sociopolitical writer. This is a must read for students of literature, critical theory, existential philosophy, philosophy in general.

George Orwell

And the Problem of Authentic Existence

Michael Carter

First published in 1985
by Croom Helm

This edition first published in 2024 by Routledge
4 Park Square, Milton Park, Abingdon, Oxon, OX14 4RN

and by Routledge
605 Third Avenue, New York, NY 10017

Routledge is an imprint of the Taylor & Francis Group, an informa business

Publisher's Note

The publisher has gone to great lengths to ensure the quality of this reprint but points out that some imperfections in the original copies may be apparent.

Disclaimer

The publisher has made every effort to trace copyright holders and welcomes correspondence from those they have been unable to contact.

A Library of Congress record exists under ISBN: 0389205788

ISBN: 978-1-032-90040-7 (hbk)
ISBN: 978-1-003-54592-7 (ebk)
ISBN: 978-1-032-90041-4 (pbk)

Book DOI 10.4324/9781003545927

GEORGE ORWELL

AND THE PROBLEM OF AUTHENTIC EXISTENCE

Michael Carter

CROOM HELM
London & Sydney

Croom Helm Ltd, Provident House, Burrell Row,
Beckenham, Kent BR3 1AT
Croom Helm Australia Pty Ltd, Suite 4, 6th Floor,
64-76 Kippax Street, Surry Hills, NSW 2010, Australia

British Library Cataloguing in Publication Data

Carter, Michael
George Orwell and the problem of the authentic existence.
1. Orwell, George–Criticism and interpretation
I. Title
823'.912 PR6029.R821

ISBN 0-7099-3442-4

Printed and bound in Great Britain
by Billing & Sons Limited, Worcester.

CONTENTS

To Bear

ACKNOWLEDGEMENTS

For permission to use copyright material acknowledgement is made to the following:

The estate of the late Sonia Brownell and Martin Secker & Warburg, Ltd. for the works of George Orwell.

Methuen & Co. and the Philosophical Library, Inc., for Jean-Paul Sartre's Being and Nothingness, translated by Hazel E. Barnes, and Existentialism and Humanism, translated by Philip Mairet.

Basil Blackwell, Ltd., for Martin Heidegger's Being and Time, translated by John Macquarrie and Edward Robinson.

T. & T. Clark, Ltd. and Charles Scribner's Sons, for Martin Buber's I and Thou, translated by Walter Kaufman.

Routledge & Kegan Paul, Ltd., for Karl Jaspers' Man in the Modern Age, translated by Eden and Cedar Paul.

Tavistock Publications, Ltd., for R.D. Laing's The Divided Self.

Excerpts from the following works of George Orwell are reprinted by permission of Harcourt Brace Jovanovich, Inc.: BURMESE DAYS; A CLERGYMAN'S DAUGHTER; KEEP THE ASPIDISTRA FLYING; COMING UP FOR AIR; NINETEEN EIGHTY-FOUR; THE COLLECTED ESSAYS, JOURNALISM AND LETTERS, Volume 1 and Volume 4; copyright 1934 by George Orwell; copyright 1949 by Harcourt Brace Jovanovich, Inc.; copyright 1962 by Sonia Orwell Pitt-Rivers; copyright 1968, 1977 by Sonia Brownell Orwell.

The real passion of the twentieth century is servitude.

ALBERT CAMUS

INTRODUCTION

Although George Orwell is indisputably a sociopolitical writer, many critics have responded to his novels in ways which suggest that his literary identity cannot be adequately expressed in sociopolitical terms.[1] In addition, even within the limits of the sociopolitical, his appeal is so various that, according to D.A.N. Jones, 'people of almost any political persuasion can find some of their political views expressed in Orwell's work, very eloquently'.[2] The aim of this book is to define an aspect of Orwell's literary identity which underlies and informs the sociopolitical content of his novels and which may account for the reason why he has come to be 'more widely read than perhaps any other serious writer in the twentieth century'.[3]

George Woodcock, one of those critics who have noted the peculiar diversity of Orwell's appeal, attributes it to an unrecognized element in Orwell's work:

> When people of widely differing viewpoints - Conservatives and Anarchists, Socialists and Liberals, ageing academics and young writers born old - find encouragement for their attitudes in a single author's work, we can reasonably assume that each of them is missing something, and that the work, considered as a whole, must be a good deal more complex than it appears at first sight.[4]

In saying that 'people of widely differing viewpoints' are 'missing something' in Orwell's work, Woodcock is implying that what they miss is precisely that element which causes Orwell to be so widely read; that the breadth of his influence derives from the undefined presence of something which is more basic to sociopolitical issues than specific ideological commitments. An element vital to Orwell's status remains undefined. To succeed in defining this, therefore, would extend our understanding of the significance of Orwell's achievement and provide a means of more accurately classifying his work. That there has been difficulty in assigning to Orwell an adequate literary classification is clear. Alan Sandison, who offers an alternative reading of Orwell by interpreting his politics as an expression of spiritual crisis, writes: 'Critics have for some time sought to establish a satisfactory provenance for George Orwell';[5] and Jeffrey Meyers: 'Orwell is a literary nonconformist whose work defies genres, a writer who is hard to place'.[6] This doubt over Orwell's placement is an issue of some importance, particularly if, as John Wain maintains, 'it is impossible to criticize an author's work adequately until you have understood what kind of books he was writing'.[7]

It is my contention that the generic indefinition noted by Sandison and Meyers derives from the inferred presence in Orwell's work of a factor which does not seem to conform to the kind of expectations with which the Orwell novel is normally approached. The error in these expectations lies not perhaps in expecting Orwell to be a socio-political writer but in the <u>kind</u> of sociopolitical writer he is expected to be. That definitional expectations may function to exclude vital aspects of an author's work has been remarked upon by Robert Lee: 'Orwell's force as a political commentator has been so pervasive that his art has suffered a unique fate: when his fiction is considered, in a curious reversal of normal critical procedure it is often used only to gloss his non-fiction'.[8]

It is not, though, with artistry that we are here concerned. It is with thematic content. This content, inferred but not defined, is, I suggest, existential authenticity. Its presence in Orwell's novels is influential in two ways. Firstly, it sufficiently obtrudes into the customary critical expectations to disrupt attempts to satisfactorily define his literary provenance; and secondly, it provides that unity of appeal among the politically diverse to which Jones and Woodcock refer. The Orwell novel reveals the effect of the sociopolitical on individual authenticity, and the effect of individual authenticity on the sociopolitical. Although the emphasis on one effect rather than the other may predominate from one novel to another, neither is ever presented in isolation. Orwell apprehended simultaneously the individual in society and society in the individual. And it is precisely this interpenetration of zones which creates the central conflict within the Orwell protagonist. Existence is experienced dualistically, the self and society coexisting irreconcilably with no definite boundary to distinguish where one ends and the other begins. The protagonist is therefore confused over what is separately and individually him, and hence anxious to perform acts which release and define the authentic self. But always this pursuit of the authentic self is burdened by the stresses of freedom and solitude, and by the opposing pressure of the inauthentic collective self. In locating this conflict as the fundamental dynamic within the Orwell novel, the existential features behind the sociopolitical content become visible and significant. George Orwell was an existential sociopolitical writer.

In this book it will be argued that Orwell's political position is the ideological formulation of a point of view established in childhood, and so Richard Rees's description of Orwell's conversion in 1936 will not be seen as signifying a sudden revolution of his ideas about the world, but only a chronological point at which he was able to relate and organize his ideas to and around democratic Socialism.[9] Certainly, if Anthony West is right in saying about _1984_, that 'the whole pattern of society shapes up along the lines of fear laid down in "Such, Such Were the Joys"' (Orwell's essay on his life at preparatory school, St. Cyprians), then the novel with most political meaning is derived from a structure of experience which was over by the time the author was thirteen.[10] A point of view sustained throughout life is therefore indicated. Orwell's own comments in 'Why I Write' encourage this notion: 'I am not able, and I do not want, completely to abandon the world-view that I acquired in childhood'.[11]

Frederick Karl, like West, notes the similarity between Orwell's description of his life at school and life in Oceania. Karl, however, furthers our understanding of the nature of this relation by characterizing it as Kafkaesque. Orwell, he writes,

> conveys, within his limitations, the pathos and terror involved in a man caught between what he wants for himself and what the political system

> has to offer him. The prison life of 1984 merges with the enclosed life of the private school he attended as a young boy, both visions of what life offers. If the reader recognizes that for Orwell, as for Kafka, the nightmare is an inner one, then he can see the political matter as secondary to the personal content. This is not to relegate Orwell's politics to a less important position, but to retain perspective on the man's talents.[12]

Karl's suggestion that the politics in Orwell's most politically intentioned novel is subordinate to the personal, and that the personal is of the type to be found both in 'Such, Such Were the Joys' and in the works of Kafka, indicates a possible departure from the customary critical approach, both to Orwell's life and to his fiction. And although connecting an author's life with his fiction has often been judged critically dubious, many Orwell critics have stressed the importance of knowing both because the novels have been heavily loaded with details drawn directly from experience. Of these, Theodorus Hooning is perhaps the most adamant: 'only in reference to Orwell's personality and life can his work be properly understood'.[13]

Karl's view of the Kafkaesque in Orwell is corroborated by Meyers, who comments that there are 'disturbing passages' in 'Such, Such Were the Joys' which 'have metaphysical implications and suggest the guilt, absurdity, confusion and anxiety of the world created by Franz Kafka'.[14] And Arthur Koestler, writing in 1950, describes 1984 as being equal in 'logical horror' to Kafka's 'The Penal Settlement'. The point of difference that he notes between these two works is of the kind which I suggested was causing a generic confusion in Orwell studies: 'Orwell's despair had a concrete, organized structure, as it were, and was projected from the individual to the social plane' (my underlining).[15] Kenneth Hamilton, who argues for the presence of Judaic-Christian patterns of thought in 1984, echoes this judgment, but provides for it a wider context:

> The form Orwell has chosen meets us at every turn in an age which has shed its illusions without achieving faith, an age which knows evil but not God. In literature its purest expression is found in Kafka's The Trial (of which 1984 reads like a revised version, in which the action is merely lifted out of the

> interior world and put into the objective plane); but it is the staple theme in the greater part of 'serious' fiction today.... In fashionable philosophy it is systematized in Existentialism.[16]

The especial importance of assserting and emphasizing the comparison between the nature of Orwell's childhood world and the world of Oceania is that it is frequently assumed that the nightmare quality of _1984_ is an expression of Orwell's final illness and the prospect of death. While _1984_ may, perhaps necessarily, be _informed_ by illness, the Kafkaesque was experienced by Orwell decades before, so its nightmare cannot be confidently thought of as a _result_ of the conditions under which the book was written. And indeed, although Lee is not proposing the type of coherence with which this book is concerned, he writes that _1984_ was not the inspiration of disease but 'the inevitable culmination of Orwell's development: that, in effect, he had been progressing inexorably towards this book since his first essay was printed in 1931'.[17] William Steinhoff also believes _1984_ to be 'a culminating work which expresses, almost epitomizes, a lifetime's ideas, attitudes, events and reading', and reckons it 'a permissible exaggeration to say that from first to last Orwell, like George Eliot, was always writing the same novel'. This sameness, Steinhoff claims, exists through the repetition of a 'central situation' which is 'a hidden or overt rebellion against a way of life accepted by most but intolerable to the protagonists'.[18] Here, we move into the zone where the specific existential problem of authentic existence can more naturally be raised, a problem implied in what Raymond Williams detects in the novels and which he describes as 'the deep Orwell pattern: the man who tries to break from the standards of his group but who is drawn back into it'. The 'pattern' neatly defines the assertion and failure of authentic resolve, thus instating the _will to choose_ at the heart of the Orwell novel. In addition, in suggesting that Orwell was aware that the flight from the group was simultaneously 'necessary but also useless', Williams implies the Kafkaesque presence of the individual anxiously choosing himself in an Absurd world.[19]

It is, then, perhaps surprizing that after a twenty-year friendship with Orwell, Rees has 'no recollection of his ever once mentioning the name of Freud or Jung, or Kafka, or even Dostoevsky'. And

Rees, after recording Orwell's indifference to 'linguistic and logical analysis', writes:

> He was equally unimpressed by the existentialist philosophies in vogue towards the end of his life and here, I think, there was a temperamental barrier; though it might nevertheless be claimed that he was in real life a better existentialist, more authentic and more 'engaged', than many philosophers whose existentialism exists mainly between the covers of a book.[20]

This description of Orwell as a man who had acquired independently the existential approach is confirmed by Woodcock. In isolating a passage from the end of *A Clergyman's Daughter* concerning Dorothy Hare's loss of faith, he writes:

> Several years before Sartre published *La Nausée*, Dorothy was in fact undergoing the classic existentialist experience of horror at the realization that the absolute is in fact only the absurd, that man stands alone, without hope, in a universe unpopulated by God or gods. Orwell never claimed to be an existentialist; in fact, he had little use for popular philosophies, literary or otherwise, and was inclined to exaggerate the coterie elements in them. By 1934 he may have read the earlier novels of Malraux, the only absurdist who had published any important works of fiction by that time, but I have seen no actual evidence of this. Certainly by the later 1940s he had read not only Malraux but also Sartre and Camus, but he had very little to say about them.... But, even if he wrote of Dorothy's experience with no knowledge of the way in which similar spiritual agonies were being treated by his French contemporaries, the revelation follows the customary pattern. What Dorothy discovers is that we give our own meaning to the world by patterns of order which we ourselves create and sustain.[21]

Perhaps the only published remark made by Orwell on existentialism is in a letter to Julian Symons (29 October 1948). Referring to Sartre's *Portrait of the Antisemite* which he had just read for review, Orwell writes: 'I doubt whether it would be possible to pack more nonsense into so short a space. I have maintained from the start that Sartre is a bag of wind, though possibly when it comes to Existentialism, which I don't profess to understand, it may not be so'.[22]

The existential perspective in Orwell was not therefore something that he adopted and consciously applied. It was no concept that had to be grafted on to an originally existing position. It was *his*, an integrated part of what he was. How Orwell developed the existential perspective, and why this perspective may plausibly be seen as the inspiration for his particular political vision, are propositions which will be engaged in the following chapter.

NOTES

1. Richard Smyer, *Primal Dream and Primal Crime* (Columbia: Univ. of Missouri Press, 1979), p. 3.
2. "Arguments Against Orwell," *The World of George Orwell*, ed. Miriam Gross (London: Weidenfeld and Nicolson, 1971), p. 158.
3. Jeffrey Meyers, *A Reader's Guide to George Orwell* (London: Thames and Hudson, 1975), p. 64.
4. *The Crystal Spirit* (1966; rpt. Harmondsworth: Penguin Books, 1970), p. 50.
5. *The Last Man in Europe* (London: Macmillan, 1974), p. 3.
6. *Reader's Guide*, p. 64.
7. "Orwell in Perspective," *Essays on Literature and Ideas* (London: Macmillan, 1963), p. 180.
8. *Orwell's Fiction* (Notre Dame, Indiana: Univ. of Notre Dame Press, 1969), xi.
9. *George Orwell* (London: Secker and Warburg, 1961).
10. *George Orwell: The Critical Heritage*, ed. Jeffrey Meyers, (London: Routledge and Kegan Paul, 1975), p. 77.
11. *The Collected Essays, Journalism and Letters of George Orwell*, ed. Sonia Orwell and Ian Angus (1968; rpt. Harmondsworth: Penguin Books, 1971), vol. 1, p. 28.
12. "George Orwell," *A Reader's Guide to the Contemporary English Novel* (1962; rpt. London: Thames and Hudson, 1963), pp. 149-50.
13. "George Orwell in His Time," *Acta Historiae Neerlandica*, 5 (1971), p. 68.
14. "Orwell's Painful Childhood," *Ariel*, 3 (1972), p. 60.

15. _George Orwell: The Critical Heritage_, ed. Jeffrey Meyers, p. 298.
16. "G.K. Chesterton and George Orwell," _Dalhousie Review_, 31 (1951), p. 205.
17. _Orwell's Fiction_, p. 128.
18. _George Orwell and the Origins of '1984'_ (Ann Arbor: Univ. of Michigan, 1975), pp. 4, 123.
19. _Orwell_ (London: Fontana, 1971), pp. 46, 39.
20. Rees, pp. 12-13.
21. Woodcock, pp. 113-14.
22. _The Collected Essays, Journalism and Letters_, vol. 4, pp. 509-10.

Chapter One

ORWELL: AN EXISTENTIAL PROGRESS

Orwell's three autobiographical essays 'Such, Such Were the Joys', 'Shooting an Elephant' and 'A Hanging' are crucial pieces. They are all about the effects of power. And although the first describes life under it, and the others describe life holding it, they conclude in the same way: power splits the personality of both oppressor and oppressed, creating a false self which is the self-for-others. It was his determination to rid himself of his self-for-others that led 'lower-upper-middle class' Eric Blair into down-and-out George Orwell.[1] To forget this, or to think it not important, would be to misconstrue Orwell fundamentally; for the concept of the inauthentic self-for-others is Orwell's primary intuition and the foundation for his attacks on all the differing forms of totalitarianism he saw.

In this chapter these essays will be examined principally from the point of view of existential psychoanalysis as developed by the Sartrean analyst R.D. Laing. I hope to make clear a connection between the experiences recorded by Orwell and the crisis of inauthentic existence which characterizes the schizophrenic. But it must be stressed that no attempt is being made to present Orwell as mentally ill. My argument is that the existential perspective can be derived from the processes involved in those situations which tend to encourage schizophrenia.

Orwell was eight, and had been in prep school 'a week or two', when he began wetting his bed: 'it was looked on as a disgusting crime which the child committed on purpose'; but 'there was no volition about it, no consciousness. You did not properly speaking _do_ the deed'.[2] He prayed earnestly for no repeats but after several more offences he is beaten by Sambo, the headmaster, with a riding crop. It breaks:

> 'Look what you've made me do!' he said furiously, holding up the broken crop.
>
> I had fallen into the chair, weakly snivelling.... Fright and shame seemed to have anaesthetized me. I was crying partly because I felt that this was expected of me, partly from genuine repentance, but partly also because of a deeper grief which is peculiar to childhood and not easy to convey: a sense of desolate loneliness and helplessness, of being locked up not only in a hostile world but in a world of good and evil where the rules were such that it was actually impossible to keep them.
>
> I knew that the bed-wetting was (a) wicked and (b) outside my control. The second fact I was personally aware of, and the first I did not question. It was possible, therefore, to commit a sin without knowing that you committed it, without wanting to commit it, and without being able to avoid it. Sin was not necessarily something that you did: it might be something that happened to you. ('Joys', pp. 382-83)

Immediately, this passage at the beginning of 'Such, Such Were the Joys' establishes in detail the existential situation. In fact the entire essay, with its concentration on freedom, determinism, responsibility, guilt, alienation, anguish, abandonment, identity and the Absurd, reads like a story devised for the demonstration of existential topics. But along with these themes, a process has begun: the emergence of a self-for-others. So far, a child, blamed and caned for an act that he 'did not properly speaking *do*', is blamed for breaking the thing he's punished with; and when he cries it is partly because he feels it is expected of him. As a result, Orwell accepts a position similar to 'doublethink'. He writes: 'this was the great, abiding lesson of my boyhood: that I was in a world where it was *not possible* for me to be good'. And yet, having denied the possibility of free choice, he continues: 'I accepted the broken riding-crop as my own crime.... *I* had broken it: so Sambo told me, so and I believed. This acceptance of guilt lay unnoticed in my memory for twenty or thirty years' ('Joys', p. 383).

According to Laing the ontological break, or the 'divided self' of schizophrenia, originates in the conflicting discrepancy between the self-definition of the child and the definition that the parents attempt to impose. It is the demand made by authority to have a false self. The child, in developing this self-for-others, develops an in-authentic self which _externally_ corresponds to the requirements of authority, while the authentic self lives _internally_ and is given no outward expression. So the young Orwell, in accepting Sambo's definition of him as _a bad and guilty person_, and in crying partly because he thinks it is expected of him, is in the early stages of developing a false self-for-others. That this description is justified becomes soon apparent, for twenty pages later Orwell mentions the possession of 'an incorruptible inner self' ('Joys', p. 402). And ten pages after this he details his schizoid predicament:

> It was their world, and the rules they made for it must be the right ones. And yet from a very early age I was aware of the impossibility of any _subjective_ conformity. Always at the centre of my heart the inner self seemed to be awake, pointing out the difference between the moral obligation and the psychological _fact_. It was the same in all matters, worldly or otherwise. ('Joys', p. 412)

This division in the self is believed by Laing to be a technique to avoid depersonalization. Of a schizophrenic patient, he remarks:

> He used two chief manoeuvres to preserve security. One was an outward compliance with the other. The second was an inner intellectual Medusa's head he turned on the other. Both manoeuvres taken together safeguarded his own subjectivity which he had never to betray openly and which thus could never find direct and immediate expression for itself. Being secret, it was safe. Both techniques together were designed to avoid the dangers of being engulfed or depersonalized.[3]

This fear of depersonalization is, in itself, a symptom of the ontologically insecure, 'whose experiences may be utterly lacking in any unquestionable self-validating certainties' (Laing, p. 39). And for Orwell, this was at the root of almost all his agony. At eight years old he had been 'taken out' of the 'warm nest' of home and 'flung into a world of force and fraud and secrecy', where he 'lived among laws which were absolute, like the law of gravity'. And in this world a child 'will accept what it is told, and it will believe in the most fantastic way in the knowledge and powers of the adults' ('Joys', pp. 392-400). Indeed, the young Orwell so lacked Laing's 'unquestionable self-validating certainties', that he became a victim to those of no sanctioned authority: 'I continued to believe that I was preternaturally ugly. It was what my schoolfellows had told me, and I had no other authority to refer to' ('Joys', p. 413). Orwell himself, then, grew to accept that his own powers of judgment were quite without value. He was precisely what he was told. He was a self-for-others. The possible outcome of this is described by Laing: 'if the individual delegates all transactions between himself and the other to a system within his being which is not "him", then the world is experienced as unreal, and all that belongs to this system is felt to be false, futile and meaningless' (p. 80).

How close Orwell came to crossing the crucial borderline which distinguishes 'normal' reality from schizophrenic unreality is suggested by the effects that his novels have had on some of his critics. Christopher Small writes: 'undoutedly Orwell felt himself an outcast, not so much from society as, much more comprehensively, from real life';[4] and John Knapp says that the reader of _Burmese Days_ 'soon discovers that he is, mysteriously enough, re-evaluating his whole sense of reality'.[5] Keith Alldritt believes that 'the crucial defect of the novels is...the lack of felt experience in them'; and although he attributes this to 'misguided efforts to write in accord with the symbolist manner', he observes a similar defect in the _autobiographical_ books, which show 'Orwell's implicit confession of the paucity, the unreality even, of his experience'.[6] That Orwell evaded the severe and persistent unreality of dissociative illness is perhaps mostly due to his arriving at St. Cyprians just a little too late for it to overwhelm existing constitutional strengths. Additionally, it seems, the schizogenic situation produces its own protective devices: 'the ontologically insecure person is preoccupied with preserving rather than gratifying himself: the ordinary circumstances of living threaten his _low threshold_ of security' (Laing, p. 42).

Pertinently Orwell says of himself that his 'sense of guilt and inevitable failure was balanced by something else: that is, the instinct to survive' ('Joys', p. 413). Indeed, throughout his life Orwell was very little concerned with 'gratifying himself'. Mary McCarthy writes that 'even when he was fairly affluent [he] seems to have been an illustrated lesson in survival techniques under extreme conditions'.[7] And John Atkins: 'everyone who has written on Orwell has noticed the constant mortification to which he has subjected himself and has tried to explain it'.[8] This point has been emphasized for what it may imply about Orwell's quest for an authentic identity. Hazel Barnes, in her study of existential fiction, comments on the life of Genet in relation to Daniel in Sartre's Roads to Freedom: 'as we saw in the case of Daniel, self-punishment seems the clearest path to self-coincidence'.[9] This insight, that a fuller sense of one's realness and distinct selfhood can be achieved through deliberate maltreatment, indicates that Orwell was a man who had to afflict himself in order to penetrate the unreality of a false external self. The body becoming an object to the self, according to Laing, is a symptom of the schizoid state. The resemblance between Orwell's situation and Laing's description is clear:

> The 'normal' individual, in a situation all can see to be threatening to his being and to offer no real sense of escape, develops a schizoid state in trying to get outside it, if not physically, at least mentally: he becomes a mental observer, who looks on, detached and impassive, at what his body is doing or what is being done to his body. (p. 79)

There has been no lack of critical confirmation of Orwell as the observer both detached from himself and the world. Small writes that 'Orwell's detachment was neither a pose nor anything to find satisfaction in but a source of continual disquiet and even itself a cause of agony'.[10] And Richard Voorhees, in terms appropriate to the present clinical context, comments: 'Here [in Homage to Catalonia], as elsewhere when he writes about himself, there is an objectivity like that in the writings of doctors who, for the sake of science, have reported their own symptoms in the impersonal terms of the medical dictionary'.[11] In Coming Up For Air we see this detached self-observation conveyed in such a way as to capture the unreality of experience: 'it was almost as if I could stand at a distance and watch myself coming down the road'.[12] This description conforms to Laing's postulate that the basic split in the schizoid personality is a cleft which severs the self from the body: 'self/ (body-world)'. The result of this is that 'the I-sense is disembodied' (p. 174). Several examples of the I-sense being disembodied are to be found in Orwell's writings, notably his early poem 'On a Ruined Farm near the His Master's Voice Gramophone Factory', a title which in itself supplies a metaphor for presence without real existence. Here, a crisis is presented. The narrator has given his 'heart to weak and stuffless ghosts,/And with the living cannot live', and, as a ghost, his estrangement from the world is total:

> There is my world, my home; yet why
> So alien still? For I can neither
> Dwell in that world, nor turn again
> To scythe and spade, but only loiter
> Among the trees the smoke has slain.[13]

Again, this illustrates the position of the schizoid, for whom 'there is a rent in his relations with the world': 'such a person is not able to experience himself "together with" others or "at home in" the world, but, on the contrary, he experiences himself in despairing aloneness and isolation' (Laing, p. 17). This not only describes the poem's narrator; it is also the situation of Orwell at St. Cyprians. Orwell at school, like Laing's schizophrenic, 'is living in what to him, if not us, is a world that threatens his being from all sides, and from which there is no exit.... For them the world is a prison without bars, a concentration camp without barbed wire' (p. 79). Orwell, who said that he had lived 'for years amid irrational terrors and lunatic misunderstandings' ('Joys', p. 419), was obviously in 'a world that threatened his being from all sides', and as he was 'locked up...in a hostile world' ('Joys', p.382) there was no sense of possible 'exit'.

This feeling of imprisonment and persecution in Orwell has an obvious relatedness to paranoia, and, as such, shows what is perhaps crucial in Orwell, insofar as the schizoid self-for-others is that part of the self which also feels itself to be under constant observation by the authority which initially produced the false self. So it is, then, predictable that the schizoid would be unusually concerned with totalitarian possibilities. This relation between the personal and the political has been noticed by Isaac Deutscher: 'I remember that I was taken aback by the stubbornness with which Orwell dwelt on "conspiracies", and that his political reasoning struck me as a Freudian sublimation of persecution mania'.[14] In Orwell, the obvious link between the psychological and the political is _1984_. But the correlation is not only a general one; the particulars of that novel are, in this context, of symptomatic value. In this novel the inquisitor of the protagonist says: '"You shall be hollow. We shall squeeze you empty, and then we shall fill you with ourselves"'.[15] The dread of the false self becoming the _only_ self permeates _1984_. It is also the dread of the paranoic. Laing, in discussing paranoia, almost exactly describes Winston Smith as he struggles for self-definition in his room with the telescreen:

> The paranoic has specific persecutors. Someone is against him. There is a plot on foot to steal his brains. A machine is concealed in the wall of his bedroom which emits mind rays to soften his brain, or to send electric shocks through him while he is asleep. The person I am describing _feels_ at this phase _persecuted by reality itself_. The world as it is, and other people as they are, are the dangers.
>
> ....[A] self is liable to develop which feels it is outside all experience and activity. It becomes a vacuum. Everything is there, outside; nothing is here, inside. (pp.79-80)

I am not arguing for the above as a description of Orwell at any time during his life; the analogy between Winston Smith and the paranoic is there to show that Orwell had detailed understanding of paranoic dread. What I am suggesting is that it is not fortuitous that Orwell showed as the principal effect of totalitarianism the ghostly unreality and hollowness which characterizes the inauthenticity of the persecuted schizophrenic. To be dispossessed of one's Being was, for Orwell, man's ultimate degradation. With no 'I' to assert, every man is any man, and any man is always a no-man, an 'unperson'. So Orwell's passionate repudiation of authoritarian structures can also be seen as a fight against schizoid living, a state which has the vicious-circle effect of both maintaining and extending filial, institutional and political power. Power, as Edgar Friedenberg has said, is the power 'to define reality' and to 'validate experience', and sanity is conferred upon those who capitulate to 'the prevailing definitions of reality on which social cohesion depends'.[16] Schizophrenic insanity, then, is a category for those who, like Winston Smith (and potentially the young Orwell) have a version of reality which does not coincide with the orthodox view of it. Thus Smith is not principally a heretic; he is described as *insane*.

One of the devices employed deliberately or inadvertently by authority which causes problems of reality, Gregory Bateson has termed the 'Double Bind'.[17] The example of this that Laing provides is of a mother who subtly conveys to her child an ambiguous command which is impossible to obey: both *Do* and *Don't*. This schizogenic situation is similar to the one in which Orwell and others were placed by Flip, the headmaster's wife. Orwell, already baffled by the impossibility of obeying the laws of his new world, and knowing that he was not the equal of most of the other boys because he had been taken on reduced fees to win prestigious scholarships for the school, 'fawned on her in the most abject way':

> Flip, although the discipline of the school depended more on her than Sambo, hardly pretended to dispense strict justice. She was frankly capricious. An act which might get you a caning one day might next day be laughed off as a boyish prank, or even commended because it 'showed you had guts'. There were days when everyone cowered before those deep-set, accusing eyes, and there were days when she was like a flirtatious queen surrounded by courtier-lovers, laughing and joking, scattering largesse, or the promise of largesse. ('Joys', pp. 400-1)

For one who was already ontologically insecure, Flip's application of the Double Bind can only have deepened the self-division and sharpened the awareness that reality is not fixed and coherent but fluctuates between two contradictory levels. If Orwell had been persistently exposed to this kind of treatment from birth, the result might have been catastrophic, for 'the possible strategies for living out this untenable position ... match the types of behaviour identified clinically as schizophrenia'.[18] As it was, he finished school divided but not psychotic, one who had collected acute insights into the psychological processes on which structures of power depend. In 1984 Orwell presented a species of the Double Bind as the crucial totalitarian device: '"Reality control", they called it; in Newspeak, "doublethink"':

> His mind slid away into the labyrinthine world of doublethink. To know and not to know, to be conscious of complete truthfulness while telling carefully constructed lies, to hold simultaneously two opinions which cancelled out, knowing them to be contradictory and believing in both of them; to use logic against logic ... to forget whatever it was necessary to forget, then to draw it back into memory again at the moment when it was needed, and then promptly to forget it again: and above all, to apply the same process to the process itself.[19]

In his 1968 Massey Lectures, Laing schematized the Double Bind to show what essentially characterized human relations in the homes of his most schizoid patients. Its similarity to doublethink is made even more eerie if it is remembered that in Oceania nothing is illegal:

> Rule A: Don't.
> Rule A.1: Rule A does not exist.
> Rule A.2: Do not discuss the existence or non-existence of Rules A, A.1, or A.2.[20]

By showing that there is an essential correlation between the principal schizogenic device and the principal totalitarian device, I hope to have demonstrated that power and the false self are inseparable, insofar as power is ineffectual if it cannot create the subordination which inauthentic life involves, and where the power to subordinate is absent no inauthentic life will be nourished. Orwell's idealistic democratic socialism, as the antithesis of totalitarianism, is therefore synonymous with non-schizoid authentic existence, for only equality can guarantee the elimination of the psychological injuries which arbitrary unelected power necessarily creates. And although it would be wrong to suggest that Orwell was familiar with either the details or the connections within the schizogenic process, he nonetheless predicted that the outcome of this process would characterize the establishment of absolute political power: 'totalitarianism ... does not so much promise an age of faith as an age of schizophrenia'.[21] This powerful and perceptive concept involved the notion that the schizoid life was also necessary for those who had the power. It was this aspect of the power structure which we see emphasized in 'Shooting an Elephant'. How the elephant came to be shot is of some importance if Orwell is to be understood existentially, for, in a sense, the rifle was cocked at St. Cyprians. I shall be arguing that Orwell, having adopted an inauthentic life, remained attached to it until he left Burma; so the shooting, as an inauthentic act, is made more probable than otherwise because it conforms to an entrenched pattern. The pattern began when the young Orwell accepted as final a definition of himself which had been imposed upon him by others. This, as we have seen, is the origin of the self-for-others. Existentially the adoption of this self is significant; in Sartrean terms it is Original Choice, which involves the deception that man has a predetermined essence which he is not free to transcend. Implicitly it is the denial that man is responsible for his life; he cannot reach beyond what he is because he is a *completed object*.

In the existential biographies, *Baudelaire* and *Saint Genet*, Sartre traces developments remarkably similar to Orwell's. If we see Sambo and Flip as surrogate parents, many of Orwell's responses can be interpreted through Baudelaire's or any child's:

> The child takes his parents for gods. Their actions like their judgements are absolute. They are the incarnation of universal reason, law, the meaning and purpose of the world. When the eye of these divine beings is turned on him ... it confers on him a definite, sacred character. Since they are infallible, it follows that they *see* him as he really *is*. There is no room in his mind for hesitation or doubt ... he realizes that his *truth* does not consist in what he can know of himself, but that it is hidden in the large, terrible yet gentle eyes which are turned towards him.[22]

In the same way, Orwell, by accepting the infallibility of Sambo and Flip, also accepted as infallible their definition of him as both bad and useless. Therefore, as Sartre says of Baudelaire, 'he was ready to appear guilty in their eyes; and "guilty in their eyes" meant absolutely guilty' (Sartre, p. 54). And because of this Orwell 'understood to perfection what it meant to be Lucifer, defeated and justly defeated, with no possibility of revenge' ('Joys', p. 412). What Orwell did with this sense of sin and general worthlessness represents his Original Choice: he chose it for his permanent definition and therefore denied his freedom to become good and valuable or whatever else it was actually possible for him to be. Like Lucifer, he was _only_ evil. Baudelaire chose for himself the identity of a solitary; but irrespective of the _kind_ of choice, the outcome is the same: a commitment to the delusion of predestination of personality. At the end of 'Such, Such Were the Joys' Orwell writes: 'I believed firmly in my evil destiny' (p. 417). This process in Baudelaire is explained by Sartre: 'in the same way that he wanted to objectify the vague flux of his inner life, he tried to interiorize the _thing_ that he was for other people by transforming it into a plan of himself' (Sartre, p. 66). And it is precisely on this basis that Orwell devises his own plan for himself:

> The conviction that it was _not possible_ for me to be a success went deep enough to influence my actions till far into adult life. Until I was about thirty I always planned my life on the assumption not only that any major undertaking was bound to fail, but that I could only expect to live a few years longer. ('Joys', p. 413)

Orwell, then, inauthentically identifying himself with failure, had accepted a pattern of life shaped for him by Sambo and Flip. And, like Original Sin, all subsequent failure could be seen as something which he could not control and for which, therefore, he could not be seen as responsible. It is the reversal of the existential dictum that existence precedes essence. Orwell had located his essence (a sinful, cowardly failure) and had determined that existence would be lived in accordance with it. Only his self-for-others was really him.

The passage seems a long one between the victimized child at prep school and the tall officer of the Imperial Burmese Police going out with his gun to engage a marauding elephant. But the Original Choice of failure, and thus the commitment to an inauthentic self-for-others, still presides, and overwhelmingly. And predictably the problem in 'Shooting an Elephant' is seen as derived from the general problem of the uses of power. Orwell, who is oppressed 'with an intolerable sense of guilt' for being part of a tyranny he loathes, can therefore 'get nothing in perspective'. But perhaps for the first time he is progressing towards an illumination about what his position means: 'one day something happened which in a roundabout way was enlightening. It was a tiny incident in itself, but it gave me a better glimpse than I had before of the real nature of imperialism - the real motives for which despotic governments act'.[23]

Orwell, getting a call about a tame elephant which has gone 'must', sets out to assess the danger. The elephant has already destroyed a native hut and killed a cow, and Orwell soon discovers that it has also crushed a coolie. At this point he exchanges his .44 for an elephant gun, knowing the elephant to be only a few hundred yards away. Then the dilemma begins: 'As I started forward practically the whole population of the quarter flocked out of their houses and followed me.... It made me vaguely uneasy. I had no intention of shooting the elephant'. With the crowd quickly accumulating around him, Orwell, looking and feeling a fool, arrives at a road alongside a large paddy field in which, about eighty yards away, the elephant is peacefully feeding, looking no more dangerous than a cow. Orwell comments: 'As soon as I saw the elephant I knew with perfect certainty that I ought not to shoot him' ('Elephant', p. 268). The elephant is not only valuable but the reason for killing it has perhaps been removed, for the 'must' seems to be passing. 'Moreover,' says Orwell, 'I did not in the least want to shoot him'. So he decides to watch for a while and then go home. The decision seems firm. Orwell is alone, facing the elephant. Then the observation occurs which causes a dramatic reversal. The self-for-others rears and asserts an unchallenged dominance:

> But at that moment I glanced around at the crowd that had followed me. It was an immense crowd, two thousand at the least and growing every minute. It blocked the road for a long distance on either side. I looked at the sea of yellow faces ... all certain that the elephant was going to be shot.... They did not like me, but with a magical rifle in my hands

> I was momentarily worth watching. And suddenly I realized that I should have to shoot the elephant after all. ('Elephant', p. 269)

At this point it is interesting to note the language. Previously Orwell had 'no intention' of shooting; he 'did not in the least want to shoot'; and indeed, he knew with 'perfect certainty' that he 'ought not'. The phrases denote both preference and choice, but one glimpse at the crowd morally flattens him. He is nothing but the crowd. He becomes a thing, a kind of weather vane which gets its direction from external influence. His choice of a life of cowardly failure shows itself here as the failure to act authentically, the failure to recognize responsibility for acts. The language therefore changes to one of choicelessness. He is compelled, so now he would 'have to shoot'. As a study in role-playing inauthenticity the passage which follows the above has classic existential status. It is one of those rare statements an author makes which can be immediately recognized as pivotal. It both captures the essence of a way of life and implicitly speaks of its end. With a sudden, cogent, and undisguisable clarity the existence of a man is seen for what it really is, and an awareness is achieved which cannot be shelved because it simultaneously becomes part of his total perspective. Life cannot be resumed on the same basis.

> And suddenly I realized that I should have to shoot the elephant. The people expected it of me and I had got to do it; I could feel their two thousand wills pressing me forward, irresistibly. And it was at this moment, as I stood there with the rifle in my hands, that I first grasped the hollowness, the futility of the white man's dominion in the East. Here was I, the white man with his gun, standing in front of the unarmed native crowd - seemingly the leading actor of the piece; but in reality I was only an absurd puppet pushed to and fro by the will of those yellow faces behind. I perceived in this moment that when the white man turns tyrant it is his own freedom that he destroys. He becomes a sort of hollow, posing dummy, the conventionalized figure of a sahib. For it is the condition of his rule that he shall spend his life in trying to impress the 'natives' and so in every crisis he has got to

> do what the 'natives' expect of him. He wears a mask, and his face grows to fit it. I had got to shoot the elephant. I had committed myself to doing it when I sent for the rifle. A sahib has got to act like a sahib; he has got to appear resolute, to know his own mind and do definite things. To come all that way, rifle in hand, with two thousand people marching at my heels, and then to trail feebly away, having done nothing - no, that was impossible. The crowd would laugh at me. And my whole life, every white man's life in the East, was one long struggle not to be laughed at.
>
> But I did not want to shoot the elephant. ('Elephant', pp. 269-70)

A completer or more perceptive statement about the dilemma of the self-for-others would be difficult to find. But what gives this passage its curiosity is that Orwell, so trenchant in his analysis of the false self, is at the same time speaking <u>for</u> the false self. In describing inauthenticity he affirms it. Instead of admitting his responsibility for being an 'absurd puppet' he blames Imperialism. Somehow he wrings out of his analysis a formidable exoneration. He is, in fact, doublethinking his way out of his freedom to choose to be other than a sahib, as if sahibs are born, not made. Strengthened by a list of obligatives ('I had got to', etc) Orwell is able to pretend that because Imperialism has destroyed his freedom it is really Imperialism which will do the killing. He is merely an instrument, a thing which has no say in how he is to be used. As such, he is re-enacting the false self of authority at St. Cyprians, a more momentous version of Sambo breaking the riding-crop on Orwell's backside: '"Look what you've made me do!"'

So while 'Shooting an Elephant' shows plainly and profoundly the link between power and the false self, it ends with no assertion of authentic resolve. The insights are made, Orwell learns, and we are left only with a sense of bulging potential. The final sentences seem to undermine, almost refute, the powerful sincerity of all that has gone before. The concluding feeling is of being spoken to by someone else, a pragmatic extrovert who rather regrets having lapsed into over-sensitive nonsense about matters of conscience and personal truth: 'afterwards I was very glad that the coolie had been killed; it put me legally in the right and it gave me sufficient pretext for shooting the elephant. I often wondered whether any of the others grasped that I had done it solely to avoid looking a fool' ('Elephant', p. 272).

Here, then, is Orwell when he was Blair, glad that a coolie had been crushed because it relieves him of the legal responsibility for an unjustified killing. With the law on his side the problem ends, even though it is the law of a system he describes as 'evil'. The moral conscience is reduced to the anxiety of being judged wrong or foolish by others, and so everything collapses into vain expediency. Orwell is a 'posing dummy' not because of Imperialism but because a sly defence of both oppressor and oppressed can produce nothing else: without defined allegiance nothing truly individual can emerge. So perhaps the kindest description of Orwell in 'Shooting an Elephant' is that of a reactionary touting for a Liberal vote.

In 'A Hanging' the form is the same, and so is the question: on what basis does man kill? Orwell, one of the officiating party, watches a Hindu being brought out for death from 'a row of sheds fronted with double bars, like small animal cages'.[24] The whole episode is written in a kind of suggestive understatement, something reluctantly but carefully hidden, the closest Orwell ever got to Hemingway. The effect is one of distance impeccably measured and maintained. As such, meaning and technique are in precise correspondence, for what is being conveyed is the contrived no-man's land between responsibility and act. The law by which the condemned is sentenced is white Imperial, the head jailer is a native in a European suit, and the hangman is a native convict: this is the hierarchy of distance, of responsibility twice removed. The structure is one of mutual exoneration. The white superintendent who authorizes doesn't do the act, and the convict who does isn't responsible for maintaining the law, and the man in the middle is, simply, the man in the middle, in this case Francis, a native in a European suit who speaks the kind of stilted euphemistic English which enables him and others to hide a little further from the purpose of their collaboration. Indeed, it is this man's ethnic indefinition that seems to neutralize the possible impact of the event. And his description of a previous hanging is reassuring because pulling at the victim's legs to '"ensure decease"' shows that it is really just a job of work in which death, as it happens, is the conclusive sign of success. And, as he goes on to tell of another condemned prisoner who has resisted being brought out to the gallows, he says that the man has to be '"reasoned with"', and this reasoning takes the inauthentic form with which we are now familiar; '"think of all the pain and trouble you are causing us!"' ('A Hanging,' p. 71). So even at the time of ultimate desperation, the condemned is being encouraged to accept responsibility. The implicit meaning of this tactic by Francis is to convey to the prisoner that if he continues to resist, then the trouble it causes can be seen as an offence which _demands_ punishment; and if, on the other hand, he ceases resistance, he is in fact _volunteering_ to die. Either way, it is the prisoner's fault.

As in 'Such, Such Were the Joys' and 'Shooting an Elephant', the system in 'A Hanging' is presented as something which has its own autonomous existence quite independent of those who have chosen to maintain it. The individual is the will-less ingredient of a self-justifying process, implacable and therefore futile to question. And so when an individual _is_ perceived he is, of course, the one about to die, for nothing individual can live in a system of collective inauthenticity. The way in which the prisoner inadvertently expresses himself as individual is through an act of such pathos that it is as if a hidden nerve has suddenly been seized. Chained to the guard, and on the path to the gallows, he steps slightly aside to avoid a puddle. This little movement of a man who still thought he had a future in which wet feet would be uncomfortable, provides Orwell with a moment of illumination similar to the one when he realized he would 'have to' shoot the elephant:

> It is curious, but till that moment I had never realized what it means to destroy a healthy, conscious man. When I saw the prisoner step aside to avoid the puddle, I saw the mystery, the unspeakable wrongness, of cutting a life short when it is in full tide. This man was not dying, he was alive just as we were alive. All the organs of his body were working - bowels digesting food, skin renewing itself, nails growing, tissues forming - all toiling away in solemn foolery. His nails would still be growing when he stood on the drop, when he was falling through the air with a tenth of a second to live. His eyes saw the yellow gravel and the grey walls, and his brain still remembered, foresaw, reasoned - reasoned even about

> puddles. He and we were a party of men walking together, seeing, hearing, feeling, understanding the same world; and in two minutes, with a sudden snap, one of us would be gone - one mind less, one world less. ('A Hanging', pp. 68-9)

Much of the power of this passage is derived from the context of the 'solemn foolery' of the Absurd in which Orwell places the life of the prisoner and his little movement around the puddle. And because the hanging has been interrupted by a barking dog suddenly bounding into the yard, there already exists the suggestion of the contingency of the Absurd which underlies the apparent absolutism of the system. So when the prisoner unpredictably moves aside, he metaphorically steps out of the system into his own individuality and can therefore be truly apprehended. Consequently he dissolves the false distance between himself, the event, and the narrator, and Orwell is now able to see that man is his own completed system, nothing less than a 'world'. No longer alienated by role-playing and false structures, everyone becomes 'a party of men' 'understanding the same world', each separate and unique but in essence all bound to the same condition. Under the pressure of the Absurd, everything divisive slides away. It was the fellowship of this radical equality which Orwell persistently sought on his return from Burma and which he was eventually able to celebrate in _Homage to Catalonia_.

During the nine years between his departure from Burma and his arrival in Spain, Orwell had battled with social class as the obstacle to be cleared before an authentic life could be gained, and, in so doing, had employed class as an excuse to justify the residual presence of his inauthentic self-for-others. In _Down and Out in Paris and London_, and particularly in _The Road to Wigan Pier_, he fulminates against class in the same way as he had fulminated against Imperialism in 'Shooting an Elephant'. In _Wigan Pier_ Orwell describes class as the determining cause of what he is, therefore apprehending himself as an _inevitable result_ of the social position to which he was born:

> Here am I, a typical member of the middle class. It is easy for me to say that I want to get rid of class-distinctions, but nearly everything I think and do is a result of class-distinctions. All my notions - notions of good

> and evil, of pleasant and unpleasant, of funny and serious, of ugly and beautiful - are essentially middle-class notions; my taste in books and food and clothes, my sense of honour, my table manners, my turns of speech, my accent, even the characteristic movements of my body, are the products of a special kind of up-bringing and a special niche about half-way up the social hierarchy. (Wigan Pier, p. 141)

But irrespective of the deterministic character of this description, a definite shift away from the false self is to be noted in Wigan Pier. Orwell no longer feels constrained to accept a socially derived self-definition as he had done in Burma. The necessary change in the self does not have to issue first from the system and then be passed on to the individual. The individual himself generates the means by which to change himself and then the system. Man is free to choose what he will be: 'I have got to alter myself so completely that at the end I should hardly be recognizable as the same person' (Wigan Pier, p. 141).

Fighting against Franco in the Spanish Civil War was an act which signified a commitment against the system he had been employed to protect in Burma; among the shabby P.O.U.M. militia he realizes his desire to be 'hardly ... recognizable as the same person'. And it was in Spain that he was given the opportunity to atone for his part in the prisoner's death in 'A Hanging'. In 'Looking Back On The Spanish War' Orwell records an event in which the symbolic value of the movement of the condemned man around the puddle achieves expression in a different way. Orwell, out to snipe at the Fascist trench, has had no success. He is about to return when he is suddenly presented with an unusual opportunity:

> At this moment, a man presumably carrying a message to an officer, jumped out of the trench and ran along the top of the parapet in full view. He was half-dressed and was holding up his trousers with both hands as he ran.... I did not shoot partly because of that detail about the trousers. I had come here to shoot at 'Fascists'; but a man who is holding up his trousers isn't a 'Fascist', he is visibly a fellow-creature, similar to yourself, and you don't feel like shooting at him.[25]

The 'Fascist', half-dressed and therefore without

uniform, has, like the condemned man, stepped out of the distance of personified abstraction into the felt presence of concrete humanity. For a moment the system has ceased to define him to others as a thing. And Orwell himself, because he is no longer the instrument of a system, either Imperialist or Socialist, is able to act in accord with values which are his own. But the paradox remains that Orwell had to kill an elephant and be involved in hangings in order to gain the perspective which would preserve a 'Fascist'.

Existentially 'Such, Such Were the Joys', 'Shooting an Elephant', 'A Hanging', The Road to Wigan Pier, Homage to Catalonia and 'Looking Back On The Spanish War' may be seen as a series of documents which record a progress to personal authenticity. They show the inception, development and consolidation of the false self, its crisis, its erosion, and its destruction. What Orwell found in Spain was an absolute contrast to the oppressive hierarchical arrangement which he had been impelled to suffer under at St. Cyprians. The 'posing dummy' into which he grew as a result of his schooling was what he finally killed when he refused to shoot the 'Fascist'. In Spain, Orwell experienced the thrill of classless community, a brotherhood in which the true self could prosper because no one had the power to split the individual, creating a false public self. He discovered 'a feeling of having suddenly emerged into an era of equality and freedom. Human beings were trying to behave as human beings and not as cogs in the capitalist machine'. Here, where the loss of power over others has temporarily eliminated servility, everyone calls the other '"Comrade and Thou"'.[26] The hierarchy of distances between people present in 'A Hanging' has now vanished, and that moment of egalitarian unity which Orwell felt when the condemned man avoided the puddle has become a condition of life. Once more he is one of 'a party of men walking together, seeing, hearing, feeling, understanding the same world'. All men are equivalently valuable in a world to which each is equivalently related. But in this world of equivalence, a man is not just anyone, just one more of the same; each is individual and special, a world in himself: when the prisoner dies, there is 'one world less'. This was the basic understanding which informed Orwell's sociopolitical position. And he saw it threatened everywhere. In Wigan Pier he writes:

'We are living in a world in which nobody is free, in which hardly anybody is secure, in which it is almost impossible to be honest and remain alive' (p. 149). And in 'Inside the Whale': 'Almost certainly we are moving into an age of totalitarian dictatorships - an age in which freedom of thought will be at first a deadly sin and later on a meaningless abstraction. The autonomous individual is going to be stamped out of existence'.[27]

Always with Orwell the difficulty of individual existence derives from the strength of the Many to define the identity of the One. It is reducible to the prevailing orthodoxy's power to demand of the private authentic individual that he generate a public inauthentic self; and it is the conflict which arises from this demand which forms the thematic centre of every Orwell novel. It is also the great theme of existential thought.

NOTES

1. The Road to Wigan Pier (1937; rpt. Harmondsworth: Penguin Books, 1966), p. 120. Henceforth cited in text as 'Wigan Pier', with page numbers to this edition.

2. "Such, Such Were the Joys," The Collected Essays, Journalism and Letters, ed. Sonia Orwell and Angus (1968; rpt. Harmondsworth: Penguin Books, Ian 1971), vol. 4, p. 379. Henceforth cited in text as 'Joys', with page numbers to this edition.

3. The Divided Self (1959; rpt. Harmondsworth: Pelican Books, 1967), p. 48. Henceforth cited in text as 'Laing', with page numbers to this edition.

4. The Road to Miniluv (London: Victor Gollancz, 1975), p. 42.

5. "Dance to a Creepy Minuet", Modern Fiction Studies, 21 (1975), p. 29.

6. The Making of George Orwell (London: Edward Arnold, 1969), p. 43.

7. "The Writing on the Wall", The Writing on the Wall (1970; rpt. Harmondsworth: Penguin Books, 1973), p. 155.

8. George Orwell (London: Calder and Boyars, 1954), p. 107.

9. The Literature of Possibility (Lincoln: Univ. of Nebraska Press, 1959), p. 327.

10. The Road to Miniluv, p. 42.

11. The Paradox of George Orwell (Lafayette, Indiana: Purdue Univ. Studies, 1961), p. 37.

12. *Coming Up For Air* (1939; rpt. Harmondsworth: Penguin Books, 1967), p. 13.
13. *The Collected Essays, Journalism and Letters*, vol. 1, p. 158.
14. "1984 - The Mysticism of Cruelty," *Russia in Transition* (New York: Coward-McCann, 1957), p. 243 (footnote).
15. *1984* (1949; rpt. Harmondsworth: Penguin Books, 1976), p. 206.
16. *Laing* (London: Fontana, 1973), p. 35.
17. G. Bateson, et al, "Toward a Theory of Schizophrenia," *Double Bind*, ed. C. Sluzki and D.C. Ransom (New York: Grune and Stratton, 1976), pp. 3-22.
18. R.D. Laing, *The Self and Others* (1961; rpt. Harmondsworth: Pelican Books, 1971), p. 147.
19. *1984*, pp. 31-32.
20. E. Friedenberg, *Laing*, p. 13.
21. "The Prevention of Literature," *The Collected Essays, Journalism and Letters*, vol. 4, p. 89.
22. J.-P. Sartre, *Baudelaire*, trans. Martin Turnell (London: Horizon, 1949), pp. 50-51. Henceforth cited in text as 'Sartre', with page numbers to this edition.
23. "Shooting an Elephant," *The Collected Essays, Journalism and Letters*, vol. 1, p. 266. Henceforth cited in text as 'Elephant', with page numbers to this edition.
24. "A Hanging," *The Collected Essays, Journalism and Letters*, vol. 1, p. 66. Henceforth cited in text as 'A Hanging', with page numbers to this edition.
25. *Homage to Catalonia* (1938; rpt. Harmondsworth: Penguin Books, 1966), pp. 230-31.
26. Ibid., pp. 8, 10.
27. *The Collected Essays, Journalism and Letters*, vol. 1, p. 576.

Chapter Two

EXISTENTIAL AUTHENTICITY

What all existentialists share is a denial of crowd identity. A crowd is always and only individuals in proximity. If the individual 'loses himself' in a crowd so that the crowd acts for him, it is still *his* life that he is living. If he is overwhelmed by the multitude, it is because he, as an individual, has permitted it. Only by deceiving himself can he be absorbed and taken over. Living is something that no one can do for him. He can never be owned, and he can never be impelled to act. He is unique, and he is free. When a man uses his freedom to deny his freedom he slips into inauthentic living, for he abdicates responsibility for himself as a uniquely existing individual. When he denies his freedom he denies possession of himself.

The chief existentialists are Soren Kierkegaard, Friedrich Nietzsche, Martin Buber, Karl Jaspers, Martin Heidegger, Gabriel Marcel, Jean-Paul Sartre and Albert Camus. All these thinkers have been concerned with the concept of authentic existence, but only in Heidegger and Sartre do we see this concept systematized and incorporated into a comprehensive description of man's being-in-the-world. Linked with Buber's account of interpersonal relations, they represent every significant aspect of existential authenticity. This chapter can therefore be confined to these three thinkers without any substantial loss to the total existential perspective. Some of the thinkers omitted here do later appear, when they are used to indicate the existential variety of the Orwell novel and to elucidate meanings that would not otherwise be captured. In this necessarily summary presentation of Heidegger, Buber and Sartre, I have endeavoured to quote rather than paraphrase, as each stylistically generates a distinctive atmosphere which conveys precisely what the existentialist most wants to reveal and preserve: the individual speaking his own experience of Being.

Existentialism is unavoidably introvert, for it stems from, and revolves around, the meaning of what it is _to be_. Existential enquiry starts from the self and always returns to it. In this Heidegger is exemplary, a classic introvert megalithically brooding over the fact that Being _is_. Why, for Heidegger, this devotion to this particular axiom is necessary is because man has 'forgotten' Being through his seduction by a collective, abstract and technical world. The consequence is dire: man has become uprooted, homeless, alienated from the sources of his Being. The path back to Being can only be achieved by ridding enquiry of the concepts that have obscured Being, thus allowing Being to reveal itself as it is. This explains Heidegger's word for truth: 'unhiddenness'.

Out of nothingness man has been 'thrown' into the world, and in the world he discovers himself as existing. This discovery involves the understanding that Being, in itself, is an issue for Being. So therefore, concern, or 'care', is the way Being manifests itself to itself. As a being-in-the-world whose primary relation with the world is care, there emerges a self, characterized by a sense of mineness:

> In each case Dasein [being-there: man] is mine to be in one way or another. Dasein has always made some sort of decision as to the way in which it is in each case mine. That entity which in its Being has this very Being as an issue, comports itself towards its Being as its ownmost possibility. In each case Dasein _is_ its possibility, and it 'has' this possibility but not just as a property, as something present-at-hand would. And because Dasein is in each case essentially its own possibility, it _can_, in its Being, 'choose' itself and win itself; it can also lose itself and never win itself; or only 'seem' to do so. But only in so far as it is essentially something which can be _authentic_ - that is, something of its own - can it have lost itself and not yet won itself. As modes of Being, _authenticity_ and _inauthenticity_ are grounded in the fact that any Dasein whatsoever is characterized by mineness.[1]

Because man's Being is basically care, and because care occurs over a region beyond the one who cares, existence means always to stand outside oneself. Therefore being-in-the-world is always being-with other people and objects; so Being is inseparably related to things that are not-self. The not-self, then, is constitutive of Being. In this region of the not-self, the most influential is the existence of the Other. But 'by "Others" we do not mean everyone else but me - those over against whom the "I" stands out. They are rather those from whom, for the most part, one does <u>not</u> distinguish oneself - those among whom one is too' (p. 154).

These Others from whom we do not distinguish ourselves comprise one's immediate community and are part of the 'everydayness' of our Being. These Others have already constituted our Being before the discovery that existence is 'mine', utterly distinct and unique. So the discovery of the self also entails, simultaneously, the discovery that the self has been penetrated by the Others. There is therefore 'constant care as to the way one differs from them, whether that difference is merely one that is to be evened out, whether one's own Dasein has lagged behind the Others and wants to catch up in relationship to them, or whether one's Dasein already has some priority over them and sets out to keep them suppressed' (pp. 163-4). In this way a 'distance' is introduced between the self and Others, and creates a disturbance in its region of care. What is recognized is that the self is in 'subjection' to the Others, and, moreover, these Others are not <u>definite</u> Others. Indeed, <u>any</u> Others can represent them. And what is decisive 'is just that inconspicuous domination by Others which has taken over unawares'; 'one belongs to the Others oneself and enhances their power':

> 'The Others' whom one thus designates in order to cover up the fact of one's belonging to them essentially oneself, are those who proximally and for the most part '<u>are there</u>' in everyday Being-with-another. The 'who' is not this one, not that one, not oneself, not some people, and not the sum of them all. The 'who' is the neuter, <u>the 'they'</u>.
>
> ....In utilizing public means of transport and in making use of information services such as the newspaper, every Other is like the next. This Being-with-one-another dissolves one's own Dasein completely into the kind of Being of the

> 'the Others', in such a way, indeed, that the Others, as distinguishable and explicit, vanish more and more. In this inconspicuousness and unascertainability, the real dictatorship of the 'they' is unfolded. We take pleasure and enjoy ourselves as they take pleasure; we read, see, and judge about literature and art as they see and judge; likewise we shrink back from the 'great mass' as they shrink back; we find shocking what they find shocking. The 'they', which is nothing definite, and which all are, though not as the sum, prescribes the kind of Being of everydayness. (p. 164)

This 'they', which is both the self and the not-self, concerns itself with 'averageness', maintaining judgements about validity and invalidity, success and failure, and the whole prescriptive network; at the same time keeping watch 'over everything exceptional that thrusts itself to the fore' (p. 165). Every kind of priority gets noiselessly suppressed. Under the dominion of the 'they', nothing anomalous or heretical can live. As a result, there is a 'levelling down' of all possibilities of Being. Distance, averageness and levelling-down are modes of publicness, and publicness controls every way in which the self and the world are interpreted. It is always right because it is insensitive to every difference of level and of genuineness; thus it never gets to the 'heart of the matter'. Publicness obscures everything, and that which has been concealed gets passed off as something familiar and accessible to everyone. The 'they', although it is everywhere, cannot be specifically located, and hence seems to have disappeared when the self presses for a decision. Yet, because the 'they' presents every judgement and decision as its own, it deprives the self of its answerability. The 'they' can be answerable for everything most easily, because it is not something which needs to vouch for anything: 'It was always the "they" who did it, and yet it can be said that it has been "no one"'. Therefore, in the self's everydayness, events usually occur through the agency of no one:

> Thus the particular Dasein in its everydayness is disburdened by the 'they'. Not only that; by thus disburdening it of its Being, the 'they' accommodates Dasein if Dasein has any tendency to take things easily and make them easy. And because the 'they' constantly accom-

> -modates the particular Dasein by disburdening it of its Being, the 'they' retains and enhances its stubborn dominion.
> Everyone is the other, and no one is himself. The 'they', which supplies the answer to the question of the '*who*' of everyday Dasein, is the '*nobody*' to whom every Dasein has already surrendered itself in Being-among-one-another. (pp. 165-6)

So the man whose Being is characterized by 'everydayness' is living in the mode of the they-self and is therefore inauthentic. In order to authenticate his Being, the self must discover the world in its own way and bring it close. This quest will necessarily involve a clearing away of concealments, obscurities and disguises, and standing in the 'clearing of Being': the unhiddenness of truth.

Heidegger identifies three significant and characterizing modes of the inauthentic they-self: Idle Talk, Curiosity, and Ambiguity. Idle Talk is merely 'passing the word along'. What is said in this talk is understood, but what the talk is about is understood only approximately and superficially. Idle Talk, which 'anyone can rake up', is the possibility of understanding everything without previously making the thing one's own, and

> it serves not so much to keep Being-in-the-world open for us in an articulated understanding, as rather to close it off, and cover up the entities within-the-world.... The fact that something has been said groundlessly, and then gets passed along in further retelling, amounts to perverting the act of disclosing into an act of closing off. For what is said is always understood proximally as 'saying' something - that is, an uncovering something. Thus, by its very nature, idle talk is a closing-off, since to go back to the ground of what is talked about is something which it *leaves undone*. (p. 213)

There is also in Idle Talk a vicious-circle effect, for it is assumed among idle-talkers that an understanding about something has already been achieved, with the result that any new enquiry is discouraged or positively suppressed. This everday mode of fatuous communication is a way of interpreting the world which Dasein, in the first instance, cannot avoid, for he has unwittingly grown into it. As such, man has been severed from the roots of his Being:

> Idle talk has been uprooted existentially, and this uprooting is constant. Ontologically this means that when Dasein maintains itself in idle talk, it is - as Being-in-the-world - cut off from its primary and primordially genuine relationships-of-Being towards the world, towards Dasein-with, and towards its very Being-in.... Far from amounting to a 'not-Being' of Dasein, this uprooting is rather Dasein's most everyday and most stubborn 'Reality'.
>
> Yet the obviousness and self-assurance of the average ways in which things have been interpreted, are such that while the particular Dasein drifts along towards an ever-increasing groundlessness as it floats, the uncanniness of this floating remains hidden from it under their protecting shelter. (p. 214)

Thus Idle Talk is the discourse of Beings alienated from their existential sources. Likewise the Curiosity of the they-self is the mode of constant movement over the surface of things, seeing without understanding. Curiosity

> seeks novelty only in order to leap from it anew to another novelty. In this kind of seeing, that which is an issue for care does not lie in grasping something and being knowingly in the truth; it lies rather in its possibilities of abandoning itself to the world .... [Curiosity] is concerned with the constant possibility of <u>distraction</u>.... [Curiosity] concerns itself with a kind of knowing, but just in order to have known. Both this <u>not tarrying</u> in the environment with which one concerns oneself, and this <u>distraction by</u> new possibilities, are constitutive items for curiosity; and upon these is founded the third essential characteristic of this phenomenon, which we call the character of '<u>never dwelling anywhere</u>'. Curiosity is everywhere and nowhere. This mode of Being-in-the-world reveals a new kind of Being of everyday Dasein - a kind in which Dasein is constantly uprooting itself. (pp. 216-7)

Idle Talk has control of Curiosity, prescribing what one must read and see. The mode of Curiosity, being everywhere and nowhere, is delivered over to Idle Talk. These two modes create Ambiguity, which is the predicament of never being able to decide what is, or what is not, genuine understanding. This Ambiguity extends not only into the world but into the self's relations with others, and, more crucially, into the self's understanding of its own Being. These interconnected modes express the way in which Being experiences its existence in the world, and, as such, are actual ingredients of the self. This three-fold alienated Being of the everyday they-self comprizes the 'fallenness' of man, his inauthenticity. The impulse towards the authenticity of one's 'own-most Being' issues from Dasein's basic constitution, his primordial state of care, that state of anxiety which inescapably attends the fact of merely being alive in the world. Dasein is not anxious in the face of anything in particular; the source cannot be located; anxiety comes from 'nowhere'. And indeed, this is the significance of anxiety, that entities within the world are absolutely irrelevant, and therefore, in moments of heightened anxiety, the world seems to collapse into insignificance. Anxiety pierces the crust of the they-self under which the self is hidden and tranquillized, and it leaves the self feeling 'uncanny' and 'not-at-home' in a world which has suddenly been rendered unfamiliar. This puts the self into flight back into the comforts of inauthentic everydayness, but 'in anxiety there lies the possibility of a disclosure which is quite distinctive; for anxiety individualizes. This individualization brings Dasein back from its falling, and makes manifest to it that authenticity and inauthenticity are possibilities of its Being' (p. 235). This disclosure bears the message that one is free, free for 'one's ownmost potentiality-for-Being', and when that is understood the realization occurs that Being is always 'beyond itself', that is, Being always comports itself towards its own possibilities. These possibilities, which have previously been submerged in the collective they-self, emerge strikingly as only _my_ possibilities. In a peculiarly religious sense, Heidegger describes these effects of individualizing anxiety as the 'call of conscience':

> In its 'who', the caller is definable in a 'worldly' way by _nothing_ at all. The caller is Dasein in its _uncanniness_: primordial, thrown

> Being-in-the-world as the 'not-at-home' - the bare 'that-it-is' in the 'nothing' of the world. The caller is unfamiliar to the everyday they-self; it is something like an *alien* voice. What could be more alien to the 'they', lost in the manifold 'world' of its concern, than the Self which has been individualized down to itself in uncanniness and been thrown into the 'nothing'? (pp. 321-2)

And so the call, which comes from the uncanniness innate to the three-fold alienation of inauthentic existence, 'speaks' to Dasein of its authentic potentiality-for-Being. This call engenders a sense of guilt, for what is realized is that one is responsible for the self; therefore, 'in understanding the call, Dasein is *in thrall to its ownmost possibility of existence*. It has chosen itself' (p. 334). Thus a sense of my own individual future is understood, and with it the understanding that Being is always, at any stage, incomplete. So if Dasein is to live in the truth of Being he must live in anticipation of the possibility of completion in death. Man, as a Being thrown into the world, is thrown towards his end. So the anticipation of death is the 'possibility of understanding one's *ownmost* and uttermost potentiality-for-Being - that is to say, the possibility of *authentic existence*'; and this potentiality must be taken over by the self alone:

> Death does not just 'belong' to one's own Dasein in an undifferentiated way; death *lays claim* to it as an *individual* Dasein.... It makes manifest that all Being-alongside the things with which we concern ourselves, and all Being-with-Others, will fail us when our ownmost potentiality-for-Being is the issue. Dasein can be *authentically itself* only if it makes this possible for itself of its own accord.
>
> .... Anticipation discloses to existence that its uttermost possibility lies in giving itself up, and thus it shatters all one's tenaciousness to whatever existence one has reached. (p.308)

Death, then, as the ultimate individuating concept, releases a truly transcendent selfhood. No longer lost among the 'they' and sheltered by its illusions, man, thrown fortuitously into the world, and standing with nothingness behind, screws himself into the comfortless resolution of looking always forward to the nothingness before. He becomes Shakespeare's 'unaccommodated man'.

Martin Buber is an existentialist who almost exclusively focuses on one aspect of being human: interpersonal relations. His appeal lies not so much in the logical structure of his argument as in that rhetoric of feeling by which the poet reveals the truth of things. For Buber, the emotions are primary; devotion to the rational falsifies man and estranges him from meaningful encounters with others.

Buber's basic premise is that the attitude of man is twofold in accordance with the two basic pair-words he can speak: I-You, and I-it (-He, -She). Always when a man says 'I' he implies either the 'It' or the 'You', but the I-You can only be spoken with one's whole Being, while the I-It can never be. The reason for this is that the world as experience belongs to the basic pair-word I-It, and the basic pair-word I-You establishes the world of relation. They therefore denote particular and contrasting modes of existence. When a man stands in the realm of the I-It he goes over the surface of things and experiences them. He brings back from them some knowledge of their condition, which is an experience. He experiences what there is to things. But it is not experience alone which brings the world to man, for what experiences bring to him is only a world that consists of 'It and It and It, of He and He and She and She and It'.[2] But whoever says I-You does not have something for his object, for wherever there is something there is also another something: every It borders on other Its. It is only It because it borders on others. But where You is said there is no something. You has no borders. Therefore, 'whoever says You does not have something; he has nothing. But he stands in relation' (p. 55). Those who stand in the experiential realm of the I-It do not participate in the world, for the experience is 'in them' and not between them and the world.

Buber describes three spheres in which the world of relation arises:

> The first: life with nature. Here the relation vibrates in the dark and remains below language. The creatures stir across from us,

> but they are unable to come to us, and the You we say to them sticks to the threshold of language.
>
> The second: life with men. Here the relation is manifest and enters language. We can give and receive the You.
>
> The third: life with spiritual beings. Here the relation is wrapped in a cloud but reveals itself, it lacks but creates language. We hear no You and yet feel addressed; we answer - creating, thinking, acting: with our being we speak the basic word, unable to say You with our mouth. (pp. 56-7)

Of these relations the most significant is the human You. Buber describes what is involved in the apprehension of the human You:

> When I confront a human being as my You and speak the basic word I-You to him, then he is no thing among things nor does he consist of things.
>
> He is no longer He or She, limited by other Hes and Shes, a dot in the world grid of space and time, nor a condition that can be experienced and described, a loose bundle of named properties. Neighbourless and seamless, he is You and fills the firmament. Not as if there were nothing but he; but everything else lives in <u>his</u> light.
>
> Even as a melody is not composed of tones, nor a verse of words, nor a statue of lines - one must pull and tear to turn a unity into a multiplicity - so it is with the human being to whom I say You. I can abstract from him the colour of his hair or the colour of his speech or the colour of his graciousness; I have to do this again and again; but immediately he is no longer You.
>
> And even as prayer is not in any time but time in prayer, the sacrifice not in space but space in the sacrifice - and whoever reverses the relation annuls the reality - I do not find the human being to whom I say You in any Sometime and Somewhere. I can place him there and have to do this again and again, but immediately he becomes a He or a She, an It, and no longer remans my You....
>
> The Human being to whom I say You I do not experience. But I stand in relation to him, in the sacred basic word. Only when I step out

> of this do I experience him again. Experience is remoteness from You. (pp. 59-60)

The I-You, then, is a reciprocal interdependent relation in which the I engages the You not as an experienced object among others but as a unique presence in its self-contained totality. This interdependence must be stressed: 'I require a You to become; becoming I, I say You' (p. 62). But 'every You in the world is doomed by its nature to become a thing or at least to enter into thinghood again and again' (p. 69). However 'exclusively present it may have been in the direct relationship - as soon as the relationship has run its course or is permeated by means, the You becomes an object among objects, possibly the noblest one and yet one of them, assigned its measure and boundary' (p. 68). This danger of the You degenerating into the It is of especial concern, for only It can be put into an order: 'only as things cease to be our You and become our It do they become subject to coordination' (p. 81). Thus, in a world increasingly penetrated by classificatory institutions, objective rationalism and philistine utility, man is increasingly threatened by 'the despotism of the proliferating It' (p. 97). If he surrenders, 'the relentlessly growing It-world grows over him like weeds and his own I loses its actuality'. He becomes a 'phantom' (p. 96).

Thus man, unless he can regain the You by recognizing and asserting his freedom for the unique particularity of the relation which defines his humanity, slides into the It-world as a 'spook', an abstraction. This fear of man losing the concrete actualness of his existence pervades existential thought.

Heidegger's 'They' and Buber's 'It' define inauthentic modes of Being. When a man lives as one of the impersonal They, his 'ownmost' possibilities are in abeyance; as one of the They he is an It, an objectivized thing which can be organized and used. When a man lives inauthentically he has taken an instrumental attitude towards himself, and to no other existentialist is this attitude more significant than it is to Jean-Paul Sartre.

In the Sartrean world there are three modes of Being: Being-for-itself (conscious Being, i.e. man); Being-in-itself (non-conscious Being, e.g. a tree); Being-for-others (man's self existing externally as an object to the Other). Man is distinguishable from all other things which exist because it is only he who is conscious of himself as a Being in the world, but his consciousness only exists because of other things. Consciousness is always consciousness _of_ something beyond itself. It cannot exist in isolation from the things of the world. Because consciousness can only appear through the existence of other things, it is perpetually aware of a distance between itself and the world. Consciousness, then, because of its absolute dependence on things beyond itself, can never be complete in itself; it is therefore experienced as a 'lack' of Being. In addition, because consciousness is always present to something that it is _not_, and depends on what it is not in order to exist, negation is constitutive of consciousness. These two aspects, lack and negation, are definitional of consciousness. Man is both irreversibly separated from the world, and, as a Being, forever incomplete. Having no way in which he can join himself to the world and have the fullness of being-in-itself, man is a 'nothingness'. But if he were able to deny his nothingness and achieve fullness, he would no longer be free. Life could have no possibilities because it would be a state of inertia. Therefore it is from man's nothingness that his freedom arises. Consciousness, as man's Being, is totally in contrast with other Beings, because its nature is perpetual flux. It cannot be captured; it never _is_. It flits from present to past and anticipates the future. Unlike the things of the world, consciousness has no substance to be defined; it exists indescribably in the mode of freedom. As freedom is fundamental to consciousness, it is imposssible for man to evade it; indeed, he is _condemned_ to be free.

Because man is free he is always confronted with possibilities from among which he is obliged to choose, and, in choosing, he is aware that he is denying all possibilities except the one he has decided on; and as freedom necessarily requires choices to be made about the direction of life, man is ineluctably responsible for himself. Thus choice is always accompanied by a degree of anxiety proportional to the importance of the decision, and it is this anxiety which pursues man throughout his life. Anxiety intensifies when it is recognized that man always chooses in isolation. Because man is the Being by whom values appear in the world, there can be no absolute sanction for these chosen values. He can only _pretend_ that he is _obliged_ to obey the rules of this State, or that God. In every instance it is man who has chosen these rules as binding. He has chosen them in the same way that he chooses his clothes: because they suit him. He can refer to nothing beyond himself in order to 'justify' what he believes or what he does. When a man provides reasons for what he does, they can never serve as excuses for his actions, for the reasons derive from the meanings and values that he has chosen. Even when a man declines to choose between one thing and another, letting life seemingly drift independently of him, his indifference denotes an attitude to life, which is a choice as significant as deciding the issues which he has spurned. Man is therefore always 'engaged', always 'committed' to making judgments of value even when he tries to be inconsequential in the world. He can never stand outside life. He is always in a 'situation'. The only thing for which man is not responsible is his very responsibility: he is 'not free to cease being free'.[3] This unalterable condition of man's existence, Sartre terms 'facticity'.

Because all the values and meanings in the world are derived from man's choice, he 'carries the weight of the whole world on his shoulders; he is responsible for the world and for himself as a way of being'; he is 'compelled to decide the meaning of being' (pp. 553,556). Even the obstacles and difficulties of the world are created by man. Adversities originate in me, for it is I alone who decide what can, and what cannot, be overcome. Degrees of difficulty are always assessed in relation to what kind of man I have decided to make myself. There are no innate cowards or heroes; only those who have decided to limit their freedom to selected definitions of Being. The kind of man I am is not something that I have been given and am obliged to accept. I have no imposed 'essence' which determines my future. I am alive in the world before I decide what I am and what I decide to be: 'existence precedes essence'.[4] That which I may call my essence is a choice about what kind of person I am. This is man's Original Choice. He defines what he is and then proceeds to live accordingly. This pursuit of fulfilling one's self-definition is his Project of Being. Having decided that I am, for example, a coward, I proceed to live a coward's life. I make a choice of myself function as a causal determinant of what I henceforth do. Of all the possibilities in the world, I restrict myself to choosing from among those which an innate coward would be obliged to restrict himself to. Thus the entire range of non-cowardly opportunities that are actually open to me I do not look upon as my opportunities. As a coward who has denied all other modes of existence, I become, to myself and others, a definite person with a predictable life. And yet nothing whatever binds me to this identity. Nothing is fixedly me. I can at any time abolish my individual Project of Being, turning cowardice into heroism. It is I who cause myself to be. Therefore I can always 'transcend' myself. But it is precisely this, according to Sartre, that we, for the most part, try to avoid. We want to be stable and identifiable, so we attempt to enslave our freedom. When we do this, we live inauthentically. We live in 'bad faith'.

Bad faith is a self-deception employed to disguise or nullify the anxiety which inevitably attends the responsibility which freedom entails. Bad faith hides us from the fact that the pattern and the meaning of life can be suddenly rendered valueless by choosing otherwise. The ontological effect of this deception is to make the self an object with a pre-determined and definitive Being, a being-in-itself. In this condition, man provides himself with the illusion that he no longer 'lacks' Being: 'what the for-itself lacks is the self - or itself as an in-itself' (p. 89). It is only because man is free to choose himself that he can pretend to himself and others that he is an enslaved being-in-itself, and it is only because he is never free to be unfree that he can never become truly enslaved.

Sartre describes two patterns of bad faith: Being a Thing, and Being a Role. The first pattern he illustrates in the following way.

> Take the example of a woman who has consented to go out with a particular man for the first time. She knows very well the intentions which the man who is speaking to her cherishes regarding her. She knows also that it will be necessary sooner or later for her to make a decision. But she does not want to realize the urgency; she concerns herself only with what is respectful and discreet in the attitude of her companion. She does not apprehend this conduct as an attempt to achieve what we call 'the first approach'; that is, she does not want to see possibilities of temporal development which his conduct presents. She restricts this behaviour to what is in the present; she does

not wish to read in the phrases which he addresses to her anything other than their explicit meaning. If he says to her, 'I find you so attractive!' she disarms this phrase of its sexual background; she attaches to the conversation and to the behaviour of the speaker, the immediate meanings, which she imagines as objective qualities. The man who is speaking to her appears to her sincere and respectful as the table is round or square, as the wall colouring is blue or grey. The qualities thus attached to the person she is listening to are in this way fixed in a permanence like that of things, which is no other than the projection of the strict present of the qualities into the temporal flux. This is because she does not quite know what she wants. She is profoundly aware of the desire which she inspires, but the desire cruel and naked would humiliate and horrify her. Yet she would find no charm in a respect which would be only respect. In order to satisfy her, there must be a feeling which is addressed wholly to her <u>personality</u> - i.e., to her full freedom - and which would be a recognition of her freedom. But at the same time this feeling must be wholly desire; that is, it must address itself to her body as object. This time then she refuses to apprehend the desire for what it is; she does not even give it a name; she recognizes it only to the extent that it transcends itself toward admiration, esteem, respect and that it is wholly absorbed in the more refined forms which it produces, to the extent of no longer figuring anymore as a sort of warmth and density. But then suppose he takes her hand. This act of her companion risks changing the situation by calling for an immediate decision. To leave the hand there is to consent in herself to flirt, to engage herself. To withdraw it is to break the troubled and unstable harmony which gives the hour its charm. The aim is to postpone the moment of decision as long as possible. We know what happens next; the young woman leaves her hand there, but she <u>does not notice</u> that she is leaving it. She <u>does not notice</u> because it happens by chance that she is at this moment all intellect. She draws her companion up to the most lofty regions of sentimental speculation; she speaks of Life, of her life, she shows herself in her

> essential aspect - a personality, a consciousness. And during this time the divorce of the body from the soul is accomplished; the hand rests inert between the warm hands of her companion - neither consenting nor resisting - a thing. (pp. 55-6)

Sartre then asks: 'What unity do we find in these various aspects of bad faith?' And he answers: 'It is a certain art of forming contradictory concepts which unite in themselves both an idea and the negation of that idea.... Bad faith seeks to affirm their identity while preserving their differences'.

In introducing the second pattern of bad faith, Being a Role, Sartre asks: 'Is man what he is?' It is clear that in some sense he is not because he exists as consciousness of Being. If man is only what he is in the way that a tree is only a tree, then authentic Being as an ideal to strive for would be impossible, for a being-in-itself has no powers to change its Being. The pretence of bad faith is only possible because the Being of man is not fixed:

> Let us consider this waiter in the cafe. His movement is quick and forward, a little too precise, a little too rapid. He comes toward the patrons with a step a little too quick. He bends forward a little too eagerly; his voice, his eyes express an interest a little too solicitous for the order of the customer. Finally there he returns, trying to imitate in his walk the inflexible stiffness of some kind of automaton while carrying his tray with the recklessness of a tightrope-walker by putting it in a perpetually unstable, perpetually broken equilibrium which he perpetually re-establishes by a light movement of the arm and hand. All this behaviour seems to us a game. He applies himself to chaining his movements as if they were mechanisms, the one regulating the other; he gives himself the quickness and pitiless rapidity of things. He is playing, he is amusing himself. But what is he playing? We need not watch long before we can explain it: he is playing _at being_ a waiter in a cafe. There is nothing there to surprize us. The game is a kind of marking out and investigation. The child plays with his body in order to explore it, to take inventory of it; the waiter in the cafe plays with his condition in

order to realize it. This obligation is not different from that which is impressed on all tradesmen. Their condition is wholly one of ceremony. The public demands of them that they realize it as a ceremony; there is the dance of the grocer, of the tailor, of the auctioneer, by which they endeavour to persuade their clientele that they are nothing but a grocer, an auctioneer, a tailor. A grocer who dreams is offensive to the buyer, because such a grocer is not wholly a grocer. Society demands that he limit himself to his function as a grocer, just as the soldier at attention makes himself into a soldier-thing with a direct regard which does not see at all.... There are indeed many precautions to imprison a man in what he is, as if we lived in perpetual fear that he might escape from it, that he might break away and suddenly elude his condition.

In a parallel situation, from within, the waiter in the cafe can not be immediately a cafe waiter in the sense that this inkwell is an inkwell, or the glass is a glass.... It is not that I do not wish to be this person or that I want this person to be different. But rather there is no common measure between his being and mine. It is a 'representation' for others and for myself, which means that I can be he only in representation. But if I represent myself as him, I am not he; I am separated from him as the object from the subject, separated by nothing, but this nothing isolates me from him. I can not be he, I can only play at being him; that is, imagine to myself that I am he.... What I attempt to realize is a being-in-itself of the cafe waiter, as if it were not just in my power to confer their value and their urgency upon my duties and the rights of my position, as if it were not my free choice to get up each morning at five o'clock or to remain in bed, even though it meant getting fired. As if from the very fact that I sustain this role in existence I did not transcend it on every side, as if I did not constitute myself as one beyond my condition. Yet there is no doubt that I am in a sense a cafe waiter - otherwise could I not just as well call myself a diplomat or a reporter? But if I am one, this can not be in the mode of being-in-itself. I am a waiter in the mode of being what I am not.

> Furthermore we are dealing with more than mere social positions; I am never any one of my attitudes, any one of my actions. The good speaker is the one who _plays_ at speaking, because he cannot _be speaking_.... On all sides I escape being and yet - I am. (pp. 59-60)

This second pattern of bad faith leads us directly into a consideration of Being-for-others. Sartre surmounts the familiar solipsistic difficulty of proving the existence of others by referring to the fact of shame, which is entirely the result of being public: 'I have acquired an identity I have not given myself' (p. 260). This new identity which the self accepts is conferred by the Look of the Other. Sartre illustrates the meaning of the Look by imagining a man who, moved by jealousy or vice, is eavesdropping, his eye against a keyhole in the door. In this position of devoted concentration the eavesdropper is aware only of his act, not of himself as a separate object. But then he hears footsteps in the hall, and everything is changed. Suddenly he becomes for himself exactly and only what he appears to the Other. He does not reject how-I-appear-to-the-Other as a strange image. On the contrary, he recognizes, in shame, the truth of this image which the Other has of him. He _is_ that object which the Other is looking at and judging. He sees himself because somebody sees him. Having become momentarily an object to himself among other objects, he is dispossessed of his freedom, enslaved by the freedom of the Other in whose world the eavesdropper exists as a thing. For Sartre this situation is basic to every encounter: all being-with-others is characterized by _conflict_. The conflict arises from the universal human desire for others to conform to the descriptions we have of them. We wish to predict their behaviour entirely, according to the role in which we have cast them. Our desire to do this with other people is even stronger than it is with inanimate objects, for other people are essentially, in themselves, and by their very existence, a danger. Once I realize that I am an object of observation of the Other, I also realize that he will have his own way of assessing me and will try to predict my behaviour. I will reciprocate and likewise try to reduce him to the status of a thing. I will attempt to dispossess him of his freedom to define me. This conflict characterizes all being-with-others, but is intensified in relations of love:

Why does the lover want to be loved? If love were in fact a pure desire for physical possession, it could in many ways be easily satisfied. Proust's hero, for example, who installs his mistress in his home, who can see her and possess her at any time of the day, who has been able to make her completely dependent on him economically, ought to be free from worry. Yet we know that he is, on the contrary, continually gnawed by anxiety. Through her consciousness Albertine escapes Marcel even when he is at her side, and that is why he knows relief only when he gazes on her while she sleeps. It is certain then that the lover wishes to capture a 'consciousness'. But why does he wish it? And how?

The notion of 'ownership', by which love is often explained, is not actually primary. Why should I want to appropriate the Other if it were not precisely a mode of appropriation; it is the Other's freedom as such that we want to get hold of. Not because of a desire for power. The tyrant scorns love, he is content with fear. If he seeks to win the love of his subjects, it is for political reasons; and if he finds a more economical way to enslave them, he adopts it immediately. On the other hand, the man who wants to be loved does not desire the enslavement of the beloved. He is not bent on becoming the object of passion which flows forth mechanically. He does not want to possess an automaton, and if we want to humiliate him, we need only try to persuade him that the beloved's passion is the result of a psychological determinism. The lover will then feel that both his love and his being are cheapened. If Tristan and Isolde fall madly in love because of a love potion, they are less interesting. The total enslavement of the beloved kills the love of the lover. The end is surpassed; if the beloved is transformed into an automaton, the lover finds himself alone. Thus the lover does not desire to possess the beloved as one possesses a thing; he demands a special type of appropriation. He wants to possess a freedom as freedom.

On the other hand, the lover cannot be satisfied with that superior form of freedom which is a free and voluntary engagement. Who would

> be content with a love given as pure loyalty to a sworn oath? Who would be satisfied with the words, 'I love you because I have freely engaged myself to love you and because I do not wish to go back on my word.' Thus the lover demands a pledge, yet is irritated by a pledge. He wants to be loved by a freedom but demands that this freedom as freedom should no longer be free.... He is and consents to be an *object*. But on the other hand, he wants to be the object in which the Other's freedom consents to lose itself.... He does not want to *act* on the Other's freedom but to exist *a priori* as the objective limit of this freedom; that is, to be given at one stroke along with it and in its very upsurge as the limit which the freedom must accept in order to be free.
>
> .... Thus to want to be loved is to infect the Other with one's own facticity; it is to wish to compel him to recreate you perpetually as the condition of a freedom which submits itself and which is engaged; it is to wish both that freedom found fact and that fact have pre-eminence over freedom. (pp. 366-68)

The hopelessness of this situation, arising from the impossible desire that the Other be simultaneously free and enslaved, may lead to behaviour of further futility: masochism and sadism. Whichever mode is adopted, being-with-others is doomed, each trying to evade becoming an object to the Other by attempting to overwhelm the Other's freedom. This conflict cannot even be overcome by solitude, for

> I cannot obtain any truth whatsoever about myself, except through the mediation of another. The Other is indispensable to my existence, and equally so to any knowledge I can have of myself. Under these conditions, the intimate discovery of myself is at the same time the revelation of the Other as a freedom which confronts mine, and which cannot think or will without doing so either for or against me. Thus, at once, we find ourselves in a world which is, let us say, that of 'inter-subjectivity'. It is in this world that man has to decide what he is and what others are.[5]

In such a world, only a decisive commitment to freedom, and therefore the utter rejection of bad faith, can provide a dignified basis for human community. Once a man recognizes the fact of his freedom, he immediately recognizes that he is the foundation of all values. Therefore, because of his inseparability from others, his free choice of values determines the conditions under which others choose. It is on this basis of inter-dependent responsibility for the human world that authenticity prospers as a universalizable ethical code. In concluding thus, Sartre has first to make a logical appeal for the abolition of bad faith:

> One can judge a man by saying that he deceives himself. Since we have defined the situation of man as one of free choice, without excuse and without help, any man who takes refuge behind the excuse of his passions, or by inventing some deterministic doctrine, is a self-deceiver. One may object: 'But why should he not choose to deceive himself?' I reply that it is not for me to judge him morally, but I define his self-deception as an error. Here one cannot avoid pronouncing a judgement of truth. The self-deception is evidently a falsehood, because it is a dissimulation of man's complete liberty of commitment. Upon this same level, I say that it is also a self-deception if I choose to declare that certain values are incumbent upon me; I am in contradiction with myself if I will these values and at the same time say that they impose themselves upon me. If anyone says to me, 'And what if I wish to deceive myself?' I answer, 'There is no reason why you should not, but I declare that you are doing so, and that the attitude of strict consistency alone is that of good faith.'.... The actions of men of good faith have, as their ultimate significance, the quest of freedom itself as such. A man who belongs to some communist or revolutionary society wills certain concrete ends, which imply the will to freedom, but that freedom is willed in community. We will for freedom's sake, in and through particular circumstances. And in thus willing freedom, we discover that it depends entirely upon the freedom of others and the freedom of others depends upon our own. Obviously, freedom as the definition of a man does not depend upon others, but as soon as there is a commitment, I am obliged to will the liberty of others at the same time as my own. I cannot make liberty my aim unless I make that

> of others equally my aim. Consequently, when I recognize as entirely authentic, that man is a being whose existence precedes his essence, and that he is a free being who cannot, in any circumstances, but will his freedom, at the same time I realize that I cannot not will the freedom of others. Thus, in the name of that will to freedom which is implied in freedom itself, I can form judgements upon those who seek to hide from themselves the wholly voluntary nature of their existence and its complete freedom. Those who hide from this total freedom, in a guise of solemnity or with deterministic excuses, I shall call cowards. (pp. 51-52)

This judgement of cowardliness on those who deny their freedom is, I believe, an appropriate way to conclude the summary of a philosophical perspective which will provide the basis for an analysis of the Orwell novel. After briefly identifying what typifies the Orwellian fictional situation, the novels will be examined chronologically. Because we are dealing with _the novel_, _Animal Farm_ will not be separately assessed, but references to that satire will be made in order to demonstrate that, even when Orwell adopts a factual historical pattern of action for his fiction, he injects it with the same existential content which informs the novels.

NOTES

1. Martin Heidegger, _Being and Time_, trans. from the 7th ed. by John Macquarrie and Edward Robinson (Oxford: Basil Blackwell, 1978), p. 68. Henceforth cited in text by page number to this edition.

2. Martin Buber, _I and Thou_. trans. Walter Kaufmann (Edinburgh: T. and T. Clark, 1975), p. 55. Henceforth cited in text by page number to this edition.

3. J.-P. Sartre, _Being and Nothingness_, trans. Hazel E. Barnes (London: Methuen, 1969), p. 439. Henceforth cited in text by page number to this edition.

4. J.-P. Sartre, _Existentialism and Humanism_, trans. Philip Mairet (London: Eyre Methuen, 1973), p. 28.

5. Ibid., p. 45.

Chapter Three

THE ORWELLIAN FICTIONAL SITUATION

As in Greek Tragedy, the protagonist of the Orwell novel is first encountered *in medias res*. Also like Greek Tragedy, the feeling conveyed is that the dice has already been thrown, that what is being witnessed is a predetermined process which is contrived to illustrate the impotence of individual endeavour. The possibility of free will and choice is always present, but, because the Pavlovian perspective prevails, the realization of this possibility never seems credible. Orwell's fiction only rarely presents impartially the problem of free will; it usually concludes by affirming a negative which has been decided before the action begins. The protagonist *has* free will, but the structure in which human life is obliged to exist is such that his freedom is profitless and usually a curse. And it is precisely this structure which overwhelms the individual which seems to engage Orwell most. Conceiving it as a jail, and the man within as an outsider, he creates a world in which his protagonists are imprisoned aliens. The protagonist doesn't temperamentally belong to the situation he feels constrained to accept, and he has the burden of deciding whether to oppose the constraint by arduously authenticating his life, or to relax utterly and gain the inauthentic comforts of normative passivity. He can only annul the vexations of a profitless compromize by either padding his cell with the rewards given to those who obey, or renounce it all and live honestly in painful isolation.

The Orwell novel always begins in an atmosphere of renunciation. The protagonist is discovered in a condition of disgust, regret and frustration, with an underlying anxiety about the tenuousness of personal identity. The protagonist's condition is always attributed to external oppressions triumphing over the urge for an authentic life. Always he is discovered in crisis, and, like Bunyan's Christian, the question which has to be answered is: 'What shall I do?' Irrespective of the Pavlovian character of the novels, the individual is seen to either stand or fall by the strength of his decision. The anxiety of choice in solitude immediately identifies this typical Orwellian situation as existential. And the choice to be made is radical. In the same way that every detail of an argument is invalid if the premise is false, life is felt to be false because it is spuriously rooted. So the choice of claiming an authentic self not only involves rejecting the validity of former life; it involves coping with the insecurity of an untested ontological status.

Chapter Four

BURMESE DAYS

Burmese Days is set in Kyauktada, 'a fairly typical Upper Burma town' with a population of 'about four thousand, including a couple of hundred Indians', 'seven Europeans' and 'two Eurasians'. The Europeans live in the open on the maidan in 'dazzling white bungalows', but the native town is set apart with the courts and the jail and 'mostly hidden in green groves of peepul trees'. All the action, all human relations, and the whole consciousness of the novel is dominated by the presence of the Club. Everything is evaluated with reference to it. What it signifies is of prime importance to everyone.

> In any town in India the European Club is the spiritual citadel, the real seat of the British power, the Nirvana for which native officials and millionaires pine in vain. It was doubly so in this case, for it was the proud boast of Kyauktada Club that, almost alone of Clubs in Burma, it had never admitted an Oriental to membership.[1]

What Orwell manages to convey in his two-paragraph description is the paradoxical strangeness, the almost surreal inversions, which underlie the apparent simplicity of British Imperialism in Kyauktada. A tiny minority of outsiders, having established absolute dominance, are resisting the intrusion of any representative of the great subjugated majority of natives. The outsiders have become the insiders, and the natives are now the outsiders, the 'foreigners'. Additionally the Club itself, because it is almost alone in rejecting Orientals, exists outside the norms. To compound this, there is an outsider within, the timber merchant John Flory. But Flory is not merely an ideological outsider. One of seven whites engulfed by blacks, his skin is 'naturally sallow', and:

> The first thing that one noticed in Flory was a hideous birthmark stretching in a ragged crescent down his left cheek, from the eye to the corner of the mouth. Seen from the left side his face had a battered, woebegone look, as though the birthmark had been a bruise - for it was a dark blue in colour. He was quite aware of its hideousness. And at all times, when he was not alone, there was a sidelongness about his movements, as he manoeuvred constantly to keep the birthmark out of sight. (p. 16)

Flory, then, is presented as an outsider both socially and physically. Accordingly, he lives on the edge of the jungle, an indeterminate region indicating his own unspecifiable identity. Each time he goes to the Club where he ostensibly belongs, he does so from the outer limits of the region inhabited by the whites. As such, Flory is closest to Kyauktada's tiniest minority, the two Eurasians, Francis and Samuel, who are '"complete outcasts"' (p. 117).

The novel opens with the ruthless, hugely bloated Sub-Divisional Magistrate, U Po Kyin. His brilliant success as a native official has been achieved by a methodical devotion to corruption. Inspired by power and prestige, he can ceaselessly conspire, betray and blackmail both native and British because people are worth nothing, just a series of levers with which to prise himself to the top of the pile. One thing remains for him to achieve before building pagodas to appease the gods: Club membership. To become a member he must first eliminate the most likely candidate, the civil surgeon Dr. Veraswami, who is Flory's only friend. That Veraswami has been befriended by a European represents Kyin's greatest obstacle, for it confers prestige. But Kyin is confident; he will use the paper Burmese Patriot to accuse Veraswami of professional malpractice and sedition; in fact, he will accuse him of everything that he himself has perpetrated. And it is this concept of disgrace through disloyalty which is at the heart of the action in Burmese Days. To disgrace a man is to make him worthless to himself by making him worthless to others. Implicitly it is a reliance on the inauthentic tendencies in man. Kyin's understanding of this as the exploitable means to power makes him the prototype for the ultimate master, O'Brien in 1984. Kyin brings shame to man by creating his public fall. But firstly, in order that authority may be convinced of Veraswami's disloyalty, Flory will have to be made to be disloyal to Veraswami by ending the friendship which would otherwise be Veraswami's protection. Kyin is not intimidated: '"Flory will desert his friend quickly enough when the trouble begins. These people have no feeling of loyalty towards a native. Besides, I happen to know that Flory is a coward"' (p. 12). This description of Flory as a coward is quickly confirmed; at the same time that Kyin begins his plotting, Flory enters the Club and is told by Ellis that the Club has received encouragement from the Commissioner to admit an Oriental. Flory says nothing while Ellis continues:

> 'He's asking us to break all our rules and take a dear little nigger-boy into this Club. Dear Dr. Veraswami, for instance. Dr. Very-slimy, I call him. That would be a treat, wouldn't it? Little pot-bellied niggers breathing garlic in your face over the bridge-table. Christ, to think of it! We've got to hang together and put our foot down on this at once.' (p.22)

Ellis, who says he would rather die than see a nigger in the Club, justifies his racism on the grounds that the Burmese are '"a set of damn black swine who've been slaves since the beginning of history"' (p. 24). Immediately afterwards the native butler appears with the drinks, saying that he finds it very difficult to keep the ice cool. Ellis is incensed: '"Don't talk like that, damn you - 'I find it very difficult!' Have you swallowed a dictionary? 'Please, master, can't keeping ice cool' - that's how you ought to talk. We shall have to sack this fellow if he gets to talk English too well"' (p. 25). Of the six whites with whom Flory mixes in the Club, Ellis's attitude towards the blacks is the most harshly inflexible, Macgregor's the most lenient: 'He had no prejudice against the Orientals; indeed, he was deeply fond of them. Provided they were given no freedom he thought them the most charming people alive' (my underlining) (p. 29). As the talk of the barely thinkable possibility of racial equality continues, the deterioration of the Empire is bemoaned and Mrs. Lackersteen proposes a way of punishing the natives for their ingratitude: '"We shall just go. When the natives come to us begging us to stay, we shall say, 'No, you have had your chance, you wouldn't take it. Very well, we shall leave you to govern yourselves.' And then, what a lesson that will teach them!"' (p. 31).

Confronting all these details arising from a dogma which an authentic life would have him oppose, Flory squirms impotently: 'It must not, it could not - no, it simply should not go on any longer! He must get out of this room quickly' (p. 31). In the Club, but not of the Club, Flory is trapped ambiguously in a contradiction between action and professed belief. Although too cowardly to live authentically, throughout the novel his position is consistently existential:

> Humanistic existentialism is unalterably opposed to the exploitation of less developed peoples. As Simone de Beauvoir has put it, any attempted justification of a 'superior' ruling class (whether benevolent or otherwise) is synonymous with a false view of the nature of the 'human'. Such a view denies that freedom which is man's essence. It pretends that a man is predetermined to be one thing rather than another, whereas each man is free to try to make of himself what he will. De Beauvoir is particularly scornful with regard to the arguments often advanced by white colonials to the effect that the natives are patently unable to look after themselves, that they would be better off under more highly civilized protectors, and that perhaps they even prefer a position of dependency.[2]

And it is, above all, this 'false view of the nature of the "human"' which has been institutionalized in the Club as a way of Being for its members. It is an organization for creating and maintaining the false view that man, black or white, has an immutable essence. Thus the blacks, because they have '"been slaves since the beginning of history"', are forever doomed to *be* slaves, that is, their future has been predetermined at birth, an inversion of the existential dictum that existence precedes essence. Orwell shows this indisputably to be a willed self-deception, for, if the blacks are essentially slaves, it would be wholly unnecessary to ensure that they are 'given no freedom'. What the Club tries to hide from is that it is *they* who have imposed an essence on the blacks. Knowing, perhaps only obscurely, that they are responsible, they attempt to justify enslavement by pretending that the blacks were discovered in such a state. This pretence is indispensable to despotism: slavery has to be created in order for the despots to realize their role-identities as masters. The members' individual and corporate identities depend on the blacks conforming to the white concept of genetic inferiority. Any black who deviates from this concept threatens not only the continuing dominance of the whites but the whites' concept of themselves. The paradox of this relation of dependence is shown in the existential farce between Ellis and the butler. The butler, in an almost obligatory act of bad faith, will modify his speech in order for Ellis to retrieve his identity, which is invested in a concept of what a black ought to be. In effect, the butler is being instructed to behave like Sartre's waiter (see above, p. 45). Ellis requires the black butler to be only a black butler, that is, a being-in-itself permanently captured in a role. It is a virulent game: if Ellis can coerce the butler into pretending, Ellis too can pretend; pretend to be only a white master. Ellis needs the butler to reconstitute his briefly lapsed sense of personal solidity.

Ellis exemplifies the man who has chosen passion for his Being: 'Ellis really did hate Orientals - hated them with a bitter, restless loathing as of something evil or unclean' (p. 23). According to Sartre, the man of passionate hatred has chosen passion in preference to reason because reason is circumspect and leaves everything in a state of possible revision; thus the reasonable man is always in a state of suspended Being. Those who hate a race irrationally do so because they want to be fixed and impervious:

> They do not want acquired opinions, they want innate ones; because they are afraid of reasoning, they want to adopt a way of life where reasoning and investigation have only a subordinate role, where one never seeks except for what one has already found, where one becomes nothing but what one was already. There is no such thing except passion. Only a strong emotional commitment can give a lightning certainty; it alone can hold reasoning by the leading-strings, it alone can remain impermeable to experience and subsist through a whole life.

> The Jew is here only a pretext: elsewhere one makes use of the Negro, elsewhere the yellow races. His [the Jew's] existence simply allows the anit-Semite to stifle his anxieties in the egg by persuading himself that his place in the world has always been marked, that it awaits him, and that he has, by tradition, the right of occupying it. Anti-Semitism, in a word, is a fear of the human condition. The anti-Semite is the man who wants to be pitiless rock, furious torrent, destroying thunder; anything but a man.[3]

And indeed, throughout the novel, Ellis is seen only as hater; his personality is utterly subsumed under the category 'racialist'. He has turned his passion into a thing by which he is wholly identified.

Flory, having denied his authentic conscience, is left with a burden of guilt to shed, and as Veraswami's chief function is that of confessor, Flory immediately goes from the Club to be shrived. It is all too easy for Flory. Absolution is certain, involving a ritual dialogue satisfyingly simple. The mild rebukes he receives are really part of a game, an opportunity for Veraswami to celebrate his delight at being allowed to censure a superior. In exchange, Flory is tranquillized, exempted from responsibility. For this role Veraswami is well chosen. Being both black and Anglophile, Flory can deviously pretend that there is much justification for white mastery.

Between Veraswami and Ellis there is a fundamental but disguised similarity. Both men's identities are invested in a passion more important than truth, and both accept obvious contradictions in order to be their passion. Orwell shows here (and throughout his work) that belief, once it is identified with Being, overwhelms all evidence which reason would use to refute it:

> It was a topsy-turvy affair, for the Englishman was bitterly anti-English and the Indian fanatically loyal. Dr. Veraswami had a passionate admiration for the English, which a thousand snubs from Englishmen had not shaken. He would maintain with positive eagerness that he, as an Indian, belonged to an inferior and degenerate race. His faith in British justice was so great that even when, at the jail, he had to superintend a flogging or a hanging, and would come home with his black face faded grey

> and dose himself with whisky, his zeal did not falter. (p. 38)

In addition, as Veraswami proceeds to defend his ideal of white superiority against Flory's contempt for it, he applies the same argument of black dependence which Flory has just heard from Mrs Lackersteen: '"Could the Burmese trade for themselves? Can they make machinery, ships, railways, roads? They are helpless without you"' (pp. 38-39). The significance of remarks of this kind soon becomes clear: Veraswami is arguing for white mastery in order to realize himself as a superior inferior. As an inferior with the advantages of white education and friendship, he is intrinsically asserting his own superiority to all the other blacks in the district. And the innatist argument by which he attempts to achieve this recognition is essentially no different from the one Ellis adopts:

> 'Behold there the degeneracy of the East,' said the doctor, pointing to Mattu, who was doubling himself up like a caterpillar and uttering grateful whines. 'Look at the wretchedness of hiss limbs. The calves of hiss legs are not so thick ass an Englishman's wrists. Look at hiss abjectness and servility. Look at hiss ignorance - such ignorance ass iss not known in Europe outside a home for mental defectives. Once I asked Mattu to tell me hiss age. "Sahib", he said, "I believe that I am ten years old". How can you pretend, Mr Flory, that you are not the natural superior of such creatures?' (p. 42).

Flory, having just come enraged from the Club because of hearing talk of this type, remains completely unconcerned, the negligence of his response seeming to actually imply agreement: '"Poor old Mattu, the uprush of modern progress seems to have missed him somehow"'.

Clearly, then, the relationship between Flory and the doctor is more complex than the flippant 'topsy-turvy' suggests. Veraswami's description says much: Mattu, as a beggar, is dependent and 'helpless' in the same way as the natives are conceived to be by the Europeans, and for the same reason Veraswami receives the white title 'Sahib'. So Orwell's comment on Veraswami becomes charged with irony: 'He was notorious for his soft-heartedness, and all the beggars in Kyauktada made him their target' (p. 42). Some of the horrifying inversions in 1984 seem to have their origins here, both in Flory's ambiguous identity and the doctor's desire to be white to the blacks and black to the whites. Ontologically, both men may be described as 'blackwhite', and the prevalent reasoning may be described as 'doublethink'. Additionally, in their predictable ritualistic discourse which almost renders their presence to one another superfluous, we discover an incipient form of 'duckspeak'. Their being-with-another is based almost wholly on memory. Existentially they ceased talking years ago, and have thus imposed limits on their lives, existing to each other as beings-in-themselves. Even when Flory seems at his most spontaneously honest ('"there's an everlasting sense of being a sneak and a liar that torments us and drives us to justify ourselves night and day"'), we are later told that this is but one part of an argument which, 'as a rule', follows 'the same course, almost word for word' (pp. 37, 39). Evidently they once communicated Being, but now even heresy has been freezed into monotonous orthodoxy. In order to secure the seductive comforts of the they-self, they have ensured that nothing out of character will occur. As with the duckspeakers, the unpredictable has been made almost impossible. Like Beckett's Vladimir and Estragon, they can only express the changeless state of their existence. Therefore, when the unpredictable does occur through the outside agency of Kyin, and Veraswami seeks nomination to the Club for protection, Flory is thrown out of that context which defines them to one another. Under this unexpected pressure to back Veraswami, Flory will nominate him but not support him: '"I'll give you my vote, but I can't do more than that. I'm sorry, but I simply can't"' (p.46). The covert reason why Flory enjoys Veraswami's company is that he is given the relief of confession without any obligation to remedy guilt by act, and this confers upon him the tranquillity of irresponsible being-in-itself. He inauthentically accepts that he is the victim of changeless circumstances, which logically permits him to say that he can't do more. To act according to his professed beliefs and fight for Veraswami's membership would cause a radical revision of his identity and entail the burden of knowing that throughout his life he had been responsible and free to change the shape of the world if he had but chosen to do so. The reason why it is possible for Flory to have such a relationship with Veraswami is paradoxical, for, while apparently finding the doctor a welcome attitudinal contrast to those in the Club, the doctor's views are obviously identical. This paradox is explicable only in terms of another, that is, Flory is a friend of Veraswami <u>only because he is black</u>. Veraswami's blackness is necessary to Flory because he can use to his own advantage a notion in which he does not believe: that black means essence, and that this essence is inferiority. Knowing that Veraswami is powerless, Flory can say what he <u>does</u> believe with impunity. Only Veraswami's blackness makes Flory's confessional relationship with him possible. If Veraswami were white, Flory would be intimidated by him and loathe him.

This 'friendship', although based on falsity and self-deception, is, however, Flory's least alienated relation, therefore indicating the desperate extent of his estrangement from everyone else. Orwell, after showing Flory's estrangement from the Club, and then his more subtle estrangement from Veraswami, moves relentlessly on to his bitter, calculating, essentially 'fallen' relation with his mistress, Ma Hla May, who is body only, a commodity with it-status, a woman 'like a doll' who has been bought from her parents for three hundred rupees (p. 50). Likewise Flory, whose it-status is that of prestigious white who can buy her things and confer upon her the distinction of 'bo-kadaw'. Theirs is the relation which precludes absolutely the possibility of the I-Thou. Her only value is that of flesh, and his only value is the colour of his flesh and what that entails socio-economically; and so in this master-slave relation there is a curious equality. It also exemplifies Flory's deadly self-defeating hypocrisy. Flory, the armchair advocate of racial equality, is, once again, using for his own advantage the notion of ethnic essence which he knows to be spurious. In submitting to this, he establishes the foundations for further inequality, inadvertently encouraging a divisive hierarchy between black and black. Therefore, when he accuses her of having a Burmese lover, she is in the position to respond: '"Urgh! To think of their horrible brown hands, touching me! I should die if a Burman touched me!"' (p. 51). Like Veraswami, she can denigrate her own race because a white man's favours have entitled her to feel special and therefore superior. So Flory, by failing to be the social democrat, does not merely leave the world in its static undemocratic condition but actively assists the suppression of the democratic principle.

Inevitably the it-world is one in which a man stands in conscious and painful solitude. With the Thou absent, the self is experienced as an incompletion, and Nature, the Romantic consolation for deficient relations, is sought. But this also fails:

> A pang went through Flory. Alone, alone, the bitterness of being alone! So often like this, in lonely places in the forest, he would come upon something - bird, flower, tree - beautiful beyond all words, if there had been a soul with whom to share it. Beauty is meaningless until it is shared. If he had one person, just one, to halve his loneliness. (p. 55)

This describes Flory's existential plight: inauthentic self-for-other relations mean personal dismemberment, a kind of pollarding which leaves him aching for self-fulfilment. What Flory has come to realize is that the human 'I', to be complete, must deliver itself to the two-fold relation of the I-Thou. And only with the solidity of this relation behind him will he acquire the strength to oppose the Club and realize his authentic possibilities. Above all, Flory wants to be accepted by another, to be discovered as he is without prior expectations, hence avoiding the manufacture of the role-playing false self. But wherever he goes he is stifled by his cowardice and by what others think he ought to be. After his failure to become united with nature, he returns home, where his servant has prepared the clothes for his sahib to wear at the Club; and once more we see that a person's prestige is derived from the status of another: 'He hated to see his master behaving differently from other white men' (p. 57). Flory obediently goes to the Club, and finding that a libellous article has appeared in the _Burmese Patriot_ which the Club attributes to Veraswami, surrenders to the power of the They and signs a notice saying that it is 'the worst possible moment to consider the election of niggers' (p. 60). Orwell comments:

> He had done it for the same reason as he had done a thousand such things in his life; because he lacked the small spark of courage that was needed to refuse. For, of course, he could have refused if he had chosen; and, equally of course, refusal would have meant a row with Ellis and Westfield. And oh, how he loathed a

> row! The nagging, the jeers! At the very thought of it he flinched; he could feel his birthmark palpable on his cheek, and something happened in his throat that made his voice go flat and guilty. Not that! It was easier to insult his friend, knowing that his friend must hear of it. (p. 61)

Here we see Flory's birthmark associated with inauthentic action. The birthmark becomes 'palpable on his cheek', as if his inauthenticity is an insurmountable fact of life. And yet the facts of the situation are clear: 'he could have refused if he had chosen'. But what follows this passage is a biographical document which, in its devious contradiction, enables Flory to think of his condition as facticity. Because the birthmark in itself is a genuine facticity, he has deceived himself into believing that the attitude he adopts towards it is predetermined:

> Flory had been fifteen years in Burma, and in Burma one learns not to set oneself up against public opinion. But his trouble was older than that. It had begun in his mother's womb, when chance put the blue birthmark on his cheek. He thought of some of the early effects of his birthmark. His first arrival at school, aged nine; the stares and, after a few days, shouts of the other boys; the nickname Blueface, which lasted until the school poet ... came out with the couplet:
>
> New-tick Flory does look rum,
> Got a face like a monkey's bum,
>
> whereupon the nickname was changed to Monkey-bum. (p. 61)

And indeed, the effects <u>are</u> genuine: the stares and the shouts and his nickname are all directly attributable to the fact of a defect over which he has no control. But, as with Orwell in 'Such, Such Were the Joys', Flory accepts defects of the body as evidence of a general constitutional inferiority, a changeless state of Being like the birthmark itself. His Being, therefore, is not what he makes it but the result of adopting what others have imposed. This acceptance of inferior self-for-others constitutes Flory's Original Choice: henceforth he will behave as if inferiority were facticity, not choice.

Thus Flory, having decided to be predetermined, achieves partial relief from the burden of being responsible for the consequences of being free to support Veraswami. The contradiction in these passages, shows both Orwell's concern with permutations of doublethink and its fundamental similarity to existential bad faith.

Sartre, in describing the 'coefficient of adversity', explains precisely Flory's problem of inherited defect:

> Even this disability from which I suffer I have assumed.... I make of it the necessary obstacle for my being, and I cannot be crippled without choosing myself as crippled. This means that I choose the way in which I constitute my disability (as 'unbearable', 'humiliating', 'to be hidden', 'to be revealed to all', 'an object of pride', 'the justification for my failures', etc.).
>
> If we have chosen humiliation as the very stuff of our being, we shall realize ourselves as humiliated, embittered, inferior, etc. We are not dealing here with _givens_ with no further meaning. But the man who realizes himself as humiliated thereby constitutes himself as a _means_ of attaining certain ends: the humiliation chosen can be, for example, identified like masochism with an instrument designed to free us from existence-for-itself; it can be a project of getting rid of our anguishing freedom to the advantage of others; our project can be to cause our being-for-itself to be entirely absorbed by our being-for-others. At all events the 'inferiority complex' can arise only if it is founded on a free apprehension of our being-for-others. This being-for-others as a _situation_ will act in the capacity of a cause, but all the same it must be discovered by a _motive_ which is nothing but our free project. Thus the inferiority which is felt and lived is the chosen instrument to make us comparable to a _thing_; that is, to make us exist as a pure outside in the midst of the world. But it is evident that it must be lived in accordance with the _nature_ which we confer on it by this choice - i.e., in shame, anger, and bitterness. Thus to _choose_ inferiority does not mean to be sweetly contented with an _aurea mediocritas_; it is to produce and to

> assume the rebellion and despair which constitute the revelation of this inferiority.[4]

The biographical passages in Burmese Days record the growing petrification of freedom and a solidification of the self-for-others. Along with this life of attrition, waste, and sterile repetitions is the developing sense of Flory's exile from England. This voluntary exile seems strange if it is not seen from the perspective of Flory's project of inferiority, for the chosen land of his adoption is one in which all those aspects which contributed to his ignominy are intensified. It becomes apparent that Flory has actually sought those conditions which extend his estranging self-for-others. His identity as outcast inferior assumes the kind of ojectivity of Being which it would not have had if he had remained in England, where 'everyone is free' (p. 66). Whereas Burma

> is a stifling, stultifying world in which to live. It is a world in which every word and every thought is censored ... even friendship can hardly exist when every white man is a cog in the wheels of despotism. Free speech is unthinkable. All other kinds of freedom are permitted. You are free to be a drunkard, an idler, a coward, a backbiter, a fornicator; but you are not free to think for yourself. Your opinion on every subject of any conceivable importance is dictated for you by the pukka sahib's code.
>
> .... You are a creature of the despotism, a pukka sahib, tied tighter than a monk or a savage by an unbreakable system of tabus. (p. 66)

So the freedoms that Flory is allowed are only those which are compatible with a life of failure and inferiority: the prohibition on freedom of speech is agreeable to a man whose project is to be an inauthentic self-for-others requiring a system of repressive social norms which can be falsely construed as an obligation to be quite without responsibility. Flory seeks a massive justification for failure: everything can be blamed on either birth or the system. He wants it to seem that his life cannot be otherwise in precisely the same way that his disfigured face cannot be otherwise. Interpreting everything as facticity, he even persists with the original image: 'eight years of Eastern life, fever, loneliness and intermittent drinking, had set their mark on him' (my underlining) (p. 65).

But what Flory cannot evade is the nausea of his perpetual self-deception: 'In the end the secrecy of your revolt poisons you like a secret disease. Your whole life is a life of lies' (p. 66). And this is not the only injurious consequence; Flory has now become a genuine exile from his homeland, which is in itself a further problem for an ontology already insecure: 'He had sent deep roots, perhaps his deepest, into a foreign country' (p. 68). Resigned to this, he sees as the only possible redemption a relation which will transcend, or at least compensate for, the worthlessness that pretence has made of his life. The relation would have to be unlike anything he had previously known, an I-Thou which would involve his whole Being:

> There was, he saw clearly, only one way out. To find someone who would share his life in Burma - but really share it, share his inner secret life, carry away from Burma the same memories as he carried. Someone who would love Burma as he loved it and hate it as he hated it. Who would help him live with nothing hidden, nothing unexpressed. Someone who understood him: a friend, that was what it came down to.
>
> A friend. Or a wife? That quite impossible she. (p. 69)

This is, of course, in fundamental contrast to Flory's current relations, in which the crucial testing element of fidelity is missing. That the bond of fidelity is crucial, the very basis for meaning among persons (as opposed to it-relations in which no other self can be betrayed), is shown when Flory receives an anonymous letter from U Po Kyin's scribe which calumniates Veraswami and warns Flory that such a friendship can lead only to personal dishonour:

> The obvious, the decent course was to give the letter to Dr. Veraswami and let him take what action he chose.
>
> And yet - it was safer to keep out of this business altogether.... With Indians there must be no loyalty, no real friendship. Affection, even love - yes.... Even intimacy is allowable, at the right moments. But

> alliance, partisanship, never! Even to know the rights and wrongs of a 'native' quarrel is a loss of prestige.
>
> .... If he, Flory, were too conspicuously the doctor's partisan, there might be hell to pay. Much better to pretend that the letter had never reached him. The doctor was a good fellow but as to championing him against the full fury of pukka sahibdom - ah, no, no! What shall it profit a man if he save his own soul and lose the whole world? (p. 75)

Fidelity for Flory, then, wholly issues from fear of the local power group, and, as such, is the fidelity of the They. If Veraswami belonged to this group, Flory would instantly cast his allegiance there. In Kyauktada fidelity is created by the abstract It of the They, and those comprizing the It are anybody, insofar as those in power are interchangeable and at any time dispensable. The individual is unspecifiable and therefore null. Flory's need for the I-Thou involves the need to break with the They and establish fidelity as the fundamental relational premise; to at least be true to someone after leading 'a life of lies'. Where betrayal is always possible, contingency penetrates all things, and where there is contingency the knowing of another is characterized by the tenuous and superficial. Thus it is that Flory understands himself to be 'drifting, rotting, in dishonour and horrible futility', desperately trying to realize 'the possibility of a decent human being' (pp. 69-70). Clearly the 'decency' is the felt quality of a life based on the fidelity of an authentic existence. Flory, having twice deceived Veraswami, knows that, in the end, the principal victim is himself; or, as Gabriel Marcel has said: 'One can betray only one's self. All treason is simply a lie'. Because 'we live in a world where betrayal is possible at every moment and in every form', 'it is fidelity which matters most', for it is a recognition of an 'ontological permanency'. Through the fidelity which exists between the 'I' and the 'Thou', the contingent world of betrayal is overcome.[5]

But not only does Flory fail in his attempt at an I-Thou through the ridiculous inappropriateness of his choice, he fails because his project of failure and inferiority remains basically unreformed. He wants the I-Thou in order to hide from his freedom, using it as a device of compromise by which he will be enabled to live less tormentedly in the world of the They. The clue to the truth of this is that, in imagining an I-Thou, he sees it as involving all the confessional elements which typify his inauthentic relations with Veraswami. Clearly Flory wishes to remain exactly as he is but have another to give him a more meaningful absolution than Veraswami is able to provide. What he really wants is a *white* woman, one who has been endowed by the They with enough status to have his secret heresy partially condoned. Flory's need for understanding is basically a need for *permission* and for someone to share the responsibility for the thoughts he is too timid to reveal except to 'inferior' blacks. Even if Veraswami were to share all Flory's opinions, Flory's problems would remain, for Veraswami can never have the authority to meaningfully sanction any opposition to the They. Flory's desire is a desire common to every Orwellian protagonist: a desire to be *inside the whale*, whether it be the leviathan of society or an immunized enclave on the edge of it. In other words, to have a *sanctioned* helplessness before the oppressive demands of the public world. The images of enclosure in the novels are all related to the desire for the suspension of the burden of responsibility which freedom necessarily entails. The protagonists search for that state which provides the *appearance* of determinism and constraint behind which they can justifiably hide their freedom (in this particular respect, Winston Smith is an exception). But this quest can only lead to 'a life of lies'.

Even the situation in which Flory first meets Elizabeth Lackersteen is based on a deception. Elizabeth, deceived about the temperament of domestic buffalo, lets out a 'terrified scream' which brings Flory to her unnecessary rescue. Being deceived about the buffalo, she is, predictably, deceived about *the kind of man* who would lunge into the jungle to save her. In fact Flory, at that moment, becomes for another an entirely different kind of man. After a long history of cowardice he is seen as a hero. Flory too is deceived about Elizabeth, inferring from the facts of her biography a life which is in radical contrast to the truth. So within half an hour both are relating on terms based on false premisses. Both *want* to believe. Both have inferred agreeable wholes from fragments: 'Paris', to Flory, means '"sitting in cafes with foreign art students, drinking white wine and talking about Marcel Proust"'; and saving her from the buffalo and killing an elephant means to Elizabeth that Flory is 'almost a hero' (pp. 81-82). In these judgments both have in fact defined a person who is the exact antithesis of what is true of the person actually encountered. Both believe the other to be what he is not. The hero is a coward, and the aesthete is a philistine. Once again there is the generation of paradoxes in the same terms as those in 1984: 'freedom is slavery' and 'war is peace'. Subsequently in their relations, the only times when Flory and Elizabeth experience their original rapture is when the original concept of the other seems the truth. When Flory can appear the hero she can almost love him, and when she almost loves him she is in that kind of excitable condition which can be associated with the 'artistic temperament', so therefore he can love her. Clearly, if it were not for the original misconceptions, they would have nothing whatever to do with one another. The last thing she wants is a cowardly, ignominious man of minimal Club status, and the last thing he wants is a snobbish, philistine, main-stream orthodox incapable of protecting him from the rancour of the They. An additional relational obstacle is that neither has enough goodwill and sensitivity to admit any argument capable of modifying their own notions about what is desirable in life. They are fixed, finished, beings-in-themselves. And although Orwell apparently expresses the formation of character deterministically, what he actually provides is a description of a process in which the choice of Being is evident. As with Flory, the crucial stage in Elizabeth's self-development occurs at school:

> There is a short period in everyone's life when his character is fixed forever; with Elizabeth, it was those two terms during which she rubbed shoulders with the rich. Thereafter her whole code of living was summed up in one belief, and that a simple one. It was that the Good ('lovely' was her name for it) is synonymous with the expensive, the elegant, the aristocratic; and the Bad ('beastly') is the cheap, the low, the shabby, the laborious.... The feeling subtilized itself as Elizabeth grew older, diffused itself through all her thoughts. Everything from a pair of stockings to a human soul was classifiable as 'lovely' or 'beastly'. (p. 86)

Here we have a description not of what Elizabeth was made to be but of what she made herself be. Her experience in an expensive girls' school not only didn't compel her into a mould to which she was henceforth 'fixed', it didn't even make her a snob. She chose the dichotomy between the 'lovely' and the 'beastly' because she already, necessarily, was a snob. The dichotomy merely gave her the terms, the rationale, which defined the way in which it was possible to live knowingly as a snob. As with Flory, what Orwell records is that phase in life during which the decision to be something was made. For them both, life was seen in terms of an either/or, and Orwell throws together a woman who has chosen the 'lovely' and a man who has chosen the 'beastly'. As for Winston Smith, the horror of life is the anarchy behind what first appeared immutable: the 'lovely' 'hero' Flory becomes the 'beastly' degenerate; the 'lovely' 'aesthete' Elizabeth becomes the 'beastly' philistine; the 'beastly' oppressor Big Brother becomes the 'lovely' benefactor. What it is important to note is that transformations are transformations of Being; thus a stress on transformations indicates an anxiety about Being, an ontological insecurity. Seen in this way, all the paradoxes and ironies evident throughout Orwell's corpus acquire an existential status, for the presentation of the ironic and the paradoxical is inseparably linked with the idea of transformation. Indeed, these categories cannot function if the concept of transformation is missing. This insistence on the alarming possibilities of one thing becoming another is a perspective which results from a concern with the problematic issues of whether or not 'truths' can be absolute, and, as such, is rooted in ontological doubt. What Orwell is really showing in Elizabeth's development of two categories by which she can assess life is the growth of ideology, the attempt to contain life in a changeless formula which provides the illusion that man is a completed Being, an object. Ideology, in Orwell's terms, is the attempt to impose definitive Being on man and thus have the same power over him as over the material world; and, as man is his views, the commitment to an ideology turns the ideologist into an in-itself form. As allegiance to dogma is choice, it is not to be separated from the desire to make of oneself a being-in-itself.

This impulse towards reductionism in order to capture Being is seen at work in Animal Farm where similar categories to Elizabeth's operate: 'four legs good, two legs bad'.[6] Here, Orwell takes a contemporary ideology to illustrate *any* ideology; it is the ubiquitous pattern which is being villified, not the *kind* of ideology. Necessarily, Orwell is saying, ideology cannot capture Being, because man is free to choose his own form and therefore escape all definitions. This is shown in the final, crucial scene of *Animal Farm*, where a transformation occurs in which the imposture of a false essence is escaped. Appropriately the context in which this is perceived is one of betrayal and deception. The man-pigs have betrayed an essence which, from the beginning, was an invention, a device which merely suited the pigs for the purposes of power. The other animals, looking in through the window, confront mutants, images of indeterminate Being which destroy the notions of absolute truth and 'fixed' character. The mutants are neither one thing nor the other: blackwhite. Flory, as a socio-physical outsider with no sense of truly belonging anywhere, is the pigs' remote ancestor, and Winston Smith represents the culmination of this tradition by undergoing a transformation in which the self is abolished and replaced. That this concept of transformation of Being is not peripheral to Orwell's understanding of the structure of reality is encouraged by what we know to be the most salient feature of his life, that is, that lower-upper-middle class Eric Blair transformed himself into down-and-out George Orwell.

Although both Flory and Elizabeth have established relations on false assumptions, it is only he who attempts to maintain her image of him. Even at their first meeting he feels obliged to pretend that his mistress is a servant's wife come to do the laundry, and within a fortnight he has paid her off and sent her away for good. So, paradoxically, in playing the role of a hero, he has to be devious and cowardly, for heroes cannot have even marginal associations with 'degenerate' races. Flory has to falsify his past to *become* a hero. But where he goes radically wrong is in his assessment of Elizabeth as an aesthete; and as she is firmly not playing this role for anyone, she doesn't conceal her disgust for his partizan social anthropology. His taking her on excursions to see the bazaar and the dance are similar to Orwell's dives into the 'sub-world', but, for Elizabeth, familiarity with the beastly does not make it more tolerable, and Flory, by association, is worsened. Flory is smitten by the *idea* of her, and strives to believe that the original conception is the genuine one; 'to recapture that easy and delightful friendship of their first meeting' is an aim which eludes him, for

> though Flory spent hours in Elizabeth's company, and often they were alone together, he was never for an instant at ease with her. They talked - so long as they talked of trivialities - with the utmost freedom, yet they were distant, like strangers. He felt stiff in her presence, he could not forget his birthmark .... After ten days they seemed no nearer the relationship he wanted.
>
> For somehow, he had never been able to talk to her as he longed to talk. To talk, simply to talk! It sounds so little, and how much it is! When you have existed to the brink of middle age in bitter loneliness, among people to whom your true opinion on every subject on earth is blasphemy, the need to talk is the greatest of all needs. Yet with Elizabeth serious talk seemed impossible. It was as though there had been a spell upon them that made all their conversation lapse into banality; gramophone records, dogs, tennis racquets - all that desolating Club-chatter. She seemed not to <u>want</u> to talk of anything but that. (p. 111)

This, then, is Elizabeth, one of the They existing by mere surface tension, mesmerized by orthodoxy and hiding from the beastly depths of Being by the flitting randomness of 'Idle Talk'. The disconnectedness of Idle Talk is her security, for it starts and finishes at any point; lacking any definite content or logical rigour, it leads nowhere and discovers nothing. And it is precisely this mode of discourse which it is necessary for her to maintain if she is to live perpetually on the phantom plane of the 'lovely'. What, therefore, outrages her is that the hero Flory threatens her with the 'beastly'. This being the case, she has to assert to excess the beastliness of the beastly. Even more unsettling is Flory's threat of transformation; he actually tries to invert the notions on which her identity and her relations with the world depend:

> She would say to Flory, as she would have said to anybody:
>
> 'How <u>revoltingly</u> ugly these people are,

> aren't they?'
> '<u>Are</u> they? I always think they're rather charming-looking, the Burmese. They have such splendid bodies!' (p. 113)

It is through exchanges of this kind that she begins to grasp that Flory's views are 'not the views an Englishman should hold' (p. 112). But it is not merely that she has a violent aversion to any suggestion of the heterodox on the grounds of prestige and propriety; like Ellis, who bifurcates mankind into black and white, she is existentially disturbed by the possibility that the world could be otherwise. The world <u>must</u> be divided and comprehended within the formula she has imposed upon it, otherwise she is displaced and lost, the structure of her life wrecked by the relativity of values and the frightening impermanence which the recognition of freedom creates.

Elizabeth is captured by the principles of bivalence and the Excluded Middle. All of the world's phenomena are ranked behind either the beastly or the lovely, so any concession to Flory about judgments of value will inevitably entail not a partial revision of judgment but a complete conversion to the opposite, that is, a transformation. And for her, the problem with Flory is that he continually offers a baffling antithesis:

> 'Those small feet are beautiful according to Chinese ideas,' said Flory.
> 'Beautiful! They're so horrible I can hardly look at them. These people must be absolute savages!'
> 'Oh no! They're highly civilized; more civilized than we are, in my opinion. Beauty's all a matter of taste.' (p. 123)

'"Beauty's all a matter of taste"' is the observation that has most horror for Elizabeth. It poses that arbitrary world which those striving for essence are compelled to deny. If the 'lovely' is relative, then Elizabeth herself might be 'beastly'. Black could be white, and white could be black. Appropriately Orwell has her confront the embodiment of this paradox, a perfect example of the Middle Included: the Eurasians, Francis and Samuel. Being examples of the Included Middle existing in a world where the pursuit of the fulness of Being is paramount, they are, understandably, '"complete outcasts"', for, ideologically, they can have no existence (p. 117). Therefore Elizabeth snubs them. She wants them not to be. She wants all the evidence for the Included Middle to be ejected, so she recommends that a subscription be collected so that they can be sent away. But given that the Eurasians have to remain, they must be allocated according to either the lovely or the beastly. There is no question of them being lovely, so, as with the Burmese, Elizabeth pursues a process which renders them predeterminedly beastly. Firstly she subsumes them under _type_: 'She had placed their type now. They looked dagoes. Like those Mexicans and Italians and other dago people who play the mauvais role in so many a film'. Then she confers upon them a kind of ultimate beastliness, an absolute fixedness of Being for which transformations are unthinkable: '"They looked awfully degenerate types, didn't they? So thin and weedy and cringing: and they haven't got at all _honest_ faces. I suppose these Eurasians _are_ very degenerate? I've heard that half-castes always inherit what's worst in both races"' (p. 117). But Flory responds characteristically, providing the reasoned case which she least wants to hear:

> 'But our attitude to them is rather beastly. We always talk of them as though they'd sprung up from the ground like mushrooms, with all their faults ready-made. But when all's said and done, we're responsible for their existence.'
>
> 'Responsible for their existence?'
>
> 'Well, they've all got fathers, you see.'
>
> 'Oh ... Of course there's that.... But after all, _you_ aren't responsible. I mean, only a very low kind of man would - er - have anything to do with native women, wouldn't he?'
>
> 'Oh, quite. But the fathers of both these two were clergymen in holy orders, I believe.' (p. 117)

So not only is Elizabeth compelled to recognize that the whites are responsible, she is faced with yet another paradox: that the whites who have made half-blacks belong to an organization traditionally dedicated to moral elevation and the purity of Being.

For the same reason that Elizabeth attempts to impose a definitive category upon the Eurasians, the Eurasians attempt to impose a category upon themselves, and in this now familiar world of paradox and irony it is predictable that the category which they attempt to impose is the opposite of Elizabeth's. They endeavour to be white; they endeavour to be only white. The further paradox here is that they endeavour to be only white because of their intense awareness of being half black. So their endeavour is inspired by the knowledge that achievement is impossible. This, of course, is doublethink; and it is significant that this form of 'reasoning' naturally issues from those who, inauthentically engaged in the pursuit of being-in-itself, are obliged to obey the principle of the Excluded Middle. The pursuit of essence, of ethnic purity, leads the Eurasians in particular to doublethink, for, unlike the blacks and the whites, they are demonstrably neither one thing nor the other. And because essence is pursued by both black and white, the Eurasians are '"complete outcasts"'. They belong nowhere because they cannot conform to the universal either/or categories of Being. Being visually anomalous, their ontological deficiency is evident to both races; so in order to capture racial essence they are obliged to re-locate the evidence for purity in an area which cannot be denied because it cannot be seen: the thickness of the skull. Perpetually they deny one half of themselves. To have a prestigious self-for-others they pretend to be white clones. Like Flory, they have chosen 'a life of lies':

> 'Their drop of white blood is the sole asset they've got. Poor Francis, I never meet him but he begins telling me about his prickly heat. Natives, you see, are supposed not to suffer from prickly heat - bosh, of course, but people believe it. It's the same with sunstroke. They wear those huge topis to remind you that they've got European skulls. A kind of coat-of-arms.' (p. 116)

The Eurasians want to be pukka sahibs, and Flory, perhaps the only white who will talk to them, does so because he is trying not to be a pukka sahib. So both Flory and the Eurasians are asserting themselves ontologically when they talk. They have conceptualized Being. Each makes the other capable of realizing themselves conceptually: Flory can't realize what he is trying to be without the presence of the Eurasians or the natives, and the Eurasians can't realize themselves as pukka sahibs without the presence of a white.

Although Flory's heretical assertions have disturbed Elizabeth, he is nonetheless still in favour, both because the misconceived glamour of their first meeting remains alive and because there is the prospect of him killing the beastly on a hunting trip. And this trip, which holds the promise of deepening relations, is enough to inject into Flory a sense of personal specialness and therefore the capacity to resist the hostility of the They. With Elizabeth apparently behind him, he can now rebel. So after a fortnight's absence he visits Veraswami and commits himself to nominate him in order to protect him from the mounting libels of U Po Kyin:

> Flory could not help laughing as he walked up the hill. He was definitely committed now to proposing the doctor's selection. And there would be such a row when the others heard of it - oh, such a devil of a row! But the astonishing thing was that it only made him laugh. The prospect that would have appalled him a month back now almost exhilarated him.
>
> Why? And why had he given his promise at all? It was a small thing, a small risk to take - nothing heroic about it - and yet it was unlike him. Why, after all these years - the circumspect, pukka sahib-like years - break all the rules so suddenly?
>
> He knew why. It was because Elizabeth, by coming into his life, had so changed it and renewed it that all the dirty, miserable years might never have passed. Her presence had changed the whole orbit of his mind.... Where is the life that late I led? he thought. Just by existing she had made it possible for him, she had even made it natural to him, to act decently. (pp. 143-44)

Fidelity, then, is now possible; but as soon as this is realized the faithless action of the immediate past works to destroy his optimism: Hla May returns in piteous abjection and implores Flory to have her back. The vicious circle of prestige and disgrace appears once more: Flory's new fidelity to Elizabeth and Veraswami was acquired at the expense of abandoning his black mistress. This he had to do in order to create the right image for Elizabeth, but because Hla May has fallen from the prestige of being a bo-kadaw she has become both alienated and disgraced among her own race:

> 'How can I go back, to be jeered at and pointed at by those low, stupid peasants whom I despise? I who have been a bo-kadaw, a white man's wife, to go home to my father's house, and shake the paddy basket with old hags and women who are too ugly to find husbands! Ah, what shame, what shame! ... I am ruined, ruined! What man will marry me after I have lived two years in your house? You have taken my youth from me. Ah, what shame, what shame!' (pp. 145-46)

Ma Hla May has, like Flory, Veraswami and the Eurasians, become an outsider. Belonging to neither black nor white, she occupies the ontologically perilous zone of the Included Middle. Repeatedly expressed in Burmese Days is the causal connection between one person's rise and another's fall, and the fall is always the shame of lost prestige. So while Ma Hla May falls from prestige into shame before the censure of the They, Flory rises to a level from which he feels able to oppose the They. The reinstatement of Ma Hla May would entail Flory's loss of Elizabeth, and his loss of Elizabeth would return him to that state of weakness which would ensure that Veraswami remained unnominated to the Club and thus vulnerable to the disgrace which is essential if U Po Kyin is to rise. It is all a struggle to acquire eminence in one's self-for-others. For the self to have validity, it must be sanctioned by the omnipotent They. As the novel progresses, Veraswami's '"prestige iss everything"' achieves the status of universal law; to have no prestige in the sight of others is to be invisible and consequently a nothing to one's self (p. 44). What emerges from these self-for-others relations is the contingency of Being. At any time a person's world can be reconstructed by the whim of another. In such a world, power is the power to modify or transform a person's conception of himself, to get him to accept the impossibility of subjective self-definition.

The immense success of the hunt is mostly due to Elizabeth's rapture over Flory's mastery. As in their first meeting, he dismisses the threatening 'beastly' from the 'lovely' white world, and assumes once more the role of hero: 'She felt almost an adoration for Flory now that she had seen how he could shoot' (p. 156). At this time of restored prestige she will marry him if he asks, but, just as he is about to, an earthquake intervenes, and he is obliged to wait until the morning. But in the morning the first person he meets is a stranger, the arrogant, militaristic, upper-class Verrall, who has just been tent-pegging with 'matchless grace' on the maidan. Flory is afflicted by a 'horrible sense of inferiority', and feels 'completely _de trop_' (pp. 175-76). Seeing Elizabeth approach, he is inspired to emulate Verrall, but his saddle slips before the horse has taken two bounds, and he falls. As he is sprawled and humiliated on the ground, with one hand hiding the birthmark, she looks at him and through him 'as though he had not existed', and walks past 'as though he had been a dead dog' (pp. 178-179). Suddenly Flory's life has reverted to its customary ignominy, having the same 'dog' status as his discarded mistress's. And this is appropriate, for it is chiefly because Elizabeth now knows about the liaison that she now snubs him. Everything seems to be lost; even his apparent mastery over beasts has disappeared.

Flory's public humiliation derives from the sudden failure in credibility of his false self-for-others. The whole act was performed _only to be judged_. Thus, what he is to himself is being delivered over to the others. He is asking to be described and is therefore committed to realizing whatever definition the others bestow. Existentially, an act of this type can create only estrangement: 'from the moment that I become preoccupied about the effect I want to produce on the other person, my every act, word and attitude loses its authenticity'.[7] In addition, the act was in itself inspired by the attempt to live in accordance with Elizabeth's false notion of him as hero, so even the confidence behind the attempt to be masterly has no grounding in the actual. There is also hypocrisy in the act, as Flory declares himself a dissenter, one who finds only vacancy and stupidity in the way of life which Verrall represents.

Verrall's unexpected appearance provides an important contrast. As distinct from Flory, Verrall is precisely the kind of man he wants to be; the despairing problematical gap between aspiration and accomplishment does not exist in him. He has self-coincidence; and it is because of this that Verrall, of all those in _Burmese Days_, is the person who most closely approximates being-in-itself. Thus the description of him sitting on his horse 'as though he were part of it' is existentially meaningful (p. 174). Wanting only to be a horseman, he is seen physically as a horse-man. Through the horse, he has gained thinghood, pure Being. Therefore Flory, who has the widest gap between existence and Being, is seen in hopeless and helpless separation from his horse. Being escapes him, 'careering away over the maidan' (p. 177). Seeing him thus separated, with all the solidity of Being lost, Elizabeth can look 'at him and through him as though he had not existed' (p. 178). The act of falling disengages him from her concept of him as a hero quite as much as the discovery of his 'beastly' relations with a native.

But in Verrall, Elizabeth finds a most exalted replacement For Flory. Verrall, of course, because he is part of the horse, cannot fall; he cannot degenerate and sully white essence by having relations with blacks which may produce Eurasians. Verrall *is* something in a way that Flory can never be. Verrall has the feeling and the appearance of full Being. Arrived in a community which craves this fulness, he is resented by all but the women, Elizabeth and her aunt, who both, in a patriarchal society, can feed off this fulness in the same way that Ma Hla May did with Flory. For the men, Verrall is a negative resource, the sublime male chauvinist whose presence enfeebles existing male authority. The Club men feel their lack of Being in his presence. Verrall has *style*, the illusion that a man's existence is not random and contingent but deliberate and justified. He makes them feel '*de trop*', like Flory.

The image of full Being which Verrall as horseman presents is repeated a week later when Verrall attends the Club for the first time and dances with Elizabeth: 'Verrall danced as he rode, with matchless grace'. Then comes the image of his fulness and the consequent vacuity of the spectators:

> Verrall and Elizabeth danced on and on, indefatigably, a pale voluptuous shape in the gloom. *They moved in perfect unison like some single animal*. Mr. Macgregor, Ellis, Westfield and Mr. Lackersteen stood watching them, their hands in their pockets, finding nothing to say. The mosquitoes came nibbling at their ankles. Someone called for drinks, but the whisky was like ashes in their mouths. The bowels of all four older men were twisted with bitter envy. (pp. 199-200) (My underlining)

Elizabeth is gratefully drawn into participating in his Being and smugly gorges there, speculating over his life in the same way that Flory speculated over hers. The ontological significance of the horse remains throughout their brief relationship. It is almost as if their medium for reality is through the horse, as if all else would dissolve without it: 'How splendid it was, that equestrian world, how splendid! And it was her world, she belonged to it, she had been born for it. These days, she lived, thought, dreamed horses, almost like Verrall himself' (p. 203).

While all this ecstasy of belonging is occurring, Flory is away in the jungle, eroding with jealousy, the world made meaningless by her absence. His fall from grace is complete. In his despairing alienation he is once again sundered from nature; he is 'alone with his thoughts among the endless, mindless leaves' (p. 204). All renovating possibilities seem closed, having 'dirtied himself beyond redemption' (p. 186). He is abandoned, solitarily pondering over his dreadful facticity: 'nothing would ever make him young again, or take away his birthmark and his decade of lonely debaucheries' (p. 215). But it is in this condition that he returns to Kyauktada and bravely executes his promise to nominate Veraswami. In a world shattered by infidelity, he dredges the strength to oppose the Club even though it is too late to save the doctor. In Flory's life, everything is too late. Cowardice and willed self-deception have deferred decisions beyond the point of any real effect. But Flory is determined. As he waits in the Club for the general meeting to begin, he watches a graphic metaphor of the burden of the One opposing the Many:

> In the channel, by the nearer bank, a huge, clumsy Indian barge struggled with desperate slowness against the racing current. At each stroke the ten rowers, Dravidian starvelings, ran forward and plunged their long primitive oars, with heart-shaped blades, into the water. They braced their meagre bodies, then tugged, writhed, strained backwards like agonized creatures of black rubber, and the ponderous hull crept onwards a yard or two. Then the rowers sprang forward, panting, to plunge their oars again before the current should check her. (p. 220)

Flory does stand up and propel himself against the mainstream. But, having proposed Veraswami, the finalizing vote is interrupted (like his proposal to

Elizabeth) by a seismic event: the barge has brought a body. Maxwell has been killed by natives. Consequently, Flory's disgrace is deepened. It seems almost 'horrible' that he was busy nominating a native while Maxwell's white body was being returned for burial. So now his rejection is overtly twofold. Both the Club and Elizabeth think him odious for different reasons, but the reasons have the same root: Flory is loathed because his association with blacks injures white prestige, for it blurs the distinction between being white and being black. He threatens to dilute the one hundred per cent whiteness of Being, undermines belief in being-in-itself. This is his only sin. Only by retrieving his heroism and therefore denying his authentic impulses can he restore the prestige which will render him desirable again. In the world of the They, the only true disgrace is the heresy of authenticity.

The opportunity for reviving his heroism quickly occurs when, the following evening, the Burmese rebel against the Club, surrounding it and throwing rocks. The club will be stormed. It is an unprecendented crisis. Word has to be passed to the military police, and the only way to do this is by the river. Flory proposes this and goes alone. Now, for once, he is acting with the whites against the blacks. In contrast to the authentic heroism of opposing the whites in favour of the blacks, this heroism is easy, and, as usual, disproportionately rewarded. Unlike swimming desperately against the current like the barge, floating in the mainstream of the They is effortless. He plunges into the river, and when he surfaces he finds 'that the swift current had floated him twenty yards already' (p. 237). Indeed, so strong is the current that he has to 'struggle out' on his arrival at the police lines.

The outcome of this act is predictable. Having apparently risked his life for the Club, it is obvious that he really is one *of* the Club; therefore his nomination of Veraswami is sound, the judgment of a true white. And although there is still the problem of Verrall, Flory has, for Elizabeth, been restored to his former position: 'He realized that his exploit of last night had made him almost a hero in her eyes. She could not know how small the danger had really been, and she forgave him everything, even Ma Hla May, because he had shown courage at the right moment. It was the buffalo and the leopard over again' (p. 245). When Verrall unexpectedly leaves, marriage once again seems probable.

But as before, and as always, it is too late. There are no more beginnings for Flory. The dream of salvation is over. The Original Choice of self as an inferior outcast destined for failure and disgrace has arranged the world in such a way that his passage to happiness is stamped with negation. Appropriately his final shaming is in church, for it is there that the They are assembled, hypocritically unified by an orthodoxy whose founding inspiration is the correction of Fallen man. During the sermon, Ma Hla May comes in, 'shrieking like a maniac' for money, and dressed to resemble a slum whore (p. 258). This is U Po Kyin's most devasting move. Elizabeth, knowing that Flory had kept a native, now knows what <u>kind</u> of native he had kept, or, rather the kind of native that U Po Kyin wants her to believe he had kept. To be the successor of the most 'civilized' native is, as has been seen, revolting enough; to be the successor of <u>this</u> native would be too gruesome to properly imagine. The 'lovely' has now transformed irretrievably into the 'beastly'; and the mark which she had previously overlooked during his brief life as a hero suddenly leaps into evidence and becomes the affirming sign of the truth of this transformation:

> Oh, the beast, the beast!.... Oh, what an unspeakable beast he was! When she thought of his face as it had looked in church, yellow and glistening with the hideous birthmark upon it, she could have wished him dead. It was not what he had done that horrified her. He might have committed a thousand abominations and she could have forgiven him. But not after that shameful, squalid scene, and the devilish ugliness of his disfigured face in that moment. It was, finally, the birthmark that had damned him. (pp. 263-64)

In the end, then, everything returns to this original problem, the birthmark which inspired the name 'Monkey-bum' and which tempted Flory to an inauthentic pattern of life dominated by the self-deception that the mark was a sign of being pre-determinedly an outcast failure. Curiously, it seems that Flory has throughout the novel tacitly encouraged Elizabeth to view the mark in this way, deviously attempting to elicit confirmation that he is justified in renouncing responsibility for what he has made of his life. The goal of his life had been to make it appear as if there had never been an alternative life. This, of course, could have had no appeal for Elizabeth; to declare that he was 'beastly', and then to lament that beastliness was his nature, an unalterable destiny, would have effected an instant and permanent breakdown in relations. As it is, she learns the truth gradually, and finally comes to judge Flory in precisely the same way as he judges himself: as 'damned' by the birthmark. And although this is precisely the recognition he desired, he wanted his damnation to be accepted and understood. He wanted someone who would make him less lonely and justify his 'life of lies', someone who, by sharing his life, would relieve him of some of the guilt that had arisen from not living in accord with the authentic impulses he found it so difficult to suppress. Elizabeth he saw principally as a means for tranquillizing his troubled conscience, but for this she was useless. For her, the authentic impulse was irreversibly beastly. She was snugly at home among the They of the Club, for the black/white dichotomy generated by an oppressive colonialism was the perfect realization of her notion that the world was exclusively divided into the beastly and the lovely. But irrespective of this, her presence stirred Flory towards authentic action because of his mistaken belief that he was no longer completely alone. He supported Veraswami on borrowed strength. Essentially, the plan of his life was never altered. The birthmark which has been the inspiration behind his life, inspires him to end it. But at the moment when he becomes the complete outcast, the reason for his suicide vanishes: 'With death, the birthmark faded immediately, so that it was no more than a faint grey stain' (p. 267).

NOTES

1. _Burmese Days_ (1934; rpt. Harmondsworth: Penguin Books, 1975), p. 17. Henceforth cited in text by page number to this edition.

2. Hazel E. Barnes, _The Literature of Possibility_ (Lincoln: Univ. of Nebraska Press, 1959), p. 75.

3. J.-P. Sartre, _Portrait of the Anti-Semite_, trans. Eric de Mauny (London: Secker and Warburg, 1948), pp. 44, 47.

4. _Being and Nothingness_, pp. 328, 472.

5. Gabriel Marcel, _The Existential Background of Human Dignity_ (Cambridge: Mass.: Harvard Univ.

Press, 1963), p. 59. *Being and Having*, trans. Katherine Farrer (London: Fontana, 1965) pp. 105, 129-30.

6. *Animal Farm* (1945; rpt. Harmondsworth: Penguin Books, 1967), p. 31.

7. Marcel, *Homo Viator*, trans. Emma Crauford (London: Victor Gollancz, 1951), p. 17.

Chapter Five

A CLERGYMAN'S DAUGHTER

Most of the problems of authenticity in _Burmese Days_ are also presented in _A Clergyman's Daughter_, but the crisis which provides the context for these problems is more immediately recognizable as existential. There is in _A Clergyman's Daughter_ the same social alienation which afflicted Flory, but in _A Clergyman's Daughter_ this is part of a cosmic lostness which raises questions about the meaning of life. Unlike Flory, there is no feeling that Dorothy's anxiety about her place in the world would be solved by marriage or liberalism; her personal and social alienation leads her to a tormenting glimpse of a picture of life whose frame is the Absurd. More so than in any other of his works, Orwell is here dealing with the problem of nothingness; Dorothy eventually sees through the tangled structure of her life and swoons at the void behind. This structure is perpetual 'bad faith', a bad faith so deep and pervasive that she can hardly distinguish the outlines of a self. Thus she lives in a complex turmoil of anxious hiddenness. Muzzled, repressed and stifled, what she is or could possibly be is almost wholly obscured by ever-proliferating obligations to others, a state symbolized by the rectory gardens:

> The front garden was choked with ragged fir-trees and a great spreading ash which shadowed the front rooms and made it impossible to grow any flowers. There was a large vegetable garden at the back.... Dorothy did the sowing, planting, and weeding in such spare time as she could command; in spite of which the vegetable garden was usually an impenetrable jungle of weeds.[1]

These images convey also the deep sense of sterility which marks her life; she resembles Gordon Comstock's loathed aspidistras in _Keep the Aspidistra Flying_. Unlike Comstock, though, she will not be saved by the sudden prospect of newly created life. Dorothy is doomed. Her life is a nightmare. In the opening sentence of the novel she wakes from a 'complex, troubling dream'. But the intervention of reality is no comfort; awake or asleep is precisely the same. All aspects of living are deadly. As for Winston Smith, there is no way out. One just persists.

It is in this, Orwell's second novel, that the relation between totalitarianism and inauthenticity is expressed domestically. The Reverend Hare's despotism can only continue because of Dorothy's submission to it, and the manner in which she submits is in the mode of inauthenticity with its concomitant leading of a double-life. And it is in this execution of a double-life that we identify the typical Orwellian situation. All his protagonists have a double-life, and they do so for the same reason: the ineludible presence of intolerable normative pressures. To locate this as characteristic of Orwell's consciousness is deeply significant, for as soon as _duplicity_ is established as his way of apprehending the world we come to understand that the Orwellian protagonist is _ambiguously situated_, and, being thus, he will, as has been seen with Flory, live with a perpetual sense of paradox and irony. Indeed, these are the terms on which life and the self are encountered; Orwellian man is not what he seems. Therefore it can be said that his sense of the world in some measure derives from a sense of his own invisibility in it, and this is to be contrasted with his overwhelming sense that what he _seems_ to be is subject to unremitting scrutiny. But of course, it is because he is so critically observed (or believes himself to be) that he has developed an inner-self, a furtive one-person world in which, as is the case with Winston Smith, the self is endangered by scary thoughts of solipsism and the indeterminability of reality. Hence, when Dorothy wakes, there is no atmospheric difference between dream and reality. This evokes the conditions of Cartèsian doubt and its consequent ontological tenuity, but God, the generous creator who would deceive no one, is only occasionally felt to be present and eventually vanishes altogether. The point of stability to which the anxious doubter could always refer for ultimate comfort is receding, and in <u>A Clergyman's Daughter</u> we see the outcome of this type of abandonment.

The significance of the novel's title is quickly made clear, succinctly conveying the fact that Dorothy's identity is derived from another's. She is a clergyman's daughter, and for her, and those who know her, this is the beginning and the end of the case. Like Eliot's Prufrock, her Being has been fixed by 'a formulated phrase'; it is her primary truth. Her self cannot be independently located. Like an object, her purpose has been defined at birth, her essence preceding her existence, and her growth, like an espalier, will be formed to create an imposed definition. She accepts this as the unalterable scheme of things partly because the shrunk nature of her life conceals alternatives, partly because of a tight complex of aversions, dreads and fears which she has for decisive and spontaneous independent action. Her life as we encounter it on the opening page resembles a behavioural experiment in stimulus-response, a type of aversion therapy in which the reward is merely the relief of imposed torment:

> As the alarm clock on the chest of drawers exploded like a horrid little bomb of bell metal, Dorothy, wrenched from the depths of some complex, troubling dream, awoke with a start and lay on her back looking into the darkness in extreme exhaustion.
>
> The alarm clock continued its nagging, feminine clamour, which would go on for five minutes or thereabouts if you did not stop it. Dorothy was aching from head to foot, and an insidious and contemptible self-pity, which usually seized upon her when it was time to get up in the morning, caused her to bury her head under the bedclothes and try to shut the hateful noise out of her ears. She struggled against her fatigue, however, and, according to her custom, exhorted herself sharply in the second person plural. Come on, Dorothy, up you get! No snoozing, please! Proverbs vi, 9. Then she remembered that if the noise went on any longer it would wake her father, and with a hurried movement she bounded out of bed, seized the alarm clock from the chest of drawers, and turned off the alarm. It was kept on the chest of drawers precisely in order that she should have to get out of bed to silence it. Still in darkness, she knelt down at her bedside and

> repeated the Lord's Prayer, but rather distractedly, her feet being troubled by the cold. (p. 5)

This Pavlovian bell-and-dog situation is marked by many of those features typical of existential fiction: solitary confinement, darkness, anxiety, decision and absurdity. But the importance of this passage is in its presentation of the human automatized, or, in the terms appropriate to this study, the human inauthenticized. The terms are, in this context, identical; man as mere mechanism is in bad faith, for, unlike the dog, in the human world mechanization is a choice; it is a position adopted. Dorothy pretends that she is *obliged* to get up. She has decided to behave *as if* she were mechanized, as if no alternative is possible. To the existentialist the decision to get up is of especial significance, for it is the moment between passivity and action, a crucial boundary met every day which could mean either the continuation or the end of a habit which patterns a life. The meaning behind the waker's positive response to the morning alarm has been discussed by Sartre:

> The alarm which rings in the morning refers to the possibility of my going to work, which is *my* possibility. But to apprehend the summons of the alarm as a summons is to get up. Therefore the very act of getting up is reassuring, for it eludes the question, 'Is work my possibility?' Consequently it does not put me in a position to apprehend the possibility of quietism, of refusing to work, and finally the possibility of refusing the world and the possibility of death. In short, to the extent that I apprehend the meaning of the ringing, I am already up at its summons; this apprehension guarantees me against the anguished intuition that it is I who confer on the alarm clock its exigency - I and I alone.
>
> .... It follows that my freedom is the unique foundation of values and that *nothing*, absolutely nothing, justifies me in adopting this or that particular value, this or that particular scale of values.
>
> .... All these ... everyday values derive their meaning from an original projection of myself which stands as my choice of myself in the world.[2]

A Clergyman's Daughter

The opening paragraphs of A Clergyman's Daughter exemplify a life: last week, last month, last year, from season to season, this is Dorothy in the morning. It is a life in which the self initiates nothing; she is a recipient, a conditioned response. She has been given a life. In the sense that most know it, in the sense of a succession of engaged possibilities, the future does not exist. It is a concept denoting endless duplication of what has been. 'Custom' has abolished time and lies upon her 'with a weight / Heavy as frost, and deep almost as life'.[3] That Orwell desired this focus is evident, for originally on the title page of A Clergyman's Daughter he had ironically quoted John Keble: 'The trivial round, the common task, / Would furnish all we ought to ask'. This 'trivial round', as Orwell presents it, is not merely the innocuous option of a million penurious middle-class spinsters but a way of life signifying both an immoral timidity before fascist control and the conditions for the emergence of existential crisis. Camus has described this emergence and where it leads, and it may stand as the pattern which Dorothy follows:

> It happens that the stage-sets collapse. Rising, tram, four hours in the office or factory, meal, tram, four hours of work, meal, sleep and Monday, Tuesday, Wednesday, Thursday, Friday and Saturday, according to the same rhythm - this path is easily followed most of the time. But one day the 'why' arises and everything begins in that weariness tinged with amazement. 'Begins' - this is important. Weariness comes at the end of the acts of a mechanical life, but at the same time it inaugurates the impulse of consciousness. It awakens consciousness and provokes what follows. What follows is the gradual return into the chain or it is the definitive awakening.[4]

Thus it is that the very condition of being mechanized produces the impulse to destroy it; as with fetters, the tighter they are, the more likely they are to break. This 'impulse' which Camus describes, and which Heidegger has termed 'the call of conscience', represents the failure of Sartre's 'guarantee'.

As with Flory, we are introduced to Dorothy at that critical point where renunciation is at its most probable, but the difference in what renunciation involves for these two shows a substantial difference of intention behind these two works. For Dorothy, the renunciation is strictly personal, in that she has only herself to save; whereas, for Flory, it extended beyond the self to the alleviation of an oppressed people. Thus the existentiality in A Clergyman's Daughter is predominantly Heideggerian in focus, in Burmese Days it is Sartrean. Orwell, having chosen to emphasize the problem of authenticity in strictly individual terms, is able to concentrate almost exclusively on the life of one person, with the result that the world of A Clergyman's Daughter is almost wholly Dorothy's. More so than in any of the other protagonists there are details in Dorothy's history which resemble a typical Freudian 'case': she has suffered a trauma over witnessing parental sex in childhood, is frigid, is afflicted by a sense of sin and guilt, and has internalized the prescriptive morality of her father's superego. She perfectly illustrates Freud's formulation of the child's response to final socialization: 'You no longer have to punish me, Father; I will punish myself now'.[5]

Dorothy's oppression has led to a split in the self, a splitting that is repeatedly evident in two ways. Firstly, in her exhortations to herself, and secondly, in her method of stifling heretical thoughts by jabbing her arm with a pin, a variant of Ingsoc's 'crimestop'. She has become both father and daughter. So profoundly is she a self-for-another that she can hardly distinguish between where she begins and where she ends. The original self and the imposed self are almost always at war, and that the imposed self always wins can be seen as attributable to its representative status. The imposed self has not merely the power of a father; being a clergyman, the self that the Reverend Hare has imposed is endowed with the power of God. Thus the original self is more bound than, for example, a colonel's daughter's; when the imposed self commands, it does so with the sanction of the absolute. It commands by right because it is Dorothy's primordial source, the actual creator of the original self. The alarm clock which rouses her to a daily renewal of her obligations to her father is, in itself, not quite sufficient to 'guarantee' the necessity of having to rise; it requires, as it does in many other circumstances during the day, the additional sense that she is being called imperatively by God. Her father's internalized command requires biblical support: 'Come on, Dorothy, up you get! No snoozing, please! Proverbs vi, 9'. The inauthentic pretence that she is compelled by the absolute obscures the sense that she is rising voluntarily to yet another futile day of drudgery and disgust, and the feeling that she is doing penance masochistically satisfies the self-hatred which stems from living inauthentically. In addition, through continually experiencing the world as depraved and wretched, the biblical description of the world as Fallen is confirmed, so her misery acquires the status of being evidence for God's existence. Dorothy needs to believe in God in order to do the work which, without God, she would not feel sufficient obligation to do. God justifies an inauthentic life. Belief in God makes her suffering an _intended destiny_, makes it _mean something_. The 'trivial round' has purpose. There _must_ be some purpose in rubbing ointment into 'large, grey-veined, flaccid legs' in a room reeking of 'urine and paregoric' (p. 52). And it is against this repellent proposition that Dorothy's enfeebled selfhood asserts its individual will. But as soon as it reveals itself it is suppressed: 'Unseen by Mrs. Pither, Dorothy gave herself a severe pinch. She had been expecting this, and - she had done it so many times before - she really did _not_ enjoy rubbing Mrs. Pither down. She exhorted herself angrily. Come on, Dorothy! No sniffishness, please! John xiii, 14. "Of course I will, Mrs. Pither!" she said instantly' (p. 52).

Around this central existential failure are all kinds of other failures, which have the effect of encouraging Dorothy to deepen her inauthenticity. Increasingly her experience of the world is that _nothing seems to work_. Everything needs her especial attention. Always she is engaged in servicing things and people that cannot function autonomously. Even the church, the house of God itself, is disintegrating. Like Boxer in _Animal Farm_, Dorothy's only way of dealing with all the multiplying demands is to 'work harder'.[6] Her chief burden, though, is money, and Orwell's use of her lack of it expresses that feeling of indebtedness which is the enduring experience of those whose self is for others. The thought of the Cargill bill sends 'a deadly pang, an actual physical pang ... through her viscera':

> At all hours of the night or day it was waiting just round the corner of her consciousness, ready to spring upon her and agonize her; and

> with it came the memory of a score of lesser bills, mounting up to a figure of which she dared not even think. Almost involuntarily she began to pray, 'Please God, let not Cargill send in his bill again today!' (p. 8)

So Dorothy, who has given all of herself away, still owes more than she can possibly repay. She is interred in a tiny gross world of materiality and flesh although ostensibly in the realm of the spirit. Her life, then, already split and therefore ambiguous, is penetrated by paradox, for the Church, whose raison d'être is the liberation of souls, creates only fatigue and constraint. The Church is disguised in the same way as the Ministries in 1984: what it seems is precisely what it is not. The Reverend himself is an example of this, belief having become totally disengaged from life and therefore reduced to a ritualized ordering of symbols. This alone is sufficient to maintain his position; he can even desert the semblance of Christian values when actually taking the service: '"This is a valid sacrament," he seemed to be saying, "and it is my duty to administer it to you. But remember that I am only your priest, not your friend. As a human being I dislike you and despise you"' (p. 10). Besides Dorothy, the only other communicant in attendance is Miss Mayfill, and through her Orwell extends the Pavlovian feeling of automatized function which characterizes his description of Dorothy rising in the morning:

> As the Rector finished the consecration Miss Mayfill began to struggle to her feet with extreme difficulty and slowness, like some disjointed wooden creature picking itself up by sections, and disengaging at each movement a powerful whiff of mothballs. There was an extraordinary creaking sound - from her stays presumably, but it was a noise as of bones grating against one another. You could have imagined that there was only a dry skeleton inside the black overcoat. (p. 12)

Miss Mayfill's condition may be seen as Dorothy's own in old age. Enfeebled and wooden, a sort of senile puppet, this is her destination, the terminal phase of those who have denied the dignity of authentic selfhood and surrendered to the deathly orthodoxy of the They. But as yet, at twenty-seven, Dorothy is anxious to preserve the link between symbol and referent, to know the meaning of the act of sacrament. Her faith remains the one point of unity in a self divided, burdened and bemused. Thus to accept the wafer sincerely is paramount. Having been distracted from the service by the distasteful prospect of taking the chalice after Miss Mayfill, Dorothy tries to pray for forgiveness so that she may receive the wafer in grace:

> But the current of her thoughts had been broken. Suddenly it was quite useless attempting to pray; her lips moved, but there was neither heart nor meaning in her prayers. She could hear Proggett's boots shuffling and her father's clear low voice murmuring 'Take and eat', she could see the worn strip of red carpet beneath her knees, she could smell dust and eau-de-Cologne and mothballs; but of the Body and Blood of Christ, of the purpose for which she had come here, she was as though deprived of the power to think. A deadly blankness had descended upon her mind. It seemed to her that actually she _could_ not pray. She struggled, collected her thoughts, uttered mechanically the opening phrases of a prayer; but they were useless, meaningless - nothing but the dead shells of words. (p. 13)

It is at moments like this when Dorothy is at her most tenuous, when the Sartrean 'guarantee', the validity of the system, seems to slide away and leave her in solitude. Suddenly there is a gap between feeling and commitment, one of those moments of disconnection which infect the 'believer' with a sense of impotence and abandonment. This loss of concentration during the service serves as a portent of the total forgetfulness she later suffers, and she is caught in the Lutheran paradox quoted at the end of the novel: '"Lord, I believe, help Thou my unbelief"' (p. 260). Temporarily she loses contact with the thing which hitherto ensured that orientation on which she has relied for definition. To no longer feel the presence of God means also to no longer feel the presence of her father, which would mean that she is no longer a clergyman's daughter; and as her identity is derived from this relation, its loss would entail an _ontological suspension_, placing her in that zone of nothingness in which the self anxiously discovers itself as free. In anxiety she would discover that the role of a clergyman's daughter is a category that she has assumed through choice. She would discover her contingency and understand that the world is not disposed in such a way that she is *necessarily* a clergyman's daughter. She would discover her life as unintended and discover also, by extension, that her father need not have been a clergyman (indeed, her father's position is based purely on the time of his birth, having entered the Church 'for the outmoded reason that the Church is the traditional profession for younger sons') (p. 19). In other words, she would face the Absurd. The application of the pin shows how desperate she is to avoid the Absurd; even though her life is one of claustral servitude, at least it diverts her from confronting squarely the 'deadly blankness' which lies behind the systems and roles. But it is this blankness which must be faced if an authentic life is to be gained. Meanwhile, her sense of role is restored through an intoxicating glimpse of sudden beauty, sunlight on the leaves of a lime: 'The flash of living colour had brought back to her, by a process deeper than reason, her peace of mind, her love of God, her power of worship' (p. 14). Dorothy is now able to pray because her essence as Christian seems affirmed. The disconnection has been repaired and she belongs once more to the they-self.

There is, however, a later time in the day when nature is restorative with the opposite effect, leading Dorothy towards the heretical region of 'half-pagan' 'pantheism' (p. 54). She finds a paradisiacal little plot on the *other side of a hedge*, indicating forbidden privacy and individualism, a place beyond the censorious gaze of the They:

> She knelt down among the tall weeds beneath the hedge. It was very hot down there, close to the ground. The humming of many unseen insects sounded in her ears, and the hot summery fume from the tangled swathes of vegetation flowed up and enveloped her.... Dorothy pulled a frond of the fennel against her face and breathed in the strong sweet scent. Its richness overwhelmed her, almost dizzied her for a moment. She drank it in, filling her lungs with it. Lovely, lovely scent - scent of summer days, scent of childhood joys, scent of spice-drenched islands in the warm foam of Oriental seas!
>
> Her heart swelled with sudden joy. (p. 53)

By the sheltered seclusion of the hedge, Dorothy

experiences the Edenesque. It is a place of suspension, a kind of secret vacuum tucked away within the oppressive gravity of the world. In it, one is closer to the unalienated primordial self, in touch with the lost time prior to the duplicity of inauthentic life. Here she can catch the 'scent of childhood joys' and the 'scent of spice-drenched islands in the warm foam of Oriental seas'. Only by the remembrance of the deep past or the perception of another kind of world can Dorothy find relief from the oppression of the present. This wishing away of the actual, which is a characteristic of her life, can only deepen her dissociation because it involves a denial of reality; the only moments worth living for are those which provide a sense of escape from typical living. Like Laing's description of the paranoid, she is 'persecuted by reality itself'.[7] And it is reality, in the mode of the prohibitive voice, which punctures her private alternative world behind the hedge:

> She checked herself instantly, and drew back. What was she doing? Was it God that she was worshipping, or was it only the earth? The joy ebbed out of her heart, to be succeeded by the cold, uncomforable feeling that she had been betrayed into a half-pagan ecstasy. She admonished herself. None of _that_, Dorothy! No Nature-worship, please! Her father had warned her against Nature-worship.... Dorothy took a thorn of the wild rose, and pricked her arm three times, to remind herself of the Three Persons of the Trinity, before climbing over the gate and remounting her bicycle. (p. 54)

Only by forgetfulness, by forgetting the existence of the multiple sources of the voice, will the voice be silenced; but by forgetting the sources she will also be losing her identity as a clergyman's daughter and step into the unfamiliar zone of selfhood.

Before impelling her towards this zone, Orwell provides her with an alternative route. via Warburton, a middle-aged dilettante painter whose affable antinomianism represents in a rather naive and stereotyped way the philistine's notion of indolent aesthete: the cultivated id cavalierly flaunting its scorn for the anachronistic provincialism of the superego. So as in _Burmese Days_ there is in _A Clergyman's Daughter_ a relation of radical contrast, although the terms are different.

In Burmese Days it was a relation involving the Beastly and the Lovely; in A Clergyman's Daughter it is the 'Pious and the Immoral', who, according to Orwell, 'drift naturally together' (p. 41). But the significance of these terms does not lie in their contrasting theological positions; respectively, piety and immorality represent the inauthenticity of the orthodox They, and the authenticity of the heterodox 'I'. Warburton is the only figure in Knype Hill who represents the value of the 'I', having defined himself through defiance of the They. Everyone else who Dorothy meets either accepts passively the fixed values of the collective, or, like her father and Victor Stone, who are both doctrinal pedants, are engaged in defining these values and enforcing their recognition in order to distinguish them from rival collectives. Both these men bifurcate and circumscribe life in accordance with the either/or of the principle of the Excluded Middle: things are either valid and prescribed, or invalid and proscribed. It is not surprizing therefore, that Dorothy, whose self is split into two irreconcilable positions, gets from Warburton, 'without being fully aware of it, a species of sympathy and understanding which she could not get elsewhere' (p. 41). Warburton is the only person she knows who speaks for the self that the imposed self suppresses; but because she exists in the binary mode, Warburton both attracts and repels. He threatens one half of her, while the others threaten the other half. Being in herself ambiguous, her relations with everyone are ambivalent.

The difficulties of their relations in public are essentially about Warburton's refusal to be a self-for-others and the effect of this on Dorothy's position as a clergyman's daughter. Having met in the High Street, they come across a procession in support of the local Conservative candidate, and Warburton points at it expressively with his stick:

> 'Look at it! Just look at it! Look at those fawning hags, and that half-witted oaf grinning at us like a monkey that sees a bag of nuts. Did you ever see such a disgusting spectacle?'
>
> 'Do be careful!' Dorothy murmured. 'Somebody's sure to hear you.'
>
> 'Good!' said Mr. Warburton, immediately raising his voice. 'And to think that that low-born hound actually has the impertinence to think that he's pleasing us with the sight of his false teeth! And that suit he's wearing is

> an offence in itself. Is there a Socialist candidate? If so, I shall certainly vote for him.'
>
> Several people on the pavement turned and stared. Dorothy saw little Mr. Twiss, the ironmonger, a weazened, leather-coloured old man, peering with veiled malevolence round the corner of the rush baskets that hung in his doorway. He had caught the word Socialist, and was mentally registering Mr. Warburton as a Socialist and Dorothy as the friend of Socialists.
>
> 'I really _must_ be getting on,' said Dorothy hastily, feeling that she had better escape before Mr. Warburton said something even more tactless....
>
> .... He was a difficult man to shake off, and though Dorothy counted him as a friend, she did sometimes wish, he being the town scandal and she the Rector's daughter, that he would not always choose the most public places to talk to her in. (pp. 38-39)

As in _1984_, there is in _A Clergyman's Daughter_ the presentation of prohibited relations being snooped upon by those who represent normative life, and, as in _Burmese Days_, the exposure of these relations is punished by the offender being shamed and shunned, to be made, in effect, an 'unperson'. As with escapers in enemy territory, visibility is death. It is the body which is the great handicap. To be relieved of the body, or to be transferred into another with which the original self cannot be identified, would therefore eliminate one of the most burdensome aspects of those wishing to claim authentic life. Dorothy, through her appearance, generates expectations in others which she feels obliged to fulfil. Mr. Twiss and others look at her critically only because they are looking at a role which is transcending its role; through her appearance they apprehend what _ought_ to be the case, and through her behaviour they are able to note the heretical disparity. So it is that essence and existence are seen to no longer coincide. The notion of essence on which normative life relies is threatened; the They detect that Dorothy is not _only_ a clergyman's daughter. The They's chief observer in Knype Hill is Mrs. Semprill:

> Entrenched behind a pile of cretonnes near the window, she had been watching Dorothy's con-

> versation with Mr. Warburton. Whenever you were doing something that you did not particularly want Mrs. Semprill to see you doing, you could trust her to be somewhere in the neighbourhood. She seemed to have the power of materializing like an Arabian jinneeyeh at any place where she was not wanted. No indiscretion, however small, escaped her vigilance. Mr. Warburton used to say that she was like the four beasts of the Apocalypse - 'They are full of eyes, you remember, and they rest not night nor day.'
> .... There was hardly a soul in the town or the surrounding country about whom Mrs. Semprill could not disclose some festering secret if you listened to her long enough. (pp. 42, 44)

This, then, is Dorothy's abiding problem in life: neither from without nor within can she escape observation. When the voice of God the Father is not exhorting her from within, the eyes of the They are staring from without. A kind of paranoid desperation pervades her life in Knype Hill. She is surrounded. Even in the dark, after Warburton has just snatched a repulsed kiss by his garden gate, she hears Semprill's window banging closed. This, together with the horror of being sexually approached, is the crowning agitation in a day fraught with tension and disgust. Her response to Warburton describes the one overwhelming desire of all inauthentic persons who have made of themselves a self-for-others: 'If only they would leave you alone! she thought as she walked onwards a little more slowly. That was how she put it to herself habitually - "If only they would leave you alone!"' (p. 75). And it is at this point that we learn that her sexual loathing has damaged her in the same way as Flory's birthmark: 'It was her especial secret, the especial, incurable disability that she carried through life' (p. 75). She had 'a deep, secret wound in her mind' (p. 77). The final scene of the chapter is of Dorothy alone in the conservatory at midnight, 'mechanically' sticking together strips of paper to make jackboots for a fund-raising play: 'Come on, Dorothy! No slacking, please! Luke ix, 62'. Strange moments of oblivion assail her, and the oilstove beneath the gluepot sings hypnotically: 'She felt, in an almost literal sense of the words, washed out' (p. 78).

The beginning of the next chapter, like the

beginning of the first, describes Dorothy waking, but the world to which she now wakes is not the familiar one of a rectory but of a London street. An unrecorded 'interregnum' of 'not quite eight days' has passed (p. 87). Though still amnesic, Dorothy is coming to consciousness for the first time since pasting the jackboots. Clearly, what has happened to Dorothy is that she has undergone a 'fugue', a psychiatric term which Charles Rycroft defines as

> the process by which a person wanders off, not knowing who or where he is. Fugues are generally categorized as hysterical and cited as examples of dissociation of consciousness. A rare condition, most of the cases cited in psychiatric text books have occurred in persons such as boys in boarding schools and conscript soldiers who feel trapped in situations in which they are no longer free agents.[8]

This describes precisely Dorothy's situation as a clergyman's daughter; also, the notion of fugue is additionally persuasive as Rycroft cites boarding schools as typical causative locations, thus evoking Orwell's imprisoned condition at St. Cyprians. In fact the idea of fugue is present in every Orwell novel; flight, memory and identity were to be basic ingredients of all the novels that followed *A Clergyman's Daughter*. The Orwellian protagonists all 'feel trapped in situations in which they are no longer free agents', and it is basically from this that the novels emerge as existential works. Fugue is a response to existential crisis. It is a desperate recoil from a situation in which the freedom of self-definition is denied, in which the authentic 'I' has been dispersed and lost among the They. And apart from the appropriateness of fugue as a symptom of existential crisis, its characteristics are such that it expresses exactly what Orwell wants to achieve in *A Clergyman's Daughter*, for fugue is a break with normative life *without* the element of conscious decision. It is therefore a kind of probationary period during which the self can recuperate and discover itself in isolation from the pressures of the They. It is a *paradoxical* situation, insofar as the wish for an alternative life has been fulfilled in the absence of conscious personal choice; so it cannot be said that Dorothy has acted in order to claim an authentic life. Indeed, although the desire for this change is obvious, fugue is something that, by definition, _happens to_ a person. Dorothy is being acted upon; it is merely a more complex and significant behavioural response than the ones she had previously been accustomed to, except that this one temporarily absolves her from self-responsibility. So whatever she does up to the time when her memory revives cannot, properly, be estimated existentially, for without memory, and therefore without an understanding of the significance of acts, she is in ontological suspension. But that Orwell is preparing her for the _possibility_ of selfhood cannot be doubted. His description of her break into consciousness is unambiguously existential:

> It was only now, after becoming aware of most of the things about her, that she became aware of _herself_. Hitherto she had been as it were a pair of eyes with a receptive but purely impersonal brain behind them. But now, with a curious little shock, she discovered her separate and unique existence; she could _feel_ herself existing; it was as though something within her were exclaiming 'I am I!' Also, in some way she knew that this 'I' had existed and been the same from remote periods in the past, though it was a past of which she had no remembrance.
>
> But it was only for a moment that this discovery occupied her. From the first there was a sense of incompleteness in it, of something vaguely unsatisfactory. And it was this: the 'I am I' which had seemed an answer had itself become a question. It was no longer 'I am I', but '_who_ am I'? (p. 81)

The existential significance of this passage can be seen by comparing it with a passage from John Macquarrie's _Existentialism_:

> An existent is not just an 'it'; the existent says 'I', and in uttering the personal pronoun lays claim not just to a unique place and perspective in the world but to a unique being. 'Mineness' is a term that has sometimes been used to express the awareness that my existence is unique and distinct from the existence of everyone else. I am not just a specimen of a class. I am I. And this last statement is not merely a tautology. It is an assertion of my unique individual being as an existent who

> stands out as this existent and no other.[9]

Dorothy, who has just escaped living the it-life of a self-for-others, rediscovers herself as a for-itself. Having been for so long 'a specimen of a class', she enters a new zone of Being in which she experiences herself as distinguishable from all others. Although bewildered, she stands self-possessed, and she has to reconstruct the world according to this new perspective. Orwell, in fact, presents her first moments of consciousness as a rebirth. She breaks into consciousness in a pre-socialized condition:

> As yet it could not properly be said that she was *looking*. For the things she saw were not apprehended as men, trams, and cars, nor as anything in particular; they were not even apprehended as things moving; not even as *things*. She merely *saw*, as an animal sees, without speculation and almost without consciousness.... She had no words, nor any conception of time or place, or of her own body of even of her own existence. (p. 80)

That the meaning of this passage is ontogenetic is later confirmed. Dorothy, who was born in Kent, comes to consciousness in the *New* Kent Road, and while she is standing there she meets a group of hop-pickers who lead her back to Kent. Having been made a child again, she no longer belongs to Knype Hill, which is in Suffolk, and that is why 'for some reason which she did not understand, it reassured her to hear that they were making for Kent. Kent, it seemed to her, was the very place to which she wanted to go' (p. 86). So the journey assumes the aspect of a quest, a quest to reinstate the original personal self that existed prior to its smothering by the imposed social self of a clergyman's daughter. And for achieving the goal of this quest she is not only prepared through having recovered the 'I', for now no one will approach her *as* a clergyman's daughter. The gold cross and Irish tweeds have vanished, and she has acquired the appearance of a slum tart. White has become black. Orwell has transformed her in the same radical way that he said was necessary if he were to abolish class distinctions: by altering himself 'so completely that at the end [he] should hardly be recognizable as the same person'.[10]

But within minutes from the time of her recovery Orwell supplies a detail which signifies the poisoning of Dorothy's authentic possibilities. Almost as if her mode of Being is constitutionally a self-for-others, she submits to the other's control. After she shows Nobby her money, he says: '"You're going to bless the day you set eyes on us lot. We're going to make your future for you, we are "' (pp. 84-85). Once again, she is accepting a situation in which giving means owing. What she might become will be what others have made of her. This acceptance indicates also the paradoxical implications of amnesia, in that, in being released from its acquired definitions, the self loses its structural supports. The same event which reveals the unconditioned freedom of the 'I' also leaves the 'I' in a condition of unprecedented passivity before the forces of the world. Dorothy, who has become a child again, has a child's dependence. She is without initiative. She is obliged to go where the crowd leads. Only by recovering her memory will she realize her freedom to choose the direction of her life, to determine what she will *be*. Only then will she be existentially tested. Only then will she be able to understand the important implications of her amnesia and maybe break the mould.

The period of about three weeks which passes before her memory revives is another kind of oblivion. Being 'everlastingly sleepy and everlastingly occupied', she is lulled into 'an almost beastlike heaviness' (p. 112). So at the point where her memory is revived by seeing her face in the scandal rag *Pippin's Weekly*, she has had no opportunity to feel her freedom and use it to extend her habitual understanding of herself. Her personal definition is still, like the photograph, a 'blurred, nebulous thing' (p. 119). There is no sense of distance between what she is and what she was. Even the means by which she is enabled to remember is due to her inauthentic self-for-others: her importance to the world is solely that she is a clergyman's daughter. Without this relation there would be nothing of interest to the readers of *Pippin's Weekly*.

Dorothy recognises the imposed 'Who' of the 'I' and is thus brought to the point where it can be knowingly denied or accepted; and it is *because* she accepts it that she refuses to return to Knype Hill and resume it. Being still a clergyman's daughter, and having the code that that role entails, she cannot return disgraced: '*Could* she, after all, go home? Dared she?'

> Could she face Knype Hill after everything that had happened?.... But when you have been plastered all over with horrible, dishonouring libels, can you go back to a town of two thousand inhabitants where everybody knows everybody else's private history and talks about it all day long?
>
> .... She knew what it means to have to live down a scandal in a small country town. The glances and furtive nudges when you passed! The prying eyes following you down the street from behind curtained windows! The knots of youths on the corners round Blifil-Gordon's factory, lewdly discussing you! (p. 121)

So Dorothy is in the position of refusing an inauthentic role for the inauthentic reason that she dare not stand individually against the power of the They. It was precisely this weakness in opposing the They's power to impose definitions on the self which so oppressively characterized her life all along.

After deciding that she won't go back, she learns that she _can't_ go back, for the Reverend too has his own self-for-others to preserve. 'Beyond all possibility of forgiveness' _she_ has disgraced _him_ (p. 168). Because she has lapsed from the socially defined prescription by which she is identified, he will not recognize her personally. She is a role, and _only_ a role; and so to break the role is to no longer _be_. She must be _wholly_ denied therefore; thus he will not even respond to her letters: 'All he wanted was to get rid of her, drop all communication with her; get her out of sight and out of mind, as a mere scandal to be covered up and forgotten' (p. 124). And if he were to have her back under present conditions, _his_ existence would be threatened, for he would no longer be seen as a proper clergyman. Dorothy, like the waiter in _Burmese Days_ who was obliged to speak pidgin in order for Ellis to maintain himself as a white master, has to maintain her identity as a clergyman's daughter for the Reverend to maintain his identity as a clergyman. Only by proving _publicly_ that she hasn't demolished her role will the clergyman be able to have her back without his role being demolished.

The message is the same as in _Burmese Days_: loyalty melts in the heat of public disgrace. True fidelity cannot exist while in the thrall of the They. The nature of Dorothy's public shame has the same element as Orwell's at prep. school. The amnesia and the bed-wetting are not intentional acts; they visit you: 'There was no volition about it, no consciousness. You did not properly speaking _do_ the deed'; 'Sin was not necessarily something that you did: it might be something that happened to you'.[11] Even though neither are responsible for their sins, both subsequently live as if they were guilty, and Dorothy, emerging from a period of vagabondage in which she had 'no standards of comparison to make her ashamed', continues now as a disgraced self-for-others (p. 89). No longer ratified in her imposed role, and yet not directed by any resolve to cultivate her original self, she is exposed and adrift. She belongs nowhere. So when her father, through his solicitor, attempts to protect himself from further disgrace by having his cousin place her respectably, she agrees reluctantly to be a schoolteacher. The cousin thinks that Dorothy has 'just the kind of face that a schoolmistress ought to have'; so '"that's the line for you, m'dear - schoolmistress. You're just cut out for it"' (p. 174).

As soon as Dorothy meets the school principal, Mrs. Creevy, it is evident that all the worst characteristics of her relations with her father are about to be restored:

> You could tell her at a glance for a person who knew exactly what she wanted, and would grasp it as ruthlessly as any machine; not a bully exactly - you could somehow infer from her appearance that she would not take enough interest in you to want to bully you - but a person who would make use of you and then throw you aside with no more compunction than if you had been a worn-out scrubbing brush. (pp. 176-77)

But additionally, Creevy is like the spiteful snoop Semprill, the one who has been feeding the scandal to the papers: 'Even when Dorothy was not actually under her eye, Mrs. Creevy had ways of making her presence felt. She was for ever prowling in the neighbourhood of the school-room, so that Dorothy never felt quite safe from her intrusion' (p. 191). So Dorothy is cornered by one who combines Knype Hill's two most personally destructive elements. And now, with the power of prayer vanished, she is caught in an intensified nightmare. Semi-starved, shabby and friendless, a utensil under constant scrutiny, and with the winter coming on, she is even denied those rare moments of exultation to be got from the Suffolk countryside. In Brough Road, Southbridge, she lives 'amid labyrinths of meanly decent streets, all so indistinguishably alike ... that you could lose yourself there almost as easily as in a Brazilian forest' (p. 175).

Situated thus, and still with an eight-day hole in her biography, her emphasis on history and geography as a teacher is significant, for history is the means for reconstructing the meaning of the past, and geography serves to specify one's place in the world. But, having broken the stupefaction of the children through her revision of the school curriculum, and feeling at last valued and respected, Dorothy sees everything collapse into misery, waste and blame, because she has discussed with the children an 'immoral' passage from Shakespeare. A consignment of parents appears and demands a return to the old ways, the copper-plate and learning by rote. Once more, Dorothy is judged, and she stands shamed and condemned. This, really, is the final beating, for like Flory, she is spurned at a time when hope and a commitment to an ideal is just burgeoning. Teaching had come to seem 'more than a mere job; it was - so it seemed to her - a mission, a life-purpose' (p. 200). Here, the relation between power and inauthenticity (and the savage fact of money, which Orwell hammers out relentlessly in his next novel, Keep the Aspidistra Flying) reasserts itself:

> The stream of mean, cruel reprimand went on and on.... Again and again she thought, 'I won't stand it, I won't stand it any longer! I'll tell her what I think of her and then walk straight out of the house! But she did nothing of the kind. She saw with dreadful clarity the helplessness of her position. Whatever happened, whatever insults it meant swallowing, she had got to keep her job. So she sat still, with pink humiliated face, amid the circle of parents, and presently her anger turned to misery. (pp. 206-7)

Dorothy, knocked back tightly into position, lingers on in the school, deteriorating steadily as she delivers the lies in the Hundred Page History of Britain and reduces geography to lists of capitals, the pupils increasingly recalcitrant and hostile: 'They hated her now, as they had hated all their previous teachers' (p. 221). It is in this state that her mind darkens and brings to the surface an attitude to life which has been gestating during the solitary months of anxiety, disillusion and abandonment; quietly, with none of the momentous clamour of Nietzsche's madman in Joyful Wisdom, Dorothy has passed into a spiritual midnight. Somewhere between Knype Hill and Southbridge, God has died: 'the whole concept of worship was meaningless to her now; her faith had vanished, utterly and irrevocably' (p. 220). And this loss, this transformation, has about it the kind of conviction that her previous faith never had, for at Knype Hill she was enmeshed in a structure and a pattern of life which derived wholly from the unchallenged assumption that God was. Thus, merely to continue with the pattern seemed to be evidence that God existed. And as the pattern was her life, to deny the pattern would be also to deny that she existed. Dorothy had generated a hidden formula: Because I am, God is. And because God was, and had created life, she had been intended. She had a necessary existence. That she was contingent was unthinkable, for the pattern which was the evidence continued. Having been meant to be a Christian, a clergyman's daughter, she had an essence, and, having accepted an essence, she was committed to a determinism of the self. Thus Dorothy's panic at Knype Hill when she had heterodox thoughts becomes more comprehensible, as any deviance would represent a departure from essence and would therefore be a crisis in identity, an ontological insecurity. All the behavioural and stimulus-response devices she submitted herself to were attempts to staunch a leaking essence and to make her Being seem to coincide with the pattern of her existence.

Clearly, then, Dorothy's pattern (the 'trivial round') had to be destroyed in order for it to be seen that it was not necessary for the continuance of life, and the way that this is achieved through amnesia is not only psychologically plausible in a clinical sense but provides the situation under which God's validity is tested existentially; furthermore, the destruction of the pattern without actual loss of life brings about the important realization that God, even if he exists, is not necessary. The process by which Dorothy loses her faith is not the familiar abstract pursuit of beating a concept into submission through the exercise of reason; it is the very antithesis of the Cartesian brain locked in a heated room pledged to a purely cerebral examination of God's validity. And the reason for this is that Dorothy is quite without motive; she doesn't set out to prove anything. God is not banished through thought but through the pressure of experience. Dorothy, unchoosing, and therefore with no anticipatory conceptions, discovered herself in an unfamiliar world, and, through experience, found herself alone there. When she awoke in defenceless solitude in the New Kent Road it was to a world absent of structure. It was a primary confrontation. As with herself, she saw the original chaos behind the imposed design; and this design was man's. God did not reveal himself. What instead emerged was the revelation of the self in its autonomous distinctiveness. No longer was the self a dependence-relation, the self-through-another of a clergyman's daughter; the self was nothing but itself: 'I am I'. Being no longer part of a design, she is contingent and condemned to freedom. Having no derived essence, she is a nothingness, and the eight-day hole in her biography which precedes her rebirth expresses the _ex nihilo_ feeling which necessarily attends the loss of faith. And in the following months Dorothy learns through destitution and sorrow the meaning of abandonment, and with icy clarity acknowledges the implications of it all. The presence which presided over her life and justified it had never been. Like Camus's Meursault in _The Outsider_, she experiences the 'indifference of the universe', but not as 'benign'.[12] The temperature of the world has fallen to zero and she cannot live there without the warmth of disguise. Quite consciously she commits herself to an enduring pretence which will blur and soften the impact of what she has discovered:

> It seemed to her that even though you no longer believe, it is better to go to church than not; better to follow in the ancient ways, than to drift in rootless freedom. She knew very well that she would never again be able to utter a prayer and mean it; but she knew also that for the rest of her life she must continue with the observances to which she had been bred. Just this much remained to her of the faith that had once, like the bones in a living frame, held all her life together. (p. 220)

The monotonous years of simulated behaviourism have left a residuum; irrespective of the fact that ritual no longer signifies she will continue _as if_ it did. Choosing this mode reduces the ex nihilo feeling, for 'tradition' connects her to what went on in the world prior to her arrival. This she feebly asserts against the anguish of 'rootless freedom'. She has become a Sisyphus figure. Although the bike has no chain, she will still pedal. She is ready to resume the habitual pattern.

And this is made possible through the exposure of Semprill's lies. Warburton brings the news that Dorothy is now 'forgiven' by her father, who, as he is no longer publicly disgraced, now wants her returned in order to look after him again. This, as she explains to Warburton, is what she wants. She wants to be 'useful'. When '"all of a sudden the whole world is empty"', to serve a purpose is paramount (p. 243). It makes the self appear necessary again, justifying her existence and therefore lessening the anxiety of her 'rootless freedom'.

On her return to the Rectory, things are so disposed that the biggest deception of all seems possible: that nothing has ever happened to Dorothy. Her father greets her 'as though she had only been away for the week-end' (p. 255). And later: 'Dorothy had been up to her eyes in work from the moment of reaching home. Indeed, things had slipped back into their old routine with astonishing swiftness. It was as though it had only been yesterday that she had gone away' (p. 254). Thus the most momentous period of her life is being reacted to as if it belonged to what Heidegger terms the 'everydayness' of life. Again, this is precisely what Dorothy wants, for now that the purpose of life has vanished, the fact of personal extinction has anxiously settled in her mind. Because death is now the end, life has become 'monstrous and dreadful', 'meaningless, dark' (pp. 258-59). And this is yet another effect of having been wrenched from her imposed clergyman's daughter's essence. As a clergyman's daughter her original self had been sheltered and tranquillized among the 'everydayness' of the They. Being just one of the collective identity, her sense of 'mineness' was smothered, and the emergence of the ultimate possibility was effectively stifled. Among the They, death had been something that one shared. Because there were no separately identifiable Who's, death was never truly felt to be a personal possibility, and, because there was God, death could always be seen as another beginning. Now that Dorothy has been stripped of her protective identity without claiming the compensatory directedness of an authentic life, she is so exposed to the prospect of _her_ death and _her_ futility that she sees in the soporific togetherness of the They the means for forgetting.

Dorothy's reason for surrendering to assimilation by the They is characterized by an extraordinary paradox: she wants to forget that she forgot. She strives through asssimilation and ritualized work to achieve another amnesia, an amnesia designed to bury the knowledge that she has been amnesic. If she can deny the blank amnesic week in her biography she can deny the sense of nothingness that grew from the abandonment which amnesia produced. So the terms descriptive of her old life once more apply, but more profoundly: duplicity and ambiguity. And the exhortations from the imposed self to the original self, which vanished during her father's absence, also return: 'Come on, Dorothy! No slacking, please!' (p. 261). But now she is consciously committed to deception. She is reconstructing a life on a deliberate denial of what she knows to be true; and it is in this mental process that doublethink and inauthenticity coincide, for, to achieve bad faith, one denies what one has affirmed. Her life, which has always been a flight from the self, has gathered further momentum through the horrified recoil from 'the deadly emptiness that she had discovered at the heart of things' (p. 258).

The final scene, disturbingly similar to the one immediately preceding her amnesia, is of Dorothy making a paper armour breastplate. It is as if she is trying to stick her broken life together and create some kind of resilience to the forces of futility and extinction. Here, at least, she finds the desired oblivion:

> Dorothy sliced two more sheets of brown paper into strips, and took up the breastplate to give it its final coating. The problem of faith and no faith had vanished utterly from her mind. It was beginning to get dark, but, too busy to stop and light the lamp, she worked on, pasting strip after strip of paper into place, with absorbed, with pious concentration, in the penetrating smell of the gluepot. (pp. 262-63)

NOTES

1. A Clergyman's Daughter (1935; rpt. Harmondsworth: Penguin Books, 1967), p. 15. Henceforth cited in text by page number to this edition.
2. Being and Nothingness, pp. 37-39.
3. William Wordsworth, "Intimations of Immortality," Poetical Works, ed. Thomas Hutchinson, new ed. rev. by Ernest de Selincourt (1936; rpt. London: Oxford Univ. Press, 1969), p. 461, ll. 131-32.
4. Albert Camus, The Myth of Sisyphus, trans. Justin O'Brien (1955; rpt. Harmondsworth: Penguin Books, 1977), p. 19.
5. Ernest Becker, The Birth and Death of Meaning, 2nd ed. (1971; rpt. Harmondsworth: Penguin Books, 1972), p. 65.
6. Animal Farm, p. 55.
7. The Divided Self, p. 80.
8. A Critical Dictionary of Psychoanalysis (1968; rpt. Harmondsworth: Penguin Books, 1972), p. 55.
9. Existentialism (1972; rpt. Harmondsworth: Pelican Books, 1973), p. 51.
10. Wigan Pier, p. 141.
11. "Such, Such Were the Joys," The Collected Essays, Journalism and Letters, pp. 379, 383.
12. The Outsider, trans. Stuart Gilbert (1946; rpt. Harmondsworth: Penguin Books, 1969), p. 120.

Chapter Six

KEEP THE ASPIDISTRA FLYING

In passing from *A Clergyman's Daughter* to *Keep the Aspidistra Flying* we shift from stoic silence to incontinent execration. And yet this apparently profound contrast is only a difference in expressive response to a condition of profound similarity, for both Dorothy Hare and Gordon Comstock have become spectators of an external process in which their selves are trapped like twigs in a stream. The differing ways in which they accept their impotence are explicable through acknowledging the difference in social position derived from the fact that Dorothy is a woman and Comstock is a man. The quietness of Dorothy's revolt is due to the personal presence of her oppressor; and this presence is part of the structure which she is constrained to accept *as a woman*. Along with this oppressor comes also the abstract oppression of society, which, *as a man*, is Comstock's *only* oppression. Comstock can fulminate against his oppression because aggressive assertion cannot be punished by an abstraction, and because, as a man, it is his right to do so. Thus Comstock is no more of a rebel than Dorothy. He is merely exercising the greater freedoms that a man inherits through the contingency of his sex.

Dorothy Hare and Gordon Comstock exemplify a significant socio-sexual distinction: the woman is in bondage to the man, and the man is in bondage to the State. The woman who rebels therefore is in a grimmer condition, for she has to overcome two forms of oppression if liberty and individuality are to be achieved. In the Orwell corpus Dorothy is especially disadvantaged because, as the only female protagonist, she is born into a world which has already pre-determined her inferiority. Her situation is distinctly a *woman's* situation. If Orwell, while reading the proofs of *A Clergyman's*

Daughter, had made the appropriate adjustments and published it as A Clergyman's Son, it would be read as an ironic farce. And while this remark may be construed as flippant, it is, existentially, a point of critical value, for A Clergyman's Daughter is understood as a realist fiction *only* because it is understood that there is a genuine distinction between a woman's being-in-the-world and a man's. Human Being is of two kinds. What we witness in A Clergyman's Daughter is the ontological poverty of womanhood. Before a woman embarks on the quest for an authentic life she has to contend with and annul her being-in-the-world as woman-for-man, and this is why Dorothy's plight is so much more serious than either John Flory's or Gordon Comstock's. Irrespective of the truth that Flory desires racial equality, his principal wish is for a cleansing of personal conscience and a shared isolation of sufficient strength to allow him to live as an outsider without being vexed by the They. He has an image of what kind of man he would like to be, and it is chiefly this that relates him to Comstock, a man who is almost paranoiacally obsessed with how he appears to the world. Through this objectivization of the self, they both make projects out of their lives, a concept utterly foreign to Dorothy. Because she is the only *real* victim, her only desire is to escape. To escape *for* something would, perhaps, seem to her an indulgence; it would definitely seem so if it meant giving up the very thing that might possibly have maintained her psychic balance: money. And yet this is what Comstock does. He renounces money. He renounces it with the same inordinateness of fervour which marks the tempted Puritan, and, like the Puritan, he detects the object of his dread and loathing in every little unlikely recess of life. Insidiously and relentlessly the money bacterium is worming itself into the heart of all things, and Comstock's scalpel intelligence drags across London's epidermal tissue and reveals its poisoned essence. In theme and atmosphere Keep the Aspidistra Flying is something like Defoe's Journal of the Plague Year grafted on to Gissing's New Grub Street and Knut Hamsun's Hunger, and if there is a general moral to be drawn from the book it is captured in the Eliot line: 'to be restored, our sickness must grow worse'.[1] But Orwell's use of money in Aspidistra differs from Gissing's and Hamsun's; the 'money-god' effects an alteration of reality in its victim, creating the familiar Orwellian world of transformation and blurred identities. Georg Simmel (1903) has described this effect:

> By being the equivalent to all the manifold things in one and the same way, money becomes the most frightful leveller. For money expresses all qualitative differences of things in terms of 'how much?' Money, with all its colourlessness and indifference, becomes the common denominator of all values; irreparably it hollows out the core of things, their individuality, their specific value and their incomparability. All things float with equal specific gravity in the constantly moving stream of money. All things lie on the same level and differ from one another only in the size of the area which they cover.[2]

In addition to the accuracy of Simmel's analysis in revealing Comstock's particular plight over money, there is a striking resemblance to Heidegger's description of the dominion of the They, even in terminology. Money, like the They, is an abstract power which homogenizes, like a sheet drawn over furniture, concealing all distinctions of quality and every individualizing characteristic. Money and the They are ubiquitous, and yet both elude any discovery which would render them tangible. Comstock, perpetually under the dominion of money, is detached both from his self's distinguishing features and the source of power which structures his life. He fits precisely Erich Fromm's description of alienation, in which 'man does not experience himself as the active bearer of his own powers and richness, but as an impoverished 'thing', dependent on powers outside himself, unto whom he has projected his living substance'.[3] This, of course, not only defines Comstock; it is true also of Flory and Dorothy. Thus Orwell's view of man in his world remains unchanged. Only his situation and his mode of response differs. Increasingly one feels that what is being enforced is the Hemingway dictum that a man can run, but he can't hide. Indeed, this would be an appropriate rubric for any Orwell novel, for it conveys the sense of the impotent victim caught in futile motion within a totalitarian scheme. But the totalitarian character of the protagonist's world in *Aspidistra* is not imposed. It is the consequence of a freely chosen attitude towards *money*, an attitude adopted in order to exempt Comstock from the strain which necessarily accompanies the pursuit of an authentic life. Thus *Aspidistra*, a novel inexhaustibly concerned with the personal and social significance of money, is a novel about a scapegoat and is therefore a study in bad faith. Additionally it follows a course of action typically existential: 'the existential writer will want to show us characters who are in the process of discovering or remaking the basic choice of themselves'.[4]

In *Aspidistra*, Orwell illustrates Sartre's premise that 'human reality . . . identifies and defines itself by the ends which it pursues'.[5] As is customary with Orwell, he provides the biographical background for these chosen ends and, in his presentation of this background, we discover the predictable: power. Power, for Orwell, is always the power to inauthenticate, and in *Aspidistra* this power is patriarchal, effecting the kind of submission described in *A Clergyman's Daughter*. Gran'pa Comstock is like an iron mould for a whole family of jelly babies:

> By the time when he died all his children were grown up and some of them were middle-aged, and he had long ago succeeded in crushing out of them any spirit they might ever have possessed. He had lain upon them as a garden roller lies upon daisies, and there was no chance of their flattened personalities ever expanding again. One and all they turned out listless, gutless, unsuccessful sort of people . . . . It was impossible to imagine any of them making any sort of mark in the world, or creating anything, or destroying anything, or being happy, or vividly unhappy, or fully alive, or even earning a decent income. They just drifted along in an atmosphere of semi-genteel failure.[6]

What has been destroyed in gran'pa's eleven children is *initiative*; in fact, so deeply have they been undermined that the instinct for survival has been curbed. Even as a boy it is noticeable to Comstock 'that they had lost all impulse to reproduce themselves' (p. 44). Deprived of all sense of choice, action and possibility, life has become merely persistence and the maintenance of the status to which they were born. Thinking of themselves as *made* by another, and hence ontologically dependent, life as a process of becoming ends when the maker dies. Thus, 'in every possible way, *nothing ever* happened in the Comstock family. Every one of them seemed doomed' (p. 44). Gran'pa's power to inauthenticate involves, by definition, the power to transform, to make another become what he feels he is not, and Comstock was born to a father who has undergone this process: 'seeing that his mind was of the literary type and he had a shrinking horror of anything to do with figures, it had seemed only natural to Gran'pa Comstock to make him into a chartered accountant. So he practised, ineffectually, as a chartered accountant' (p. 45). It is appropriate, then, that Comstock, born to a man who has surrendered his will, should be an 'unintended child' (p. 44). It is a comforting origin for one whose basic position in the world is that he is not responsible for himself.

In their biographical understanding of self-development, Sartre and Orwell are almost identical, and Keep the Aspidistra Flying is the novel in which this connection is particularly apparent, for Gordon Comstock's predicament in life is presented as being explicable through a self-created Project derived from an Original Choice made in bad faith.

The terms in which Comstock's family are described convey the impression that he was born in a neglected allotment, and it is against this background of decline that he asserts his own rather impoverished vitality. Because all members of the family have the passivity of victims, existence must seem as if it is something done against them. With no challenge seeming to be effective against the forces of the world, it would seem also that these forces are insuperable, and therefore function as determinative laws: 'Every one of them seemed doomed, as though by a curse, to a dismal, shabby, hole-and-corner existence. None of them ever did anything. They were the kind of people who in every conceivable activity, even if it is only getting on a bus, are automatically elbowed away from the heart of things' (p. 44).

Comstock's family, then, has an in-itself existence; they have renounced all hope of individual endeavour with its insecurities and anxieties, and settled for the featureless stability of genteel poverty. Their only hope is the possibility that the 'clever' Gordon will do the living for them and restore their lost status, a status that they had not originally made for themselves but had been given them by gran'pa. So what they are is not what they have made, and what they aspire to be they invest in the power of another; and with this prospect in mind they spend unaffordable sums on Gordon's education. But it is at school that he develops the heretical attitudes which will soon be used as a way of spuriously justifying the conviction that he is bound to fail. His 'crawling reverence for money' results initially from the fact that his comparative poverty at school leads him to feel inferior to the others (p. 47). Thus the desire to belong, to be normative, is, paradoxically, the motive for his eventual position as an outsider. As an outsider, he puts himself beyond shame. For Comstock, to be judged is always to be found guilty of inadequacy. In the capitalist middle-class world he is sub-standard, personally incomplete. Thus his pursuit of socialism is comprehensible as a drive to compensate for a sense of feeling deficient. The inspiration behind his socialism is, then, no different from what inspired his envy of riches: either would serve his purpose if it provided that sense of self-significance to be got from a sense of parity and belonging. Comstock's desire is to _be_ something, and as the ordinary route to Being seems closed, he adroitly converts his lack into a fulness; and it is at this point that the old formula of the either/or of the Excluded Middle is engaged: 'Gordon thought it all out in the naive selfish manner of a boy. There are two ways to live, he decided. You can be rich, or you can deliberately refuse to be rich. You can possess money, or you can despise money; the one fatal thing is to worship money and fail to get it' (p. 50). As with Elizabeth Lackersteen's the 'beastly' and the 'lovely', the world is bifurcated in order to exclude any shading of identity, for the quest to be something tolerates nothing but plenitudes. It is on this basis that Comstock establishes his Original Choice, but in order to conceive of himself as immutable essence he must deceive himself on the point that it is he alone who does the choosing. He provides the semblance of this by developing a self-for-others:

> He took it for granted that he himself would never be able to make money. It hardly even occurred to him that he might have talents which could be turned to account. That was what his schoolmasters had done for him; they had rubbed it into him that he was a seditious little nuisance and not likely to 'succeed' in life. He accepted this. Very well, then, he would refuse the whole business of 'suc-

> ceeding'; he would make it his especial purpose _not_ to 'succeed'.... Already, at sixteen, he knew which side he was on. He was against the money-god and all his swinish priesthood. He had declared war on money; but secretly, of course. (p. 50)

What Comstock is accepting is a description of himself which suits his purpose, which is to fail, but to fail without being seen as responsible for it. He welcomes the notion that success is impossible because failure would then be inevitable, a _destiny_. As a destiny, failure becomes essence; as an essence he _is_ a failure in the same way that a cripple is a cripple. Not being able to transcend his condition, he can never be blamed for not 'succeeding'. And it is, above all, the blame and guilt that he wants to elude. He wants to be morally stainless before the world, otherwise he cannot live as the bitter victim of it. Planning to be an outsider _by necessity_, he will henceforth interpret his isolation as the result of exclusion. He will see the world as cause, and himself as effect, and thereby all his hatreds and disgusts will carry an implicit accusation. As a result, his whole experience of the nature of the world will organize itself in conformity to his original choice of self-as-failure. He will, in Karl Popper's phrase, perpetually detect 'confirming instances' of his theory of Being.[7] In this way it can be said that, for Comstock, like Winston Smith, the objective state of things is everywhere disguised. He is estranged from the actual. And nowhere in _Aspidistra_ is this estrangement more despairingly expressed than in the opening chapter, where we encounter Comstock in his maturity, frustrated and impoverished, living out the logical conclusion of his Original Choice:

> He gazed out at the graceless street. At this moment it seemed to him that in a street like this, in a town like this, every life that is lived must be meaningless and intolerable. The sense of disintegration, of decay, that is endemic in our time, was strong upon him. Somehow it was mixed up with the ad-posters opposite. He looked now with more seeing eyes at those grinning yard-wide faces. After all, there was more than mere silliness, greed, and vulgarity. Corner Table grins at you, seemingly optimistic, with a flash of false teeth.

> But what is behind the grin? Desolation, emptiness, prophecies of doom. For can you not see, if you know how to look, that behind that slick self-satisfaction, that tittering fat-bellied triviality, there is nothing but a frightful emptiness, a secret despair? The great death-wish of the modern world. Suicide pacts. Heads stuck in gas-ovens in lonely maisonettes. French letters and Amen Pills. And the reverberations of future wars. Enemy aeroplanes flying over London; the deep threatening hum of the propellers, the shattering thunder of the bombs. It is all written in Corner Table's face. (p. 21)

The clue to the interpretative nature of this vision of hopelessness is the rhetorical interpolation, 'can you not see, if you know how to look'. Appearances have to be seen through in order for significancies to be revealed: 'what is behind the grin?' Objective forms bear codes which have to be broken for the 'real' to emerge: 'It is all written in Corner Table's face'. The world has to be bent into a new shape in order for it to conform to, and therefore justify, the view of the world that he established when he made his original choice. Comstock doesn't uncover anything in the world that he doesn't want to see. Through a fixed programme of selected perception he invents reality. He makes what he sees. This, and the deception it involves, is given a more tangible presence in the advertisement, for, when Comstock looks into Corner Tables' face he does so as one who has been responsible for creating similar advertisements at the New Albion. He, like Winston Smith working in Minitrue, has been involved in fraud, and, also like Smith, he has become the victim of his own deceptions. But Comstock incessantly denies that he is deceived about the nature of the world; it is he, almost alone, who understands the truth of things. He denies that the 'desolation, emptiness, prophecies of doom' 'behind the grin' are the outcome of his own personal project of failure. This, he endlessly repeats, is what the world objectively <u>is</u>. That he is in these kinds of clothes, with this kind of wage, in this kind of shop, on this kind of street; that he has this kind of past, and this kind of present, and this kind of future; that he hates like he does and rages with all kinds of frustration: all these are symptoms of a sociopolitical plague with which he has been helplessly infected.

Comstock, although nearly thirty, decided the structure of his self and the world when he was sixteen; and this explains much about his temperament as we see it throughout the novel. Comstock behaves like an adolescent because, by dogmatizing a reductionism, he has frozen himself into the world-view of an adolescent. Having decided definitively what was and what wasn't, further emotional and intellectual development in any substantial sense became unnecessary. Discovery was at an end. Everything was explained. Money was the First Cause, the fundamental deterministic law which shaped the self and the world. Therefore resistance was futile. One was only free to complain, to harangue the prison governor through the bars of the cell. And it was through submitting to this scheme that living, for Comstock, transformed into dying: '"My poems are dead because I'm dead. You're dead. We're all dead. Dead people in a dead world"' (p. 90). He can feel no real engagement with life because all sense of volition and spontaneity is lost. He lives on the surface of things, estranged by his own concepts from the feeling of being consequential. Everything in and around him is lifeless because the automatism he has adopted deprives him of the sense that it is *his own life* that he is living. The quality of 'mineness' has been flattened by determinism. Like a puppet, he moves only by being moved. As with his family before him, he has lost all feeling of being able to initiate. He has become a *thing*. The consequence of Comstock's lacking a sense of mineness is realized in his sense of feeling superfluous, and, feeling superfluous, he continually feels the pain of being disregarded. In believing that money is everything, in poverty he is nothing.

This money-maketh-man dogma has its most biting and humiliating effect in his relations with others, of whom there are few and only two that count: Ravelston and Rosemary. Ravelston, upper middle-class and wealthy by inheritance, owns the left-wing journal *Antichrist*, in which Comstock gets most of his poems placed. He both functions in the same confessional role as does Dr. Veraswami in *Burmese Days*, and, more importantly, his presence establishes the same invidious contrast with Comstock as does that of the horseman Verrall in relation to Flory. Verrall appeared in *Burmese Days* as an exemplary figure, not in moral terms, but as one who had achieved coincidence in what he was and what he desired to be. He had *style*, the illusion of being solid and personally identifiable. In contrast, Flory felt empty and insignificant. Comstock, although he 'adores' Ravelston, envies him for the same reason Flory envied Verrall: his style, his self-possession. Ravelston has maintained his upper middle-class style independently of his renunciation of upper middle-class life. His style, derived from class, continues to exist even though he has rejected class. Thus he presents Comstock with the illusion of having essence, the thing for which Comstock strives but cannot achieve. Style has the appearance of being intrinsic to Ravelston and not something that he has acquired. Comstock's envy of this is expressed in his habit of emphasizing its pecuniary origin; and because money is something which Ravelston inherited, Comstock is able to explain Ravelston's virtues in terms of contingency. So Comstock, who explains his own negative attributes through this same contingency, is adroitly able to make it seem that these negativities don't belong to him, are not really part of him. He has been visited by his defects. His defects are not symptoms of personal inferiority but inevitable effects of causes beyond his control. In this way Comstock gains parity with Ravelston. Qualitatively they are the same. But this is not enough. Ravelston must be shamed. But in order to shame him Comstock is logically obliged to adopt a contrary position in which monetary determinism is denied. He encourages Ravelston to feel guilty for being born into a specific class and for inheriting money as a result of this. In all things related to money, Comstock attempts to make Ravelston feel guilty, and the reason why he is so successful at this is because Ravelston doesn't accept the deterministic mode from which Comstock himself has fashioned a life. Ravelston is a man who accepts that he is free and responsible for his effect on the world and can always do more for it. And it is by virtue of this honesty that Cosmtock can procure the appearance of a moral advantage, and he extends this by deliberately arranging both conversation and situation in such a way that Ravelston's income comes to seem increasingly unjustified and reprehensible. Thus Ravelston is a hypocrite. It is Comstock's meanest and most dishonest streak that he encourages his only real male friend to feel guilty about the very things that Comstock most envies. He wants to make it seem that he himself has given up money and position through a moral disgust with capitalism, and, as a result of having given up these comforts, has additionally sacrificed himself as a writer (he can't write because he was morally obliged to surrender those things which make writing possible). Thus he is able to project himself as morally fine, a kind of martyr and an honourable idealist. In this way he comes close to achieving an image of himself which is not merely false but diametrically in opposition to what is the truth. But the relational dynamic behind this is that Comstock has created a false image of himself through falsifying another. Like Ellis's attitude to the waiter in Burmese Days, Comstock needs Ravelston's tacit assent to the kind of identity he wishes to secure. With the waiter, assent is given because his living depends upon it; with Ravelston, assent is given through the very thing that Comstock is trying to subvert: Ravelston's moral generosity of spirit. Comstock relies on Ravelston's good will. He relies on his not asserting that, of the two, it is only he, Ravelston, who can be called idealistic and sacrificial. Ravelston's comparative moral worth is indicated by the fact that he still feels guilty even though 'his whole life' is 'a struggle to escape' the 'fatty degeneration of spirit which goes with wealth'. Although he gives up 'his time and a large part of his income to editing an unpopular Socialist monthly', and distributes money 'in all directions', he still feels guilty and 'acutely ashamed' (p. 89). In contrast, Comstock has given up nothing except responsibility, and his project of deterministic failure ensures a guiltless passivity before human misfortune.

So self-absorbed is Comstock that he fails to apply his monetarist dogma to others, continuing to cadge from his poor spinster sister even though '"a man's whole personality is bound up with his income. His personality is his income"' (p. 102). Thus, in his own terms, he is gradually eroding his sister's personality in order to maintain his own. From this point of view, Comstock becomes politically very strange indeed, a kind of parasite feeding on other people's ontological capital. Comstock is a text-book capitalist, one of the few who really believe in the existence of homo economicus. The value of man, according to Comstock, resides not in what he is but in what he owns; ontologically, man is a dependence-relation. Cash brings him into Being; he is discovered through money. Money has the magic property of conferring visibility on its owner, both in the sense that the owner becomes tangible to himself and in the sense that he becomes something to others. Thus when Comstock is out pacing the streets, the eyes of the girls who pass go 'over him and through him as though he had not existed' (p. 79). It is through this kind of detail that we understand what a torment his project has become. What initially was to provide him with both a sense of ontological fulness and an easy device for justifying inadequacy has delivered him over to abjection and vacuity. This he never imagined. What he never predicted was that the original choice created a style of choosing which increasingly led him beyond the desired limits of his projected determinism. He wanted to circumscribe his life, not kill it. But, having adopted the deterministic structure, it bound him in all things. Curiously, Comstock confused an escape from freedom with freedom. The movement of flight had the radiance of liberty, and through this observation we arrive at the most crucial aspect of Comstock's conflict: it is because his flight into bad faith involves the rejection of the norms of the They that he interprets his consequent isolation as the proof and manifestation of liberty. In becoming free of the They, he assumes the burdens of freedom without actually living it, because the specific purpose of the flight was bondage. Thus, in one movement, he inherits the incarceration of a deterministic life together with all the anxious uncertainties of an authentic life. So the solidity of self which was the aim of determinism is perpetually eroding because his experience of the self is characterized by the dread and flux of having been thrown into the world a free man.

Comstock's position is such that life is incomprehensible both logically and emotionally. He is caught by the Ingsoc paradox, 'freedom is slavery'. In thinking of slavery he evokes freedom, and in thinking of freedom he evokes slavery. Antithetical categories have lost their mutual exclusivity and merged. Life has become a riddle for which there is no forseeable solution, not, anyhow, if it requires individual decision. Existence, it would seem, can only be altered from the outside: another scapegoat. And this is discovered in war:

> Money, money! Corner Table! The humming of the aeroplanes and the crash of bombs.
>
> Gordon squinted up at the leaden sky. Those aeroplanes are coming. In imagination he saw them coming now; squadron after squadron, innumerable, darkening the sky like clouds of

> gnats. With his tongue not quite against his teeth he made a buzzing, bluebottle-on-the-window-pane sound to represent the humming of the aeroplanes. It was a sound which, at that moment, he ardently desired to hear. (p. 26)

This desire to see the money-world bombed indicates Comstock's dissatisfaction with money as a comprehensive determinant of his life. Money, which has been used as an excuse for all things, is no longer powerful enough to stifle the sense of his own 'horrible freedom' (p. 112). Freedom, because it implies responsibility for the self, is the enemy, and money is the means for imprisoning it. But freedom eludes prolonged capture; it requires a more formidable constraint: a war. Besides destroying Comstock's failing scapegoat and replacing it, war will seem to do so <u>irresistibly</u>, hence avoiding the too flagrant sense that it is he who is freely choosing a new kind of deterministic device to imprison his freedom. It is the ultimate scapegoat. He would need to change nothing except the blame, but the new object of blame would have the fabulous status of universal credibility. Instead of blaming money, which convinces only the few, he would blame war, which everyone will understand. Comstock would be swept inside the whale by the storm of a great event. Along with millions of others he would be granted thinghood. Henceforth, whatever needed to be justified in himself, he will be able to say: 'Then the war came and changed everything. It's not my fault. It was the war that did it'.

This characteristic of its not being his fault is triumphantly present in his relations with his other friend, his girlfriend, Rosemary. And it is because of this that his relations with her are, as is also true with Ravelston, marked by the absence of progression. It is as if he meets them both in order to affirm that nothing in his life has changed: the same excuse equals the same person.

Comstock wants Rosemary to undertand absolutely the causal hub of his life. If she were to understand the ontological significance of money she would then be able to understand that he has no control over what he is. It is only when this is accomplished that he will feel the satisfaction of having being-in-itself. But Rosemary, like Ravelston, believes in freedom and the importance of individual decision: 'It was against her code to interfere - "You've got to live your own life," was always her attitude' (p. 61). This is Rosemary's response to Comstock giving up his 'good job' at the New Albion, she believing, of course, that what he is doing is exercising his freedom in order to establish his 'own life', whereas it is the mineness of 'own life' that he seeks to elude. Subsequently, the fact that it was a free decision will be something to deny, to bury; indeed, all his excuses depend on the suppression of this fact. Far from wanting his *own* life, he wants to be the helpless *spectator* of a process. But Rosemary, like Ravelston, is too generous to remind him of the origins of his project. She accepts his will to be determined because, irrespective of the contradiction, it is still *his* decision to be so. She persists in this liberalism to the end, without any hint of self-advantage. In fact, her libertarian stance brings her nothing but woe, for much of their conflict is reducible to her refusal to surrender her self to Comstock's own notions about what women are *in general*, even though this generalized woman is, ostensibly, the object of his contempt and the woman he would least like her to be. But his desire for her to be a woman in general is rooted in his desire to have her reluctance to 'sleep' with him explained in causal terms. He wants it to seem that she won't sleep with him because, as a woman in general, she is *obliged* to obey the money-code. In this way, if his sexual hunger goes unfed he can attribute it to being an effect of a cause over which he has no control: money. He can bear the pain of sexual rejection if he can construe her resistance as involuntary. But meanwhile, before becoming convinced that she won't, he tries to nag her into submission:

> 'Say "yes," Rosemary! "Yes" - it's such an easy word. Go on, now; say it. "Yes!"'
> 'Anyone would think you were teaching a parrot to talk, Gordon.' (p. 119).

Up to this point Comstock has given her the freedom to say either Yes or No, but on understanding that No is final, he deviously attempts to devastate her individuality by attributing to her the same determinism which he has imposed upon himself: '"Of course it all comes back to money"' (p. 120). *Her* determinism becomes *his* scapegoat: 'he did not even want to be fair. His sexual disappointment still pricked him. With a sort of melancholy triumph he reflected that, after all, he was right. It was money that stood between them. Money, money, all is money!' (p. 122).

At bottom, Comstock cannot comprehend the otherness of the Other, cannot even begin to concede that the Other is not really himself in disguise. Thus his interpretation of her is merely what we already know about Comstock:

> 'It's women who worship it. A woman's got a sort of mystical feeling towards money. Good and evil in a women's mind mean simply money and no money.... It's not because you're mercenary. You don't want me to _pay_ you for sleeping with me. It's not so crude as that. But you've got that deep-down mystical feeling that somehow a man without money isn't worthy of you. He's a weakling, a sort of half-man - that's how you feel.... Women!'
>
> 'Women!' echoed Rosemary on a different note. 'I hate the way men are always talking about _women_. "_Women_ do this," and "_Women_ do that" - as though all women were exactly the same!'
>
> 'Of course all women are the same!' (pp. 122-23)

By asserting that all women are the same, Comstock voids Rosemary as a particular and gives her the status of a specimen. But as yet he hasn't demolished the idea that she may have adopted by choice this status. However, the chance to annihilate is soon to come, when Rosemary offers to pay for their meal:

> 'What! Do you think I'd go to a restaurant and let you pay for my food?'
>
> 'But why not?'
>
> 'Because one can't do that sort of thing. It isn't done.'
>
> 'It "isn't done"! You'll be saying it's "not cricket" in another moment. _What_ "isn't done"?'
>
> 'Letting you pay for my meals. A man pays for a woman, a woman doesn't pay for a man.'
>
> 'Oh, Gordon! Are we living in the reign of Queen Victoria?'
>
> 'Yes, we are, as far as that kind of thing's concerned. Ideas don't change so quickly.'
>
> 'But _my_ ideas have changed.'
>
> 'No, they haven't. You think they have, but they haven't. You've been brought up as a woman, and _you can't help behaving like a woman_ [my underlining], however much you don't want to.'

> 'But what do you mean by <u>behaving like a woman</u>, anyway?'
> 'I tell you every woman's the same when it comes to a thing like this. A woman despises a man who's dependent on her and sponges on her. She may say she doesn't, she may <u>think</u> she doesn't, but she does. <u>She can't help it</u> [my underlining]. If I let you pay for my meals <u>you'd</u> despise me.' (pp. 126-27)

The extraordinary element of this dialogue is what has initiated it. For Comstock, any absolutist prescriptivist device will suffice to establish the sense of constraint that he wants to impose, even the rejected code of the They: '"one can't do that sort of thing. It isn't done"'. Deviously, Comstock explains this constraint on his life as caused by the constraint on women: thus Comstock is constrained because women are constrained. But if women are constrained by choice, then, logically, he is too, which is unbearable. In order to eliminate this choice he has to eliminate her as an individual, for one is only an individual through the possession of the possibility of free independent action. In effect, whatever ideas she may have are not <u>her</u> ideas. What he is compelled to assert, then, is that <u>she is not herself</u>; she, like he, is merely a spectator of that chimera called self. It is in this way that Comstock urges upon her the status of an <u>It</u>, of an object. In order to overwhelm her belief in his freedom he overwhelms <u>her</u> freedom; thus it is true that, as with Ravelston, he attempts to falsify another for the purpose of falsifying himself. From this he derives a confirmation of his Being, and also, because his causality issues directly from hers, he can be seen as <u>her victim</u>, a position Comstock obviously favours as it will excite Rosemary's compasssion. And Rosemary shows her compassion in precisely the manner that a person reduced to a thing would: she makes it seem that she is <u>possessable</u>. She becomes body only: 'The hard defensive feeling had gone out of her body. She shut her eyes and sank against him and into him as though her bones had grown weak.... And suddenly, as he felt her body yielding, he seemed to know with certainty that their struggle was ended. She was his now when he chose to take her' (p. 129).

These chill manoeuvres by Comstock to gain both self-justification and control involve the attempted inauthentication of Rosemary through the pressures of doublethink, for what is sought is repentance for causality. What he wants to hear her say has the logical status of: 'I'm sorry I'm responsible for not being able to help making you my victim'. As it is, she says something similar through gesture; she rewards him by *allowing* her body to seem a helpless thing. The situation exemplifies what Sartre says of love: 'In love it is not a determinism of the passions which we desire in the Other nor a freedom beyond reach; it is a freedom which *plays the role of* a determinism of the passions and which is caught in its own role'.[8]

Living in an it-world of his own making, Comstock is deprived of the possibility of creating relations with another to whom he can say Thou and by whom his own Thou-ness is felt. He, like the Other, is an It among Its. The uniqueness of the self and the Other is dispersed among *things*, and the specificity essential to love is lost. In this way people are expendable because they are replaceable. *Any* Other will do. The feeling of having a life which is *mine* vanishes when all of one's actions are felt to be inevitable. The concreteness of self fades to abstraction and consequent powerlessness. Action becomes reaction. With no sense of the self, life is a record of what is *done to* you; and it is this, above all, which Comstock captures in the poem that he is currently writing:

> The lord of all, the money-god,
> Who rules us blood and hand and brain,
> Who gives the roof that stops the wind,
> And, giving, takes away again;
>
> Who spies with jealous, watchful care,
> Our thoughts, our dreams, our secret ways,
> Who picks our words and cuts our clothes,
> And maps the pattern of our days;
>
> Who chills our anger, curbs our hope,
> And buys our lives and pays with toys,
> Who claims as tribute broken faith,
> Accepted insults, muted joys;
>
> Who binds with chains the poet's wit,
> The navvy's strength, the soldier's pride,
> And lays the sleek, estranging shield
> Between the lover and his bride. (pp. 162-63)

The world thus described is a complete expression of the extent and nature of power in 1984, and with the understanding that this is a world whose adversity is of Comstock's own choosing, it may be asserted that Orwell's explanation for the existence of totalitarianism involves the desire to create a determinism in order to elude the anxieties of a contingent world in which man is responsible for what he becomes. But the consequences, as has been shown, are dire and paradoxical: the pursuit of essence through determinism affects the hunter with a sense of deadness, of unreality, of despair (p. 21), so that the ontological fixity which was the aim of the pursuit is rendered less likely because of the pursuit. Caught in this spiralling attrition, Comstock's one remaining stability (indeed, his self-definition) is his dogma, to which he is obliged to cling with an ever-increasing tenacity.

But there is one interlude in the novel where redemption seems possible, and that is when Comstock and Rosemary leave the city for a day in the country. The very terms in which this outing is described suggest an emancipation from Comstock's iron view of being-in-the-world. Nature temporarily suspends the it-world of money because it is not obviously the scene of man's projects. Comstock, brought up in London, and almost never out of it, enters a world quite unassociated with the forlorn pursuit of Being. Entering the natural world, he is impressed by the contrast and impelled to take a view of himself not possible in the city. He feels 'shrunken and out of place', 'as though he had been living underground for a long time' (p. 135). As with those in Plato's cave, what he has always construed as reality might merely be shadows of the real thing. Perhaps the dogma is false. Perhaps the world can be otherwise, or, at least, the gutter may be no more 'real' than the grass. Certainly there is an alteration of consciousness in Comstock. Especially significant is his sudden relish for 'similes and metaphors', indicating a transformational perspective; and important too, in one instance, is the manner in which metaphor is employed. Previously the advertisements on the hoardings were blatant symptoms of civilization's desolate heart. Now, they are joyfully ridiculed, the autumn leaves being '"Thick as the Breakfast Crisps that strow the plates / In Welwyn Garden City!"' (p. 138). It is 'great fun'. The 'shrunken' feeling vanishes; he has grown to fit the new openness, and he is alive in a world from which he is not estranged. There is a feeling of prelapsarian belonging: 'They pressed their bodies together in a sort of sexless rapture, like children' (p. 136). At last, it is their world. The grip of urban calculation has eased. He can look at Rosemary now as not the means for something; she is an end in herself. Feelings peculiar to the I-Thou relation are generated:

> Here in the open air he could see the marks of time quite clearly upon her face. She was nearly thirty, and looked it, and he was nearly thirty, and looked more; and it mattered nothing. He pulled off the absurd flat hat. The three white hairs gleamed on her crown. At the moment he did not wish them away. They were part of her and therefore lovable. (p. 136)

They are 'extravagantly happy', falling into 'absurd enthusiasms' over everything they see (p. 137). Here, alone together in the country, there is 'hardly a breath of wind' (p. 138). They are becalmed, a constrast to the opening line of his poem about the irresistible powers of the money-god: 'Sharply the menacing wind sweeps over / The bending poplars, newly bare' (p. 161). Without the wind, there is self-direction, the possibility of 'mineness'. Everything seems set for a cheerful restoration. But of course, this is what Orwell denies. Typically, he provides the possibilities of a restoration during a brief remission from the conflicts of life, but only to create a sharp contrast with what follows. It is almost as if one ascends merely in order to go down deeper and more quickly.

Having passed over the chance to eat in a cheap pub, Comstock and Rosemary arrive at the only alternative, The Ravenscroft Hotel: 'It did look expensive. It was a vulgar pretentious place, all gilt and white paint - one of those hotels which have overcharging and bad service written on every brick.... Gordon quailed. The money in his pocket seemed to shrink to nothing. This was the very opposite to the cosy pub they had been looking for' (p. 141). The significant word here is 'shrink'. Comstock, having come 'shrunken' from London, expands to fit the sudden new dimensions of the world and becomes full; now, confronting a building of blatant falseness, his money, with which he totally identifies, shrinks, and thus he with it.

He is reminded of his project, of what he _is_. Although resolved to eat cheaply the They reasserts itself: 'In such a place as this you couldn't possibly say "Bread and cheese and beer"; "Lunch" was the only thing you could say. There was nothing for it but "Lunch" or flight' (p. 142). Since the creation of his choice between 'success' and 'failure' at school, this has been the permanent feature of Comstock's life. He asserts only one antithetical option, an utterly inflexible either/or. According to the Comstockian code, everything is either fully one thing or fully another; any compromise, any hint of the Middle Included, jeopardizes his theory of Being. Comstock, not taking flight, is _bound_ to have lunch, and, having lunch, is bound _also_ to pay for Rosemary, because 'a man pays for a woman' (p. 126). Coming in from the unselfconscious, non-prescriptive, projectless countryside, he falls instantly into a type of conduct where actions become inevitable, freedom is denied, and mineness is lost. No longer will Rosemary's three white hairs be lovable because they are _hers_.

Comstock, by ordering 'lunch', _commits_ himself to dissimulation, at the same time knowing that credible dissimulation is _not possible_. In fact, by ordering lunch to protect himself from shame, he creates the major reason for his ridicule, for he demonstrates to the waiter that he is not even capable of playing the role which the ordering of lunch commits him to. The paradox about Comstock's pretence of having more money than he has is that it stems from the belief that the waiter _knows_ that he is poor. So convinced is he of this that he has the 'hateful feeling that the man could actually see through the cloth and count the money in his pocket' (p. 142). The pretence actually functions as a means of revealing what the pretence is trying to hide, as Comstock is not able to buy all the other things that the ordering of lunch would normally entail. Additionally ludicrous, Comstock is pretending to a man who is himself perhaps pretending: 'probably he was an Englishman and had assumed a foreign accent because this was proper in a waiter' (p. 143). But, unlike Ellis instructing the waiter in _Burmese Days_, Comstock, because of his penury, does not have the power to enforce a deferential pretence in the waiter. Indeed, the roles are reversed, and the waiter feels his power and uses it to reveal Comstock's inadaequacy as an actor. Comstock, having offered himself as an actor, is left with nothing when his role is blown. So it can be seen that it is Comstock's acquiescence to the norms of the They which makes his humiliation by the They possible.

Even the rejection of the chilled red wine doesn't 'win back his prestige' (p. 144), and not merely because it is too cheap to warm but because it lacks the courage of an individualistic assertion: '"That's not the way to serve red wine"' (p. 145). Even if this comment had had the effect of humbling the waiter, it would have still occurred in the context of Comstock's general submission, for, in ordering wine, he has already surrendered to the waiter's power. The victory over Comstock was complete when he failed to order beer. Having ordered wine in conformity to the pressure of the They, he is, in returning it, still in conformity, for returning the wine is something 'one can do'. It is permitted. Far from being a challenge to the They, it is upholding the They's standards, and, of course, Comstock is exercising his entitlement to restore his credibility as an actor. His aim is to be treated like everyone else. The last thing he wants is to be seen as aberrant. Whatever his individual preferences, he will use every opportunity to exist for himself and the waiter as an average diner, as one of the anonymous They. As such, he is a nobody whose only power is that of the regulations; he can say '"That's not the way to serve red wine"', but not 'I don't like chilled red wine'. The regulations speak for him; he is not responsible. But as he hasn't earned sufficient credibility as an actor, the waiter can treat him with disdain for making the false assumption that he was making a complaint under the protection of the They.

Comstock's hypocrisy of values becomes sharply obvious when he eventually tips a shilling to the waiter, a man whom Comstock hates: 'He thought he had never hated anyone so much as he hated this waiter' (p. 144). The shilling is a desperate measure, given as a last hope of having his identity affirmed as one of the They, a cash gamble aimed at procuring by some small gesture of the Other an acknowledgement of one's orthodoxy. Believing that money creates the self, he naturally believes that the self can be bought. This also fails. The way in which the waiter responds to the shilling represents his opinion of Comstock: suspect, offensive, ridiculous, to be ignored: 'The waiter balanced it for a moment on his hand, flicked it over, and then slipped it into his waistcoat pocket with the air of covering up something unmentionable' (p. 147). In addition, the giving of this shilling is an act of betrayal, as it belongs to Comstock's impoverished sister Julia, who is a _waitress_. Thus Comstock's hypocrisy is double-edged, for the value that he has maintained of the man paying for the woman is harshly negated. Indeed, it is the 'loan' from Julia which has made the whole outing possible. Comstock has reduced Julia in order to pay a man he hates merely to gain a false prestige. He has decided to use a woman's money so that he can maintain in front of the Other the image of the man paying for the woman. His values, then, are entirely concerned with self-image; they are for the outside alone: the principle of the self-for-other. Truth, or any kind of probity or fidelity, is valueless. He wants to be _seen to be_. It is for this alone that his 'code' exists.

The outcome of this session of multiple pretence is that Comstock has driven the It between the incipient I-Thou. Released once more into the countryside, Comstock and Rosemary feel their distance, a distance which generates calculation and objectivity. All the prelapsarian, unselfconscious unity of their relation is lost. Rosemary becomes a body, a thing to be used, and, being a thing, she becomes unfamiliar. They both feel their estrangement and are intimidated:

> Rosemary walked ahead of him, rather nervous, not speaking. She was half frightened now by the thing she had resolved to do. He watched her strong delicate limbs moving. There was her body that he had wanted so long; but now when the time had come it only daunted him. He wanted her to be his, he wanted to _have had_ her, but he wished it were over and done with. It was an effort - a thing he had got to screw himself up to. It was strange that that beastly business of the hotel bill could have upset him so completely. The easy care-free mood of the morning was shattered; in its place there had come back the hateful, harassing, familiar thing - worry about money. In a minute he would have to own up that he had only eightpence left; he would have to borrow money off her to get them home; it would be squalid and shameful. (pp. 147-48)

What would have been natural, thoughtless and

spontaneous before lunch takes on the aspect of a formal agreement, a sex-pledge which guarantees availability irrespective of emotional change. Rosemary's tacit promise, won by extortion on a previous occasion, was an attempt by Comstock to have her surrender her freedom. The meaning of the promise is that she will, at a certain time, become instrumental. It makes action seem to be inevitable, turns his defloration of her into her destiny. Under such conditions, sex is a mechanical act performed by Its. With no feeling of choice and personal involvement, the participants become spectators of what their bodies are doing, almost like voyeurs. For this kind of event Comstock finds the appropriate place: behind barbed wire at the far edge of a 'dead and empty' copse (p. 148). Rosemary is the prisoner of her promise:

> She lay under him, yielding rather than responding. She did not resist when his hand sought her breasts. But in her heart she was still frightened. She would do it - oh, yes! she would keep her implied promise, she would not draw back; but all the same she was frightened. And at heart he too was half reluctant. It dismayed him to find how little, at this moment, he really wanted her. (p. 149)

But Comstock never gets properly under way. Appropriately for an 'unintended child' who denies responsibility for his deeds, he has brought no condoms, and this stirs Rosemary to the freedom to resist. And although she later relents, Comstock, having cited money as the reason for having no condoms, is captured in full-flight determinism:

> 'Don't you understand that one isn't a full human being - that one doesn't <u>feel</u> a human being - unless one's got money in one's pockets?'
>
> 'No. I think that's just silly.'
>
> 'It isn't that I don't want to make love to you. I do. But I tell you I can't make love to you when I've only eightpence in my pocket. At least when you know I've only eightpence. I just can't do it. It's physically impossible.' (p. 156)

Comstock is now talking as if copulation had not initially been possible, whereas, still with only eightpence in his pocket, he had been about to accomplish it. He wants to make it seem that it wasn't Rosemary's freedom which stopped him but the perennial scapegoat. Thus he can feel that he wasn't actually rejected by her as a person but was himself rejecting her through something for which he is not responsible. This, of course, is a compensation for her not being so overcome by desire for him that she would risk a pregnancy. He is innocent.

Comstock's next fiasco is also the final one, and it shows, irrespective of wealth or poverty, that his project of failure leads him always to the same humiliation. Elated by an unexpected cheque from a poetry magazine, he invites Ravelston and Rosemary to Ravelston's favourite restaurant, Modigliani's. The big coup is that he will be seen to pay for them _both_, and then, with much more than eightpence in his pocket, have a night with Rosemary in a hotel. Everything which went wrong at the Ravenscroft will be excessively corrected. He will see the fulness of his Being reflected in the bought eyes of the waiter. And for a while he does. He even becomes 'interesting' to another woman (p. 172). Then drunkenness begins, and the sudden bright splendour of his life fades into squalor. Rebuffed by Rosemary in the street for treating her just as a body, he ends the night in a brothel. But now that he can actually pay his way and buy a body, his impotence is genuine: 'No. No use. Impossible. The will but not the way. . . . the booze, it must be' (p. 189).

Apart from the final chapter, the remainder of the novel records Comstock's descent and occupation of the 'sub-world', and follows the same pattern of experience as Dorothy Hare's. Both slide into an abyss after a period of oblivion. But for Comstock, there is nothing unexpected about this. Even before his sudden elevation to temporary wealth, he had seen clearly the outcome of his original choice:

> At this moment he saw himself and his life without saving disguises. Every night the same - back to the cold lonely bedroom and the grimy, littered sheets of the poem that never got any further. It was a blind alley. He would never finish _London Pleasures_, he would never marry Rosemary, he would never set his life in order. He would only drift and sink, drift and sink, like the others of his family; but worse than them - down, down into some dreadful sub-world that as yet he could only

> dimly imagine. It was what he had chosen when he declared war on money. Serve the money-god or go under; there is no other rule. (p. 160)

The sub-world is, in fact, the logical destination of his project. What the period of oblivion marks is the extinction of any remaining resistance to his chosen destiny: 'In his heart he didn't want to be helped. He only wanted to be left alone. He was headed for the gutter' (p. 204). His ultimate resting place is 'the jail', the place of definitive bondage, a symbol of determinism. The jail would be a place of rest, for in it he would find _freedom from freedom_. He imagines 'quiet worlds where money and effort and moral obligation did not exist' (p. 209). He wants it to seem that he is being dragged underground, irreclaimably out of reach of the They. And this is crucial to an understanding of Comstock's existential position. Instead of surrendering his freedom to the norms of the They and becoming one of them, he buries his freedom in a deterministic plan in order to elude the They's condemnation. Being, at heart, one of the They, he believes his revolt to be unjustifiable. Feeling traitorous, he evokes a determinism in order to have himself justified. Thus, his attitude towards the They is always ambivalent, a position which achieves its most evident expression in his relations with Ravelston and Rosemary. While he incessantly fulminates against the They's money-code, he simultaneously accepts absolutely the They's economic definition of man. He is the kind of man who he purportedly defines himself _against_.

It has already been noted that Comstock is frustrated by the failure of his project and almost permanently discontent, and it was suggested that his desire for war was rooted in a wish to have his scapegoat replaced by one which would more effectively justify his life. The descent into the sub-world is a measure of Comstock's desperation over the inefficacy of his project. In the absence of any effective alternative, he merely lets go and sinks into a deathly insensibility. Floundering on the bottom, he discovers something very ordinary, a desire for the easy vitality of common life. But he smothers this and drifts, a thing without purpose or meaning, the very last of the Comstocks. It is in this condition that he is visited by Rosemary on a mission of mercy: 'Simply because he was penniless and a failure she had got to yield to him, even if it was only once' (p. 235). At last he is rewarded, but the manner in which the consummation occurs is a most fortunate reversal of their previous attempt in the country, for the pregnancy which ensues can almost be seen by Comstock as the result of rape:

> 'This isn't wise,' he said.
> 'I don't care. I wish I'd done it years ago.'
> 'We'd much better not.'
> 'Yes.'
> 'No.'
> 'Yes!'
> After all, she was too much for him. (p. 236)

And it is the child which is his salvation. Within minutes of being told of her pregnancy, he discovers a ghastly either/or of obvious partiality. In response to Rosemary's 'you've got your own life to live', Comstock, obviously hating this notion, says:

> 'It comes down to this. Either I marry you and go back to the New Albion, or you go to one of those filthy doctors and get yourself messed about for five pounds.'
> At that she twisted herself out of his grasp and stood up facing him. His blunt words had upset her. They had made the issue clearer and uglier than before.
> 'Oh, why did you say that?'
> 'Well, those _are_ the alternatives.' (p. 243)

Putting the alternatives in this way instantly produces an almost insurmountable aversion to the alternative that Comstock has no intention of considering. Thus he can feel obliged, almost impelled, and the pregnancy begins to function as a really viable scapegoat, with the additional advantage that it will be seen by Rosemary as a sacrifice of his treasured 'code'. She will think him a better man as a result.

As used by Comstock, the either/or is a deterministic technique which disguises the fact of decision. The either/or, when tendentiously uttered, produces the favoured choice as if it were the only one possible. The other partner, by acquiescing in the impossibility of there being other alternatives, becomes an unconscious collaborator in the scheme. With neither party wishing it to be otherwise, reality becomes an agreement between two people. Once the sleight of consciousness of there being only two routes is established, the second sleight is to make it seem that one of the two routes is blocked (paying a filthy doctor a fiver to mess you about). In this way the illusion is created that there is no choice at all. Comstock _must_ go back to the New Albion and marry Rosemary, and he will do so with the contentment of being a _victim_. Thus, after a short period in which it would seem that he is deciding, he phones Rosemary and says: 'It's the only thing I can do' (p. 251). Once more, Comstock has transformed a desired choice into a destiny, and, having adequately replaced his failing scapegoat, he no longer wants there to be a war: 'He did not any longer want that war to happen. It was the first time in months - years, perhaps - that he had thought of it and not wanted it' (p. 246). Calmly, and without difficulty, Comstock can now return to the womb of the They as one who has been _driven_ there. And, in a passage in which his new choice is seen as but an inevitable twist within a predestined plan, we see explicitly the confusion between freedom and slavery which has characterized his life since the formation of his original choice at school:

> Now that the thing was done he felt nothing but relief; relief that now at last he had finished with dirt, cold, hunger, and loneliness and could get back to decent, fully human life. His resolutions, now that he had broken them, seemed nothing but a frightful weight that he had cast off. Moreover, he was aware that he was only fulfilling his destiny. In some corner of his mind he had always known that this would happen. He thought of the day when he had given them notice at the New Albion.... Yet it was foredoomed that he should come back and he had known it even then. And it was not merely because of Rosemary and the baby that he had done it. That was the obvious cause, the precipitating cause, but even without it the end would have been the same; if there had been no baby to think about, something else would have forced his hand. For it was what, in his secret heart, he had desired. (p. 253)

Keep the Aspidistra Flying is a study of the way in which a man can fashion a life from the devices of bad faith, and of how bad faith can survive in disguised form after its apparent abolition. From the rather severe perspective of existential authenticity, Comstock alters nothing. The project which inspired his flight from the They was deterministically founded, and he evoked determinism to justify his return. The goal is different, but not the mode of pursuit. Comstock's victory is that he becomes a happier man through discovering a scapegoat which creates a way of life appropriate to his temperament and his genuine beliefs. His greatest self-deception was the conviction that he was a rebel; whereas, from the beginning, he was the money-god's most obedient servant.

NOTES

1. T.S. Eliot, "East Coker," Collected Poems 1909-1962 (London: Faber and Faber, 1974), p. 202.
2. Sociological Perspectives, ed. K. Thompson and J. Tunstall (Harmondsworth: Penguin Books, 1971), p. 87.
3. The Sane Society (1955; rpt. London: Routledge and Kegan Paul, 1963), p. 124.
4. Hazel E. Barnes, The Literature of Possibility, p. 17.
5. Being and Nothingness, p. 557.
6. Keep the Aspidistra Flying (1936; rpt. Harmondsworth: Penguin Books, 1966), p. 43. Henceforth cited in text by page number to this edition.
7. Bryan Magee, Popper (London: Fontana, 1973), p. 25.
8. Being and Nothingness, p. 367.

Chapter Seven

COMING UP FOR AIR

Coming Up For Air is Orwell's first great novel. Much of this achievement is due to his at last succeeding in what he was always attempting: the creation of total life. If fictional excellence can be judged by the credibility of its illusions, then George Bowling is a masterwork. At times he has the supreme actuality of Joyce's Bloom, even though there is no stream-of-consciousness to realize his presence. But this fulness, so striking to the reader, is precisely what Bowling feels he lacks. Indeed, *Coming Up For Air* is a record of the process by which the self is engulfed and lost, drowned by the river of time which courses down from the bright uplands of a country childhood into the darkening cul-de-sac of an urban middle-age. The meaning of Bowling's life is lodged in a self which has died, and he lives on, as it were, posthumously, a bereaved anachronism afflicted by a sense of ghostly unreality. The real Bowling is entombed within a stranger.

This feeling of the self-as-riddle, of the truth of Being existing either incognito or being removed to a quarter no longer accessible, was first presented by Orwell in *A Clergyman's Daughter* and gave that novel its peculiar characteristic of being an existential detective story. And, like Dorothy Hare, Bowling's ontological mystery derives from having grown into a state of thinghood. But in *Coming Up For Air* the element of choice in the creation of personal thinghood is peripheral; man becomes dismembered and de-personalized through the grinding powers of world history. And this represents a crucial shift in Orwell's comprehension of man's being-in-the-world. George Bowling is the first of Orwell's characters to be historicized. He is therefore immediately distinguishable from Flory,

Dorothy, and Comstock, who, though individuals of time and place, were not *necessarily* symptomatic of their age in a general sense. The external forces which gave shape to their lives were local: their family, their work, their community. These forces had their source in things that were known and were, therefore, potentially controllable. In this sense, the powers which oppressed them were intelligible. Power did not come suddenly and unpredictably from the *outside*, from beyond the zone of customary experience. It was something you either grew up with or gradually came to understand as a condition of existence. You were not suddenly uprooted and transformed by the gale of the world. Being had its boundary. It never collapsed under a siege of otherness. The Great War in *Coming Up For Air* is such a siege. It effects an ontological violation by destroying the traditional division between the inner 'I' and the outer 'They', and creates the Copernican understanding that one's place in the world is not at its centre. Temporality and relativity have arrived; suddenly man's place is nowhere, and time leads him implacably towards the Nothing. And additionally, the War, annihilating at random, penetrates life with a contingency never before imagined. This is the Bowling background. What we first encounter is the result:

> The idea really came to me the day I got my new false teeth....
>
> I was trying to shave with a bluntish razor-blade while the water ran into the bath. My face looked back at me out of the mirror, and underneath, in a tumbler of water on the little shelf over the washbasin, the teeth that belonged in the face. It was the temporary set that Warner, my dentist, had given me to wear while the new ones were being made. I haven't such a bad face, really. It's one of those brick-red faces that go with butter-coloured hair and pale-blue eyes....
>
> Making a mental note to buy razor-blades, I got into the bath and started soaping. I soaped my arms (I've got those kind of pudgy arms that are freckled up to the elbow) and then took the back-brush and soaped my shoulder-blades, which in the ordinary way I can't reach. It's a nuisance, but there are several parts of my body that I can't reach nowadays.... I'm not what they call 'disgustingly' fat, I haven't got one of those

> bellies that sag half-way down to the knees.... Do you know the active, hearty kind of fat man, the athletic bouncing type that's nicknamed Fatty or Tubby and is always the life and soul of the party? I'm that type. 'Fatty' they mostly call me. Fatty Bowling. George Bowling is my real name.
>
> . . . . As I stood up to soap my crutch I had a look at my figure. It's all rot about fat men being unable to see their feet, but it's a fact that when I stand upright I can only see the front halves of mine.[1]

This is Orwell at his most impressive, achieving great symbolic force without diverging from the realist mode. The ordinary external facts are presented in such a way as to express the experience of a man profoundly self-estranged. The manner in which Bowling relates to his body signifies an utterly depleted sense of 'mineness'.

To enter Bowling's world is to become instantly detached from the origins of things. The 'idea' in the opening sentence, which is the recovery of original identity through a return to the place of birth, is asssociated with false teeth, suggesting that the idea is also false. But principally the 'idea' is a response to the false, an urge towards the recovery of a time when the self felt its authenticity because it was rooted in the primordial. The teeth, having no roots, are not his own; they have no foundation in his Being. They come from the _outside_, replacing the _inside_. That Bowling can find no access to his roots is captured in the act of shaving with a _bluntish_ razor. His ontolgical severance is expressed in his feelings of being disembodied; the face, which is the self's primary means of recognition, seems to exist beyond him in the mirror, above the teeth which belong to it. The face and the teeth have become objects among other objects, existing independently on the outside like equipment, interlocking pieces suggestive of an identity puzzle. In this vein Bowling proceeds to present other parts of himself. He seems incapable of describing what he is individually; only by reference to type can he provide a picture of himself. He's got '_one of those_ brick-red faces'; he's got '_those kind_ of pudgy arms'; he hasn't got '_one of those_ bellies'. As a fat man he is a '_kind_' of fat man. The overwhelming impression that Bowling conveys is of one who has not grown organically into what he is but has been assembled from a Fatty

Bowling Kit. In this sense, the body described does not belong to him. The body he is obliged to live in is an alien construction, a foreign body from the outside with which he is objectively familiar but which he cannot _feel_ he fully possesses: 'there are several parts of _my_ body which I can't reach nowadays'. Thus the fatter he becomes the more alienated from himself will he be. Ontologically Bowling is diminishing through expansion.

The fat in which Bowling is interred symbolizes the false self which was generated by the vast cleavage of the War and which obscures the self's authentic origins. As a symbol it is perfect, for, because of the swollen belly, when Bowling looks down _he can hardly see where he comes from_. Only the front halves of his feet are visible, and these remains are in themselves symbolic of the only means by which his origins are known: his memory. Memory is his existential umbilical cord. Jettisoned from the enclosed unitary world of authentic selfhood in which he could touch all the distinct corners of his Being, he is now encrusted and assimilated by the inauthentic they-world to the extent that his sense of selfness has become indefinite; it is amorphous and flaccid like his body. Some of himself he can no longer reach, and what he can get hold of doesn't seem to be his. He cannot determine where he begins or ends. He is mass-man, sucked into the indiscriminate generality of world-being. Like his teeth, he has become an object to himself, and an object which is false. He exists as a specimen, and, appropriately for a specimen, he lives in a specimen house:

> Do you know the road I live in - Ellesmere Road, West Bletchley? Even if you don't, you know fifty others like it.
>
> You know how these streets fester all over the inner-outer suburbs. Always the same. Long, long rows of little semi-detached houses ... as much alike as council houses and generally uglier. (p. 13)

> There's the same back garden, same privets, and same grass, behind every house in Ellesmere Road. (p. 7)

The house, like the self, is _anyone's_. Additionally the house, like the self's body, is not really owned by the occupant: 'we don't own our houses, even when we've finished paying for them. They're not freehold, only leasehold' (p. 15). The Cheerful Credit Building Society provides the tenants with the 'illusion' of possession. Bowling, because he has no possession of himself, has therefore no self by which it is possible to possess anything else. As an object, he can only be owned, and owned he is: 'We're all bought, and what's more we're bought with our own money' (p. 16). He can make no permanent claim on the world. Existentially, he is homeless. And yet Bowling, as an insurance agent, deals in claims and securities. When things fall apart, when the centre no longer holds, he is mankind's solid guarantor. He provides the very thing that he himself lacks: self-security. So insecure in himself has he become that a gulf has appeared between Being and existence, between what he feels himself to be and what he can see that he has externally become. His subjectivity has become detached from his objective state and he has come to see himself in the same way as the Other does: as pure outside:

> I had no illusions about myself that morning. It was almost as if I could stand at a distance and watch myself coming down the road, with my fat, red face and my false teeth and my vulgar clothes.... Even if you saw me at two hundred yards' distance you'd know immediately - not, perhaps, that I was in the insurance business, but that I was some kind of tout or salesman. The clothes I was wearing were practically the uniform of the tribe. (pp. 13-14)

What the Other sees and relates to is a collection of acquired characteristics which conceal the essential man: 'I'm fat, but I'm thin inside' (p. 23). Thus Bowling is situated existentially where he is situated geographically: in the 'inner-outer suburbs'. His house, his street, and the estate and its location all accurately reflect his condition, and this condition is that of the schizoid, who

> experiences his self as being more or less divorced or detached from his body. The body is felt more as one object among other objects in the world than as the core of the individual's own being. Instead of being the core of his true self, the body is felt as the core of a false self, which a detached, disembodied, 'inner', 'true' self looks on at with tenderness, amusement, or hatred as the case may be.[2]

As with Dorothy Hare, Bowling's prevailing sensation is that of living his life in the third-person. The life of the man described is not experienced as his. Existence and Being no longer coincide. Bowling, the 'Fatty' Bowling, lives in the unreal they-world of self-for-others. Uprooted, he exists on the surface of things, on the outside. It is almost as if the fat of his false self has provided him with an insurmountable buoyancy. He cannot penetrate to the underside and let the authentic self come up for air. Both physically and existentially he cannot shake off

> That burthen of my own unnatural self,
> The heavy weight of many a weary day
> Not mine, and such as were not made for me.[3]

So lost is Bowling in his role of a 'Fatty' that even in moments of anguish the role will not burst. The thin man will never weep through the fat man's eyes. He will only let himself be known for what he is not. The fat self-for-others, generated by the acquiescence to be what others prescribe for one who is fat, will even stifle the thin man when the others are not present. Bowling, remembering a scene from a romantic novel in which the hero flings himself down in 'a paroxysm of weeping' after discovering that 'his girl has gone off with another chap', comments: 'There you have it, you see. That's how people - some people - are expected to behave. But how about a chap like me? Suppose Hilda went off for a weekend with somebody else... would I fling myself down in a paroxysm of weeping? Would anyone expect me to? You couldn't, with a figure like mine. It would be downright obscene' (p. 22). The comicalness of this passage disguises the grave truth that Bowling continues to behave as a self-for-others even though there are no others to show the self to. He has become a closed system. The Other is no longer necessary for the perpetuation of the false self. Like Winston Smith, Bowling conducts himself as if he were under incessant observation. Even in solitude he cannot hide. The others have transformed the self into an object. So impressed is Bowling by the ontological importance of fat that he doubts 'whether a man who's never been anything but fat, a man who's been called Fatty ever since he could walk, even knows of the existence of any really deep emotions' (p. 21). The congenital Fatty is nothing but what others believe him to be. But this is not the case with

Bowling. In his life he's been both fat and thin, and is therefore familiar with two ontological states, which can be categorized and elaborated thus: Contemporary Being (inauthentic, external, objective); Historic Being (authentic, internal, subjective). Here we have once again the Orwellian bifurcation of modes of Being denoting the antithetical consciousness of the principle of the Excluded Middle. The identification of these two modes, the Contemporary succeeding the Historic, leads to another familiar term: Transformation. Bowling has been transformed from the inside of the past to the outside of the present, from being-<u>in</u>-the-world to being-<u>on</u>-the-world.

The dereliction of this transformation to the outside is nowhere more evident than when Bowling, having arrived too early to collect his new false teeth, goes to eat in a milk bar. It is the climax of Part 1 and is Bowling's moment of epiphany:

> There's a kind of atmosphere about these places that gets me down. Everything slick and shiny and streamlined; mirrors, enamel, and chromium plate whichever direction you look in. Everything spent on the decorations and nothing on the food. No real food at all. Just lists of stuff with American names, sort of phantom stuff that you can't taste and can hardly believe in the existence of. Everything comes out of a carton or a tin, or it's hauled out of a refrigerator or squirted out of a tap or squeezed out of a tube. No comfort, no privacy. Tall stools to sit on, a kind of narrow ledge to eat off, mirrors all around you. A sort of propaganda floating round, mixed up with the noise of the radio, to the effect that food doesn't matter, comfort doesn't matter, nothing matters except slickness and shininess and streamlining. (pp. 25-26)

Bowling is surrounded by surfaces, as he was in his bathroom. Like Bowling himself, the world of the bar is outside only. Nothing can be looked <u>into</u>, everything <u>reflects</u>. The world is reduced to the seen, to a collection of optical observations in which one's own outside also appears. The subjective things, privacy, comfort, taste, have no objective existence and are therefore invalid. The names of the foods, being American, are not indigenous; they come from the outside; and the food itself has been processed, transformed. It is 'unreal' 'phantom stuff' because its original sources are untraceable. Between the eater and the edibles is a veil of alienation. The elimination of origins and the consequent impossibility of ontological definition is reinforced by the presence outside the bar of a newsboy with a poster flapping against his knees: 'LEGS. FRESH DISCOVERIES' (p. 26). This, already referred to while Bowling was breakfasting off marmalade containing 'neutral fruit-juice' (p. 12), concerns a pair of legs found in a parcel in a railway waiting-room. As a murder case involving the mystery of identity, it parallels in detail Bowling's plight, for he too has lost sight of his legs, through the fat which is symbolic of the false self. As has been suggested, legs mean roots. To look down and see one's legs is to know where one stands and to know what one is existentially. One does not come from _anywhere_; one's place in the world is assured. One's roots are _my_ roots; they are originative and unique. To be legless, to have no roots, is to have _thrown Being_. To be severed from one's roots is to develop _necessarily_ a not-self, a false self. To be rootless is to be cast onto the outside and live on the surface as a thing without history. The 'legs', suddenly appearing in the world, with no known connection to anybody, illustrate man's thrownness, his fragmentariness and his contemporary status as a thing, the antithesis of full Being that Bowling experienced prior to the shattering of the War. The police, like Bowling, are searching for a person whose remains are their only guide. Both want to fit the legs to the body, and make a whole person. Bowling, a torso only, wants to recover his legs and have the depths of his Being restored. For both he and the police the quest is to discover the Who, the specific identity. This fragmentation and sense of assembly echoes the opening page of the book where Bowling is making a kind of inventory of his body.

The 'fresh discoveries' concerning 'legs', that is, _roots_, occur for Bowling when he eats. Falsity meets falsity:

> The frankfurter had a rubber skin, of course, and my temporary teeth weren't much of a fit. I had to do a kind of sawing movement before I could get my teeth through the skin. And then suddenly - pop! The thing burst in my mouth like a rotten pear. A sort of horrible stuff was oozing all over my tongue. But the taste!

> For a moment I just couldn't believe it. Then I rolled my tongue round it again and had another try. It was _fish_! A sausage, a thing calling itself a frankfurter, filled with fish! I got up and walked straight out without touching my coffee. God knows what that might have tasted of.
>
> Outside the newsboy shoved the _Standard_ into my face and yelled, 'Legs! 'Orrible revelations!' (pp. 26-27)

Here, physical and existential nausea combine, for, as Sartre has said, food 'reveals to me the being which I am going to make my flesh'.[4] Cooking, according to Lévi-Strauss, is in itself an 'agent of transformation', a process by which Nature is assimilated into the Social.[5] Natural Being becomes artificial Being, a process fundamental to an understanding of Bowling's personal development. Thus, in eating cooked food, one is transforming a transformation, and, in Bowling's case, he is transforming a transformation which is offered in an external disguise. Additionally, he is doing so with temporary artificial teeth. That moment of biting, or sawing, is dense with significancies which reveal to Bowling in disgust and horror the hard insurmountable fact of alienated rootless existence. Like Bowling himself, the frankfurter is not what it appears. Both biter and bitten are inauthentic. Bowling cannot engage reality.

These ''Orrible revelations' about the nature of things come to assume the same sinister, nightmarish aspect as the Ingsoc Ministries, whose names belie their functions:

> I remembered a bit I'd read in the paper somewhere about these food-factories in Germany where everything's made out of something else. Ersatz, they call it. I remembered reading that _they_ were making sausages out of fish, and fish, no doubt, out of something different. It gave me the feeling that I'd bitten into the modern world and discovered what it was really made of. That's the way we're going nowadays. Everything slick and streamlined, everything made out of something else. Celluloid, rubber, chromium-steel everywhere, arc-lamps blazing all night, glass roofs over your head, radios all playing the same tune, no vegetation left, everything cemented over, mock-turtles grazing under the neutral fruit-trees. But when you

> come down to brass tacks and get your teeth into something solid, a sausage for instance, that's what you get. Rotten fish in a rubber skin. Bombs of filth bursting inside your mouth. (p. 27)

The world thus described is de-naturized through transformations made possible by uprootedness. Bowling, having been made rootless, is severed from the depths of Being and exists on the surface where he can be moved about and reshaped by the arbitrary pressures of the They, a piece of ontological flotsam. The fish, which belonged under the surface, now turns up anywhere on the surface in mutant form. Everything, either animal, vegetable or mineral, is trapped in a process which hides origins. Identity, like the food, is 'phantom stuff'. Being is not 'something solid'. Having nothing to call 'mine', and having no predetermined place, Bowling feels the draught of nothingness, the *horror vacui* which attends the discovery that *there is nothing which is essentially anything*. Man is an onion.

Thus Bowling, leaving the milk-bar, is in the Emersonian mood:

> Give me truths;
> For I am weary of the surfaces,
> And die of inanition.[6]

And soon, symbolically equipped with new razor-blades and teeth which now sit 'nice and smooth over the gums' (both items bring him closer to his roots), he moves into a period of long retrospect precipitated by another poster which creates an image of the truths he has lost: 'KING ZOG'S WEDDING POSTPONED' (p. 30). Juxtaposed as it is to the 'legs' poster with all its attendant meanings, it is clear that what is being presented is a contrast. The significance of Zog is that he recalls for Bowling the biblical Og, who, with Sihon, was mentioned in a psalm sung in church during Bowling's infancy: 'I saw them as a couple of . . . great Egyptian statues . . . enormous stone statues thirty feet high . . . their hands on their knees and a faint mysterious smile on their faces' (pp. 32-33). The remembrance of the biblical Og and his imagined existence as an Egyptian statue, speaks of a *lost time*, both from Bowling's own life and from the centuries before; so in remembering childhood he is also engaging religious traditions in history which offered explanations for the origins of the world.

Through memory Bowling identifies his own creation within a tradition of uninterrupted continuity which provided the feeling of ontological fulness. Life had coherence.

The meaning of Og as a statue becomes apparent when compared with how Bowling understands himself: 'I'm fat, but I'm thin inside. Has it ever struck you that there's a thin man inside every fat man, just as they say there's a statue inside every block of stone?' (p. 23). The statue, then, represents the real man, the authentic self. The human statue is solid, _all of one piece_. It is complete, self-possessed, a radical contrast to the fragmented self-for-others symbolized by the 'legs'. A statue is not composite in the way that Bowling feels himself to be; it is on the inside what it is on the outside. It is unaffected by existence and therefore incapable of transformation. The statues will not lose their legs; indeed, being fashioned from single blocks, and with 'their hands on their knees', they are examples of the irreducible integrity of independent Being. Such is the actuality of the pre-war world which Og evokes that Bowling speaks of the present as 'less real': 'For a moment I didn't merely remember it, I was _in_ it'. 'I belong to it', he says (pp. 33-34). Being _in_ and _belonging_ were possible in the past because the world, like the statue, was three-dimensional; enclosure and insidedness created a sense of place and rootedness. One's life had _depth_, and it is the absence of this quality which typifies the modern world and which is Bowling's despair. He is obliged to be an outsider because, in a world that expresses itself in surfaces only, there is nothing to get within. Without roots there is only the one-dimensional surface of the present. Thus the posters of LEGS and OG represent two radically different ontological epochs in English life: the cheap superficial modern world on which man exists as a fragment, and the rich deep Edwardian world in which man was whole, solid and immovable. Historically, the division between these two states is the First War. Bowling's fear is of a Second, for after that what then would man be? Now there are bombs. Whatever remains of a man's insides will be dispersed irretrievably.

Almost as if Bowling has assumed the density of the statue (as opposed to the buoyancy of the false fat self which keeps him afloat on the surface), he sinks into the depths of his past to his beginnings. He is 'actually _in_ the past' (p. 30). Immediately we are in a world of specific place, of particulars, of relations, of belonging. The Being-ness of things is restored, and the record of the discovery of one's self in one's world is comparable to Dorothy Hare's recovery from oblivion and the revelation that existence is <u>mine</u> ('I am I'):

> When you're very young you seem to suddenly become conscious of things that have been under your nose for a long time past. The things round about you swim into your mind one at a time, rather as they do when you're waking from sleep. For instance, it was only when I was nearly four that I suddenly realized that we owned a dog. Nailer, his name was, an old white English terrier of the breed that's gone out nowadays. I met him under the kitchen table and in some way seemed to grasp, having only learnt it that moment, that he belonged to us and that his name was Nailer.... All these things dropped into place in my mind one by one, like bits of a jig-saw puzzle. (p. 36)

Here, Bowling records the genesis of the 'I' through its recognition of its place in the scheme of things. The world is understood through the I's relation to it, not as something which stands in separation against the 'I'; and the things in the world present themselves in specific identifiable forms which cannot be confused with other things in the way that they are when transformations are rife.

The pre-transformational mode of being <u>in</u> the world is everywhere celebrated by Bowling, and often amounts to a rapture over the easy comprehensibility of things. The world is real, and the world is known, and he provides exhaustive lists as evidence of his mastery over the world that is now lost, the first of which, in its emphasis on stasis and harmony, contrasts with the flux and discord which have made contemporary life so fearful. Being did not shift; it had its place. If the appropriate cosmology for the middle-aged Bowling is Copernican, then the enclosed eternity of his childhood is Aristotelian. Indeed, these two differing world-pictures serve as models for the present self-for-others and the self-possession of the past. Bowling, flung from the centre to the outside, has no stable positions of reference by which it is possible to derive a scheme analagous to that of his childhood:

> I'm back in Lower Binfield, and the year's 1900. Beside the horse-trough in the market-place the carrier's horse is having it's nose-bag. At the sweet-shop on the corner Mother Wheeler is weighing out a ha'porth of brandy balls. Lady Rampling's carriage is driving by, with the tiger sitting behind in his pipeclayed breeches with his arms folded. Uncle Ezekiel is cursing Joe Chamberlain. The recruiting-sergeant in his scarlet jacket, tight blue overalls, and pillbox hat, is strutting up and down twisting his moustache. The drunks are puking in the yard behind the George. Vicky's at Windsor, God's in heaven, Christ's on the cross, Jonah's in the whale, Shadrach, Meshach, and Abednego are in the fiery furnace, and Sihon king of the Amorites and Og the king of Bashan are sitting on their thrones looking at one another - not doing anything exactly, just existing, keeping their appointed places, like a couple of fire-dogs, or the Lion and the Unicorn. (p. 34)

In the modern world where a sausage turns out to be a fish, Christ could be puking behind the George, and a drunk would be on the cross. In the old world, people, animals, and things all have 'appointed places', and these places are inseparable from their definitions; they are interconnected plenitudes. Uncle Ezekiel in a recruiting-sergeant's uniform would not <u>be</u> Uncle Ezekiel. Partly because the past naturally reveals itself in such a way, and mostly because Bowling experienced it as such and yearns for that experience again, it is expressed as essence. As essence, no person or thing can be transformed and consequently misrepresent itself. Dissimulation is impossible. Because of this there is also no possibility of the development of the self-for-others, which relies on the existence of the potential for a man to have both an inside and an outside. One cannot be split in accordance with the Laing formula 'self/(body-world)', as exemplified by Bowling observing himself in the inner-outer suburbs.[7] Self, body and world had seamless coincidence: 'I can feel the grass round me as tall as myself, and the heat coming out of the earth' (p. 39).

In such a world of belonging, it is not surprizing that Bowling can recall a mode of eating in which falseness and alienation are absent, a type of eating which is natural and authentic because the food is not severed from its origins and anonymized by the transformations necessary for social consumption. Going to the roots of your food and picking it is to feel your authenticity in a way not possible in a milk-bar where 'everything comes out of a carton or a tin, or [is] hauled out of a refrigerator or squirted out of a tap or squeezed out of a tube':

> I do remember different seasons, because all my memories are bound up with things to eat, which varied at different times of the year. Especially the things you used to find in the hedges. In July there were dewberries - but they're very rare - and the blackberries were getting red enough to eat. In September there were sloes and hazel-nuts. (p. 38)

And so the list goes on: 'crab-apples','beech-nuts', 'haws', 'hips', 'angelica', 'grasses', 'sorrel', 'pig-nuts', 'wood shamrock' and 'plantain seeds', each one having its time and place and its own distinctive flavour, a contrast to the milk-bar in which one not only doesn't know where the foods originate but has no sense of their chronological place in the cycle of the seasons. But food has not only become placeless and timeless; one expects it 'to taste of nothing' (p. 26).

The fruit-eating of the past, then, is the antithesis of eating a frankfurter in the present. Bowling remembers the seasons because all his memories 'are bound up with things to eat'; so to recall a food is to recall a time. Food is an ingredient of the past and serves as a mnemonic. To remember eating a dewberry is to know that it was eaten in July, but to remember having eaten a modern food is not sufficient to know when. There is no necessary connection any more. The frankfurter comes from anytime, just as the eater is anyone from anywhere. Food, the eater and his home are all generic categories; there is no sense of this food, this eater, this home. The Who, the What, the Which, and the When have all been either abolished or reduced to the point were interchangeability would be undetectable, a condition remarked upon by one of the 'commercials' in the train: '"'Ow could you identify a pair of legs? They're all the bleeding same, aren't they?"' (p. 24) The frankfurter is the food of the neuter, the They. But the suggestiveness of the frankfurter is not exhausted by this conclusion. The milk-bar food of Bowling's description carries implications which show just how subtly cohesive Orwell's mind really was, for the food, in being rendered timeless, _has been deprived of the possibility of becoming anachronistic_. It exists, therefore, in that endless present which characterizes the despair of _1984_. For Orwell, the evidence of there being a past (and therefore a self) is the present existence of things which are not products of the present; and these must be 'something solid', like Winston Smith's paperweight. Contemporary food is 'phantom stuff' because it has about it no evidence of having a history. Without this, nothing can have fulness of Being, for time past is ontologically constitutive of the self, providing that sense of three-dimensionality which Og's statue embodies. One only knows what one is through knowing what one was. The only meaning to be derived from the present is derived from the past: the present only _is_ because the past _was_. The present is only made real to the existent because its origins are traceable. Alone, it is a phantom, merely a surface.

The significance of pre-war food in _Coming Up For Air_ is that all Bowling's memories are 'bound up' with it, and as it is only memory which can recapture the experience of the authentic primordial self, all things which relate to food assist to reveal the nature and meaning of Bowling's pursuit. Going to the sources of food is identified with the quest for the source of the self, and this is so because it eliminates the possibility of a transformation into fraudulence and unintelligible ambiguity. The frankfurter is the image of this ambiguity, for it is, like Bowling himself, a composite form which resists a specific unalloyed definition. Only terms like 'doublethink' and 'blackwhite' can account for such phenomena, and, if this is so, it may be seen that Newspeak is a way of dealing with the logical perplexities which arise from the ontological changes consequent to the abolition of essence, that is, roots. The coincidence between names and their referents are becoming detached. Things and people have lost their 'appointed places': fish get into sausages, and legs are found in waiting-rooms. Without roots, it is a contingent world; and it is precisely the absence of this which Bowling records when he remembers his mother:

> It would be an exaggeration, but not a very big one, to say that I never remember her when she

> wasn't cooking. When you look back over a long period you seem to see human beings always fixed in some special place and some characteristic attitude. It seems to you that they were always doing exactly the same thing....
>
> I used to like to watch Mother rolling pastry. There's always a fascination in watching anybody do a job which he really understands. Watch a woman - a woman who really knows how to cook, I mean - rolling dough. She's got a peculiar, solemn, indrawn air, a satisfied kind of air, like a priestess celebrating a sacred rite. And in her own mind, of course, that's exactly what she was.... When she was cooking, all her movements were wonderfully precise and firm. In her hands egg-whisks and mincers and rolling-pins did exactly what they were meant to do. When you saw her cooking you knew that she was in a world where she belonged, among things she really understood.... So far as the meals and so forth went, ours was one of those houses where everything goes like clockwork. Or no, not like clockwork, which suggests something mechanical. It was more like some kind of natural process. You knew that breakfast would be on the table tomorrow morning in much the same way as you knew the sun would rise. (pp. 47-50)

This description serves as a catalogue of all the things which Bowling has been deprived of: place, belonging to place, wholeness of self, understanding of world and certainty of continuation. Bowling's mother is part of the process of life; organic, not mechanical; a contrast to Bowling's description of himself as one who has been assembled. So deeply is she _in_ the world that the notion of there being an _outside_ beyond the immediate and understood reality hardly exists:

> Except through the Sunday papers and an occasional bit of gossip the outside world didn't really exist for her.... She certainly couldn't have told you whether Ireland was east or west of England, and I doubt whether any time up to the outbreak of the Great War she could have told you who was Prime Minister. Moreover she hadn't the smallest wish to know such things.... In reality she lived her life in a space that must have been as small and almost as private as the average zenana. (p. 49)

Bowling's mother, then, along with all the other two thousand inhabitants of Lower Binfield, lives in a world within a world within the world. And in the context of the meanings which issue from the 'legs' case it is significant that Bowling remarks: 'I think Mother thought of the world outside Lower Binfield chiefly as a place where murders were committed' (p. 52.). The 'outside', on the rare occasions that it is thought about, is a threat to life, and her way of dealing with this threat is to seal off the inside by pulling down the shutters of the shop. The case of the 'little American doctor who dismembered his wife' upsets her so badly that 'the tears actually came into her eyes' (p. 53).

The world Mrs. Bowling shuts out is the world that her son now occupies, and it is the ache to be once more behind the shutters on the inside and be whole again which drives the dismembered Bowling towards the recovery of his past. Now, as a fragment, he looks back to the time behind the shutters when the parts of the world were all in place 'like bits of a jigsaw puzzle' (p. 36). Once, he had the completed picture; then the War came, shattering the puzzle, and he lived on, an estranged piece of the whole. In the past he could connect one thing to another because everything had its 'appointed place' (p. 34). Nothing demonstrates this ability to connect more than his passion for fishing, and his yearning to do so again may be construed as the desire to find a route from the present outside to the past inside, to find the lost whale from which he has been expelled. And it is appropriate that it is Bowling's <u>mother</u> who supplies the image from which this conclusion is drawn, for it is she who is Bowling's <u>original appointed place</u>, the <u>primordial inside</u>. It was in her that he had an absolute immunity to all the fragmenting forces that now typify contemporary reality. A container who is contained, for Bowling she represents the innermost inside, the fabulous, inviolate once-visited pool which burns in his memory and irradiates his quest. Thus the basic fact of birth is to be considered as a powerful intensifier of Bowling's sense of sundered unity, for it is with birth that the child is delivered over to irreversible separation. At birth, <u>the child becomes only part of what he was</u>, and this occurs as a result of <u>the inside becoming the outside</u>. That Mrs. Bowling can exclude the outside where dismemberments occur expresses the pre-natal atmosphere in which she, Bowling, the family and all those in Lower Binfield lived during the pre-war years. Binfield was a second womb, an inside on the outside like the marsupial pouch, and the War came as a second birth which ripped open the pouch and delivered man over to existence as a self-for-others among the alienating forces of the world. Thus fishing, for Bowling, becomes comprehensible as a fishing for roots, the means to become whole again. The line is an existential umbilical cord, cast onto _the surface of the present_ with the intention of reconnecting Bowling's contemporary existence with his primordial Being. But it is all too late for Bowling. The fish-womb of the depths, if it is there, can no longer contain him. The fat of the inauthentic self prohibits re-entry, and he floats for ever on the outside.

By citing the mother as important to Bowling's wish to return to the beginnings, we approach an interpretation which seems more naturally to belong to the psychological than the existential. But this is true only insofar as the psychological is of ontological relevance. Hazel Barnes's description of the distinction between the psychological and the existential serves to show the ontological unity behind these differing concepts, and, in so doing, provides an explanation for the meaning of the past as it is presented in _Coming Up For Air_. One of 'the fundamental themes of existentialism', she writes, is

> the nostalgia for a return to nature, a forbidden longing more basic in the eyes of the existentialist than the Freudian yearning for the lost security of the womb. Just as the return to the foetal state symbolizes rest, security, and absolute belonging to an all-embracing mother-home, and freedom from the burden of being a separate individual, so the return to the womb of nature represents a oneness with the environment in which man is no longer responsible for himself, where he has the certainty of instinctual living and the security of belonging so completely that the question of being wanted or being necessary cannot even arise.[8]

To believe that a passion for something is only explicable through the existence of something else less obvious can perhaps only be justified if the details of that passion coincide with a consistent pattern of images which have revealed the vital meanings of a work. _Coming Up For Air_ reveals such a pattern through the reiterated dichotomy of inside and outside, surface and depth, and the urge to unite these opposites. Additionally, corroboration for the permanence of this presence in a structural sense is to be found in the previous novels, all of which are informed by an inordinate awareness of the principle of the Excluded Middle. Fishing (Bowling's 'passion'), as an activity which unites opposites (surface to depth, present to past), shows a time when the principle of division did not exist, when there was neither a split in the self nor a split between the self and the world; the time, in fact, before the self becomes conscious of itself and becomes <u>an object with an outside</u>. The classic expression of this is the Christian Fall of Man in which Adam, alienated from his origins, understands his separate objective existence and covers his body. Thus an ontological change occurs as a consequence of the severance from roots. Perhaps the appeal of this myth arises from the truth that it is every man's destiny within his own lifetime to experience such a break, both through the break with the mother and with the more memorable transformation of adolescence. Significantly, fishing, as a ritual re-enactment of belonging to one's origins, is, for Bowling, only performed up to the time of adolescence. Adolescence is a definitive ontological rift. The ritual loses its magic power, and the blissful state of belonging becomes only a memory. So, if man forgets his Being, existence becomes unreal, 'phantom stuff'. On his eventual return to Binfield, Bowling, on the outside where murders and dismemberment occur, feels a 'ghost' (p. 197). The fat of the false self, which he does not feel to be his, assumes a new meaning: that of reincarnation. From this position of utter detachment, 'fishing', Bowling says, 'is the real thing' (p. 69). He could connect: 'I felt the rod tighten in my hand. Christ, that feeling! The line jerking and straining and a fish on the other end of it!' (p. 61). This ecstasy over the fish 'biting' creates a powerful contrast to the inauthentic 'unreal' connection of Bowling biting into the frankfurter skin and recoiling in disgust at his contact with 'rotten fish'. Here we have the kind of contact typical of the post-transformational world; or, to use a term more appropriate to this stage of the discussion, post-lapsarian.

That fishing as a mode of primordial contact was a sacramental act may be inferred from a selection of Bowling's descriptions. Fishing is to

Bowling what cooking is to his mother. He can hardly 'remember a time when she wasn't cooking', and when he looks back 'the whole of my boyhood from eight to fifteen seems to have revolved round the days when we were fishing' (p. 69). While cooking, his mother is in a world which she 'really understands', and therefore she was in 'a world where she belonged'. Belonging through understanding provides her with the status of 'a priestess celebrating a sacred rite'. Bowling too has this understanding: 'I could write a book on the technique of fishing' (p. 69). And he shares the same sense of the mystical: fishing is 'not a thing that you can explain or rationalize, it's merely magic' (p. 57). Through cooking and fishing, both seem to exist in a state of mediumistic contact. What is plain is that both, through a performance similar to ritual, achieve oneness with the world. But with Bowling the ritual evokes the Edenesque, and during it he breaks with profane time and enters the sacred: 'time stretched out and out' (pp. 60-61). In thinking of his brother and friends fishing without him, he says 'it was as though they were in paradise and I'd got to join them' (p. 59). After initiation he studies the Gamage's fishing catalogue 'as though it had been the bible!' (p. 70). He remembers the still summer evenings with a 'kind of passion', 'hoping and praying (yes, literally praying)' that he would get a bite before dark (p. 72). And after not having fished for thirty years, he says 'I've still got, I've always had, that peculiar feeling for fishing' (p. 74). He explains this lapse by saying that 'there's some devil in us' (p. 80). The impossibility of resuming the ritual is, of course, due to the present loss of 'understanding' the self and world. Bowling cannot understand the post-transformational (post-lapsarian) world, so therefore he cannot 'belong'. When things shift from their 'appointed places' and mutate, understanding is at an end. The 'magic' no longer works. The transformation of the Fall has brought ontological ambiguity into the world. The umbilical cord has been cut and there is no connection left between inside and outside. The univocal world of essence is finished.

The way in which Bowling's adolescence ends conforms to the present notion that adolescence is to be interpreted as an expression of the Christian Fall. Bowling, at sixteen, makes a discovery in the grounds of the derelict Binfield House. After having struggled through fifty yards of 'jungle' he enters a clearing in which there is a pool which he 'had never known existed'. It is completely new territory, and the fish he sees there is the biggest he's ever seen, 'dead or alive'. It makes him 'almost jump out of [his] skin'; it is 'as if a sword [has] gone through' him. He explains the hugeness of the fish in a way that corresponds to his own developing alienation from his origins: 'I knew what had happened. At some time this pool had been connected with the other [the one he normally fishes from], and then the stream had dried up and the woods had closed round the small pool and it had just been forgotten' (p. 78). The umbilical cord of the stream is now but a trace, and the fish, portents of the contemporary Fatty Bowling, are now anyway too large to pass through to the mother pool; they have grown to 'monstrous sizes'. Bowling thrills to the idea of their capture, but their weight is too great for the strength of his gear. Other equipment is necessary. He can no longer properly connect. The 'magic' techniques of childhood are passing away. The world is transforming.

The discovery of the forgotten pool, then, may be seen as symbolic of Bowling's discovery of his estrangement from origins due to the transformation of adolescence, and the first fish he sees there is suggestive of the reason for this estrangement: 'It was almost the length of my arm. It glided across the pool, deep under the water'; 'in a moment another huge thick shape glided through the water' (p. 78). Bowling has become trapped inside his own swollen carnality. To grow is to grow <u>from</u>. Growth and alienation are inseparable. Growth destroys the sense of human essence, and it was this sense of essence which united Bowling's world and made fishing efficacious as a holistic ritual. That the meaning of fishing derived from this experience is enforced by the fact that, at the point where Bowling is given the greatest opportunity for his greatest catch, he stops fishing altogether. He has become aware of his own separate existence. He no longer belongs to nature. And it is appropriate that, four years later, he only returns to the pool in order to use the carnality that he discovered there. He returns to the vicinity as an outsider, one who is conscious of himself as separated from nature and therefore not dressed for it. Having now accepted his object-state he has increased his estrangement from the authentic self within, and this is expressed when Bowling fails to overcome the obstacles of nature which divide him from the pool:

> It suddenly struck me that for years I'd meant to come back here and had never come. Now I was so near, it seemed a pity not to go down to the other pool and have a look at the big carp .... Practically they were _my_ carp. I actually started wandering along the bank in that direction, and then when I'd gone about ten yards I turned back. It meant crashing your way through a kind of jungle of brambles and rotten brushwood, and I was dressed up in my Sunday best. Dark-grey suit, bowler hat, button boots, and a collar that almost cut my ears off. (p. 105)

De-naturized and de-spiritualized, he is left only with the flesh. And this he immediately uses. It is his 'first time' (p. 106). In Elsie he finds a new inside. This new connection signifies the passage from relations of essence to relations of existence, which, according to Paul Tillich, describes the nature of the Christian Fall.[9]

Because the decline of the Binfield community begins at the time of the discovery of the hidden pool, there is an implicit suggestion that the discovery is _causal_: 'About three days after I'd seen the big carp at Binfield House, Father came in to tea looking very worried and even more grey and mealy than usual' (p. 91). Trade has suddenly slumped. It is as if the microcosmic insideness of the village has been breached and the outside has been let in: 'Sarazins', the big retail seedsmen ... had stuck a tentacle into Lower Binfield' (p. 92). The unprecedented has happened, and the comprehension that is necessary for 'belonging' to the world is threatened: 'He couldn't understand what was happening to him. For years his profits had gone up ... and now suddenly they'd gone down with a bump. He couldn't understand it.... None of us had any grasp of what was happening' (pp. 93-94). And for reasons that have already been discussed, it is significant that this intrusion from the outside makes Mother 'less lordly in the kitchen'; she begins to use margarine, 'a thing which in the old days she'd never have allowed in the house'. And she, whom Bowling had seen as 'a sort of great opulent creature like the figure-head of a battleship', shrinks with anxiety and comes to look older than her age (p. 100). Bowling's brother, as though the breach of the inside has given him the means of access to the outside, deserts the family with the money from the till, and goes off to the 'new world', America, and is never heard of again. Everything is changing. Essence has transformed into existence, and all is contingent. With nothing any longer in its 'appointed place', the continuity that is essential for a sense of understanding disappears. Life becomes 'a race between death and bankruptcy, and, thank God, death got Father first, and Mother too' (p. 102). Mortality has arrived, but death is preferable because

> at least they never lived to know that everything they'd believed in was just so much junk. They lived at the end of an epoch, when everything was dissolving into a sort of ghastly flux, and they didn't know it. They thought it was eternity. You couldn't blame them. That was what it felt like. (p. 109)

> And yet what was it that people had in those days? A feeling of security, even when they weren't secure. More exactly, it was a feeling of continuity. All of them knew they'd got to die ... but what they didn't know was that the order of things could change. Whatever might happen to themselves, things would go on as they'd known them.... But it's precisely in a settled period, a period when civilization seems to stand on its four legs like an elephant, that such things as a future life don't matter. It's easy enough to die if the things you care about are going to survive.... Individually they were finished, but their way of life would continue. Their good and evil would remain good and evil. They didn't feel the ground they stood on shifting under their feet. (pp. 107-8)

This assessment of the age which was finally destroyed by the Great War coincides precisely with the existential interpretation of history. 'There were periods', writes Karl Jaspers, 'in which man felt his world to be durable', when 'the world was his own world'; but

> compared with man in those eras, man today has been uprooted, having become aware that he exists in what is but a historically determined and changing situation. It is as if the foundations of being had been shattered. How self-evident to the man of old seemed the unity of life and knowledge has become plain to us now

> that we realize that the life of our fellows in the past was spent under conditions in which reality was, as it were, veiled. We, on the other hand, have become able to see things as they really are, and that is why the foundations of our life quake beneath our feet.[10]

The 'veil' of which Jaspers speaks is that which divides the inside from the outside in Coming Up For Air. Already breached, its total removal is accomplished by the Great War, and the inside is destroyed. In identifying the War as the final phase of transformation for Bowling, his family and the Binfield community, Orwell is evoking the profane time of secular history which leads to death, and the depravity of the natural world. Henceforth Nature and Time are postlapsarian. The future becomes something to be 'terrified of', and the natural world undergoes an accelerating process of despoliation (p. 106).

The depth of Bowling's estrangement from the world of childhood, and the intensity of his longing for it, are explicable through the binary sense of the Fall due to his adolescence ending at the time when the War was beginning. Adolescence deprived him of his unity with the world, and the War both disrupted the only community he knew and expelled him from it. So firstly he becomes ontologically displaced, then geographically. And this, of course, is the path of Adam, whose alienation from his spiritual home is followed by an alienation from his material one. Bowling's own understanding of his own prohibition from Eden he expresses in terms that we have learned to expect: 'you can't put Jonah back into the whale' (p. 223). This approach to Bowling as Fallen Man endows the scene in the milk-bar with a further significance: the ''Orrible revelations' which issue from biting the frankfurter is the moment when the sinner suddenly realizes the corrupt nature of things, and all of Bowling's subsequent eschatological dreads and warnings acquire the status of an urge for universal salvation.

If it is true that Bowling has passed from essence to existence it is to be expected that this vital transformation into rootlessness be recorded, and in such a way as to express the helpless contingency of 'thrown Being'. This expectation is fulfilled through the effect of an army at war:

> It was like an enormous machine that had got hold of you. You'd no sense of acting of your

> own free will, and at the same time no notion of trying to resist.... The machine had got hold of you and it could do what it liked with you. It lifted you and dumped you down among places and things you'd never dreamed of, and if it had dumped you down on the surface of the moon it wouldn't have seemed particularly strange. The day I joined the Army the old life was finished. It was as though it didn't concern me any longer. (p. 112)

Because inauthenticity in Orwell's fiction always occurs in situations where some form of totalitarianism is present, it is important to identify the totalitarian character of the above passage and observe that Bowling's experience of 'thrownness' leads irresistibly to inauthenticity. In _1984_ we see that Winston Smith, if he is to assert himself against the system, has to recover the past _in order to have something on which to base the assertion_; and that base is the continuity of self from its origins to the present. In this way it can be seen that it is Smith's sense of having thrown Being that must be eliminated if power is to be effectively opposed. One cannot feel the substantiality of one's will if it is not demonstrably derived from a self that is identifiably _mine_. And this is precisely Bowling's situation. His overwhelming sense of thrownness deprives him of the 'sense of acting of his own free will'. His self is not _his_ any more. _It belongs to the system, to the others on the outside_. And thus it is from this phase in his life that what we recognize as Fatty Bowling emerges. His old authentic self has been destroyed, and he is reincarnated with a new inauthentic self which is the self-for-others. Without will, he experiences himself as a thing, an instrument for the Other's use. Being now rootless, he can be turned into anything, and, having no roots to his Being, there is no self left to resist the change. Thus, through this process, he has been re-born as _anybody_. He is one of the They.

That Bowling is both thrown and fallen existentially is graphically illustrated when he gets shelled in France, and it is to be noted that this scene involves both fragmentation and injuries to the legs:

> I felt as if an enormous hand made of air were sweeping me along. And presently I came down with a sort of burst, shattered feeling among

> a lot of old tin cans, splinters of wood, rusty barbed wire, turds, empty cartridge cases, and other muck in the ditch at the side of the road. When they'd hauled me out and cleaned some of the dirt off me they found that I wasn't very badly hurt. It was only a lot of small shell-splinters that had lodged in one side of my bottom and down the backs of my legs. (p. 110)

The result of the War is that it leaves Bowling 'with a feeling of disbelief in everything'. Society is no longer 'something eternal and unquestionable, like a pyramid'; it is 'just a balls-up' (p. 123). He is the baffled and forlorn survivor of prolonged existential exposure. That Orwell located Bowling's transformations at this particular point in world history and urges this history as specifically and uniquely causal is a matter of some importance in a book whose intention is to reveal a philosophical perspective which is described by William Barrett as being determined by the same historical period. What can be inferred from the following assessment is that Orwell's presentation of the crisis of man in _Coming Up For Air_ is in precise concord with that of the existentialists':

> August 1914 is the axial date in modern western history, and once past it we are directly confronted with the present-day world.... August 1914 shattered the foundations of [the] human world. It revealed that the apparent stability, security, and material progress of society had rested, like everything human, on the void. European man came face to face with himself as a stranger.... The individual is thrust out of the sheltered nest that society has provided. He can no longer hide his nakedness by the old disguises. He learns how much of what he has taken for granted was by its own nature neither eternal nor necessary but thoroughly temporal and contingent.... He has come to feel himself an outsider even within his own human society. He is trebly alienated: a stranger to God, to nature, and to the gigantic social apparatus that supplies his material wants. But the worst and final form of alienation, toward which indeed the others tend, is man's alienation from his own self.
>
> _The whole problematic of Existentialism_

> unfolds from this historical situation. 11 (My underlining)

The decades after the War record Bowling's complete urbanization, his almost total forgetfulness of origins and his marriage to Hilda, who, as the custodian of everything quotidian, ephemeral and material, deserves the title of Queen of the They, and who, within three years, transforms from a young and pretty girl 'with beautiful movements' 'into a depressed, lifeless, middle-aged frump' whom Bowling has 'serious thoughts of killing', confirming Mother Bowling's opinion that on the outside murders happen (pp. 135-6). And in conformity with his new ontological status of thrown self-for-others, he works for the Flying Salamander Insurance Co. as a travelling salesman. Life has become featureless and therefore unmemorable: 'When I look back I realize that my active life . . . ended when I was sixteen', which was his age when he discovered the hidden pool. 'Everything that really matters to me had happened before that date' (p. 131). In contrast with the rural boy, the urban man lives in a road which is 'just a prison with the cells all in a row' (p. 14). And in this prison he is afraid: 'Fear! We swim in it. It's our element' (p. 19). Fear is the outcome of the Fall from essence, for fear is anxiety over the possibility of being changed and having no control over that change, a thing not experienced by those who have essence. Fear is always anticipatory and is therefore symptomatic of the recognition of one's being in time, of having a future in which one is menaced by change. And this marks a crucial distinction between the world as it was and the world as it is: 'people then had something that we haven't got now. What? It was simply that they didn't think of the future as something to be terrified of' (p. 106). Having so acutely experienced change himself, and sensing the eruption of a second war which will further transform a world already corrupted by its alienation from origins, Bowling now generalizes his condition and falls into an apocalyptic mood in which he can see

> that the old life we're used to is being sawn off at the roots. I can feel it happening. I can see the war that's coming and I can see the after-war, the food-queues and the secret police and the loudspeakers telling you what to think. And I'm not even exceptional in this.

> There are millions of others like me. Ordinary chaps that I meet everywhere . . . have got a feeling that the world's gone wrong. They can feel things cracking and collapsing under their feet. (pp. 157-58)

Bowling diagnoses contemporary man's condition in terms that suggest both an organic and a spiritual depravity: 'There's something that's gone out of us in these twenty years since the war. It's a kind of vital juice that we've squirted away until there's nothing left.... Nerves worn all to bits, empty places in our bones where the marrow ought to be' (p. 168). This expression of a vital loss is inspired by an experience which Bowling has just described, when, stopping by the roadside one fine day in early spring, he leans across a five-barred gate and sees the embers of a fire and a tiny pool covered with duckweed. The embers give him a feeling of life: 'There's something about it, a kind of intensity, a vibration'; 'it's a feeling inside you, a kind of peaceful feeling, and yet it's like a flame'; 'it let's you know you're alive yourself. It's the spot on the picture that makes you notice everything else'. He slides his false teeth out, and his body and everything it represents becomes of no importance: 'it doesn't matter'. All he wants is to be alive with the flame within. And when he looks into the rich density of the pool with all its creatures, he senses the 'mystery of their lives, down there under the water'; if you spent 'ten lifetimes' watching them you'd still not know everything the pool contains. With 'the peculiar flame inside' him, he watches with a 'feeling of wonder'. He says it's 'the only feeling worth having, and we don't want it'. He is at peace, which is 'a feeling in your guts' (pp. 163-65). So here, for a moment, Bowling recaptures the 'magic' feeling of fishing. He can reconnect. Even the umbilical feeling in his guts remains.

Neither the experience nor the geography that compose this scene are anomalous in the Orwell novel. Every protagonist finds a paradisiacal plot off the thoroughfare of a hostile reality, divided by an obstacle suggestive of prohibition: an enclosed place on the 'outside' like the marsupial pouch. In such a place Dorothy Hare has a moment of blissful unity with nature and is temporarily regenerated. Thus the attainment of unity with the sources of life is curative. As a man who has been disconnected from these sources, Bowling expresses his condition in a way that illustrates this disconnection: he has 'squirted away' a 'vital juice' 'until there's nothing left'. Without his connection with his ontological sources he has therefore become incapable of generating _seminal_ fluid. He has lost the means of regeneration which his connection through fishing once ensured. This relates to his rejection of the hidden pool in favour of Elsie, into whom, for the 'first time', he expended his seminal juice without returning to the pool to be replenished. From that time onwards his connections are entirely carnal. He has denied the spiritual sources of life. He has Fallen. But his experience with the embers and the duckweed pool act on him like a 'call' to original unity.

By returning to Binfield in order to fish in the hidden pool ('I thought of it in the dark place among the trees, waiting for me all those years' (p. 170)), Bowling exemplifies the mythic behaviour of archaic man as described by Mircea Eliade:

> The radical 'cure' of the suffering of existence is attained by retracing one's footsteps in the sands of memory right back to the initial _illud tempus_ - which implies the abolition of profane Time.
>
> .... The man of the archaic society is trying to transport himself back to the beginning of the world in order to re-absorb the initial plenitude and recover, intact, the reserves of energy in the new-born babe.... The 'cure' and, consequently, the solution of the problem of existence, becomes possible by the Remembrance of the primordial deed, of that which came to pass _at the beginning_.[12]

This quest, according to Eliade, attempts to transform, or reverse, the 'chaos' of existence (war, fragmentation) into 'cosmos' (harmony, essence). Fishing, which is described by Bowling as being 'the opposite of war', is the ritual by which he will restore the wholeness of self (p. 83). The embered fire, and the pool 'covered over with duckweed' and swarming with life, are images of what Bowling must recover if he is to be regenerated; respectively, the spiritual flame and the self-contained harmony of a cosmos in which everything is in its place and inseparably inter-related. Clearly, these objectives, and the reasons for having them, disclose Bowling as a figure whose missionary task is the redemption of a world 'gone wrong', and, as such, indicate a literary tradition which includes Langland, Bunyan and, especially, the Eliot of The Waste Land: 'I sat upon the shore / Fishing, with the arid plain behind me'. And Bowling, like Eliot, finds that he 'can connect/Nothing with nothing'.[13]

The return to Lower Binfield is Bowling's doom. If he had but resisted the visit he might have been able to maintain the peaceful illusion that at least one place in his world had somehow eluded transformation. The past has been devoured by the present:

> The first question was, where was Lower Binfield?
>
> I don't mean that it had been demolished. It had merely been swallowed.... All I could see was an enormous river of brand-new houses which flowed along the valley in both directions and half-way up the hills on either side. Over to the right there were what looked like several acres of bright red roofs all exactly alike. A big Council housing estate, by the look of it.
>
> But where was Lower Binfield? Where was the town I used to know? It might have been anywhere. All I knew was that it was buried somewhere in the middle of that sea of bricks.... As I looked a fleet of black bombing planes came over the hill and zoomed across the town. (pp. 176-77)

So Bowling, the thin man buried in the fat man, looks down on the thin man's village and discovers it buried in a 'manufacturing town' which resembles the fat man's Hesperides Estate.

It was suggested at the beginning of this chapter that Bowling's physical condition is an expression of his existential condition, and also that his geographical location in the inner-outer suburbs functions as an affirmation of this correspondence. Bowling, having arrived now in Binfield, enters the same situation. The village, like Bowling, has 'spread', and, also like Bowling, has spread into anonymity. It has lost its specificity and become any town, one of those 'new towns that have suddenly swelled up like balloons in the last few years' (p. 180). 'Looking down' on the 'swollen' Binfield, Bowling re-enacts the scene in the bathroom at the beginning of the novel, in which he looks down at 'one of those bellies'. Bowling cannot escape from images of what he has physically and existentially become. Everything seems to deny what he feels he is inside. Therefore, to find the village inside the town becomes a quest for ontological proof, for evidence of the continued existence of the thin authentic man. It is as though if the village no longer exists, then the authentic self which belonged to it has also ceased to exist. Thus the importance of place to personal identity is asserted. In that lost world of childhood where place and self were indivisible, where one implied the other in a mutually inclusive relation, to lose one part of the relation means the loss of both. To continue to have existence under these conditions is to experience the self and the world as ghostly, and this is precisely what characterizes Bowling's experience. The feeling of having an after-life, of being reincarnated, which has been intermittently hinted at throughout the novel, begins to achieve a definite and pervasive presence; and simultaneously generated is the sense of the frankfurter's composite ontology:

> Queer! You can't imagine how queer! All the way down the hill I was seeing ghosts, chiefly the ghosts of hedges and trees and cows. <u>It was as if I was looking at two worlds at once</u>, a kind of thin bubble of the thing that used to be, with the thing that actually existed shining through it. There's the field where the bull chased Ginger Rogers. And there's the place where the horse-mushrooms used to grow! But there weren't any fields or any bulls or any mushrooms. It was houses, houses everywhere, little raw red houses.... And blokes walking up and down, and women shaking out mats, and snotty-nosed kids playing along the pavement. All strangers! They'd all come crowding in while my back was turned. And yet it was they who'd have looked on me as a stranger, they didn't know anything about the old Lower Binfield. (My underlining) (pp. 178-79)

Like the frankfurter, Binfield has, in losing its essence, transformed and become ghostly: 'phantom stuff'. It has become <u>ambiguous</u> and therefore incomprehensible. Once more we find that Bowling doesn't 'belong' because he lacks 'understanding', and this lack of understanding is derived from things seeming to have lost their 'appointed places' through the invasion of the 'outside'. As Bowling says, the real Binfield might be 'anywhere'. Even the dead have been displaced from their customary place at the centre. Now they are laid on the outside:

> It wasn't only that the town had grown so vast that they needed twenty acres to dump their corpses in. It was their putting the cemetery out here, on the edge of the town. Have you noticed that they always do that nowadays? Every new town puts its cemetery on the outskirts.... It wasn't so in the old days. We had our churchyard plumb in the middle of the town, you passed it every day, you saw the spot where your grandfather was lying and where some day you were going to lie yourself. (p. 178)

The new town, then, all the accretions which have collected around the essential village, is a metaphor for the metaphor of the false fat self which has encrusted the true thin self. Bowling's baffled journey through this false outside towards the true inside expresses his sense of his own unintelligibility. Not understanding himself, he doesn't belong to himself, so loses his way. Figuratively journeying through the 'fat' of the town, he loses his way, finds it again, regains confidence and then is once more lost. The outside now penetrates the core; the authentic and the inauthentic are now inextricably mixed. What comes from where is impossible to discern: 'I could remember nothing. I couldn't even remember whether it was hereabouts that the town used to begin. All I knew was that in the old days this street hadn't existed' (p. 179). Bowling has wandered into an ontological labyrinth, into that 'jigsaw puzzle' which in youth was whole but which has been shattered by the Falls of adolescence and war. Nothing fits. There is no map of the self wherein existential boundaries are shown. And when he does eventually find the old centre it is with the old dead in the old churchyard. In pursuing an understanding of his beginnings, he arrives only at an understanding of his end. Only here does he find man's changeless state. All the riddles of the self have been played out in the context of the most tangled riddle of all. Here, in the churchyard at the centre, he grasps man's essence as a nothingness. He confronts the ultimate thin man: the fleshless man, the man of bone. Over his parents' graves he feels 'nothing'. All the permanent giants of childhood have vanished: 'All gone to dust'; 'nothing left of any of them except a slab of stone and God knows what underneath' (p. 188). The sense of nothingness, fragmentation, discontinuity, incoherence, deletion of memory and the puzzle of Being are all captured when Bowling reads an epitaph from one of the slabs. It is an image of the broken jigsaw, in which the pieces that once integrated a life have now lost their 'appointed places':

> Here....................son, Gent.,
> of this parish................. his just &
> upright............................... etc.
> (p. 189)

With the name gone, nobody knows who it is who is to be remembered. It is the grave of <u>any</u>man; the grave of an anyman from an anytime in the last remnant of a village lost in an anytown. Bowling, dehistoricized, and having already experienced confirmation of his anonymity in the hotel where his name is not recognized, squats down over this 'pattern' of words opposite the family pew. Bowling confronts his own mortality in the midst of a world that makes no sense. It is another ''Orrible revelation'. The final 'veil' has been whipped away, and what lies behind is the Absurd.

After this, the ghostliness intensifies:

> Two days I spent just wandering round the old landmarks, such of them as I could identify. And all that time I never ran across a soul that knew me. I was a ghost, and if I wasn't actually invisible, I felt like it.
>
> . . . . For hours on end I'd be walking through a world that wasn't there. I'd count my paces as I went down the pavement and think, 'Yes, here's where so-and-so's field begins.' . . . . It was as though the countryside had been buried by a kind of volcanic eruption from the outer suburbs. (pp. 197-98)

Only traces of reality are left in a world of accelerating metamorphosis. Anything can become anything: 'That petrol pump is really an elm tree' (p. 197). Without essence, no ontological certainty can exist. Everywhere there are images of ersatz and self-for-others. The self and the world are in the process of an arbitrary and irreversible reconstitution. This is the inspiration behind Bowling's brooding eschatology.

All of Bowling's significant discoveries in Binfield possess this feature: there is no observable connection between what a thing was and what it now is. Binfield, the place of peace, now manufactures bombs; Elsie, Bowling's first lover, once 'deeply feminine', with 'a delicate, curiously gentle face' (p. 103), had become 'a kind of soft lumpy cylinder, like a bag of meal' (p. 204); his father's old seed shop is now an 'arty' tea shop which makes 'home made cakes' out of 'margarine and egg-substitute' (p. 187); and, most drastic of all, the hidden pool, which is the object of his quest, is now a rubbish-dump. Significantly, it is now 'outside the grounds' of Binfield House, which is now a Mental Home (p. 211). The new reality is an unintelligible sequence of ahistorical transformations leading to death. The bomb that accidentally falls on Binfield makes 'a noise like the Day of Judgement'. Bombs are things which become fragments through the process of the inside becoming the outside, an image of the new world. The sound of the explosion gives Bowling

> a vision of bursting metal. You seem to see great sheets of iron bursting open. But the peculiar thing is the feeling it gives you of being suddenly shoved up against reality. It's like being woken up by somebody shying a bucket of water over you. You're suddenly dragged out of your dreams by a clang of bursting metal, and it's terrible, and it's real. (p. 219)

This is immediately followed by a scene similar to the one at the end of Animal Farm. It is as if the explosion, by exposing the inside to the outside, actually creates mutant forms:

> And then I saw an extraordinary sight. At the other end of the market-place the High Street rises a little. And down this hill a herd of pigs was galloping, a sort of huge flood of pig-faces. The next moment, of course, I saw what it was. It wasn't pigs at all, it was only the schoolchildren in their gas-masks.... But I tell you that for a moment they looked exactly like a herd of pigs. (pp. 219-20)

The bombed house captures exactly Bowling's forlorn recognition that his childhood world is now lost for ever. The inside mineness of individual life has been obliterated by the invasion of the anonymous outside mass. One wall of the house has been 'ripped off as neatly as if someone had done it with a knife'. It is '*just like looking into a doll's house*' (My underlining). The ground floor is a 'smashed-up mess'. Now that everything is on the outside, insides can mix with insides, to form part of the *ersatz surface of the world*, *like the frankfurter*. But whereas in the milk-bar Bowling had the comforting presence of King Og's solid wholeness, he is left now with only the 'legs':

> A jar of marmalade had rolled across the floor, leaving a long streak of marmalade behind, and *running side by side with it there was a ribbon of blood*. But in among the broken crockery there was lying a leg. Just a leg, with the trouser still on it and a black boot with a Wood-Milne rubber heel. This is what the people were oo-ing and ah-ing at.
>
> I had a good look at it and took it in. *The blood was beginning to get mixed up with the marmalade*. When the fire-engine arrived I cleared off to the George to pack my bag.
>
> This finishes me with Lower Binfield, I thought.
>
> (My underlining) (p. 221)

So Bowling returns to Ellesmere Road with nothing behind him, a mortal fragment on the surface of the present caught in a process of transformations leading to 'God knows what'. In searching for the thin authentic man he has gained four pounds, thus adding more fat to the outside and contributing to his existence as a self-for-others.

Coming Up For Air records an attempt to enrich an impoverished life by reviving the wholeness of original self which has been estranged by adolescence, severed by war, and then buried for decades by the amnesic everydayness of the They. The characteristic of this original self which Bowling most wanted to secure was its fulness, but it is crucial to note that this fulness is not that fixed state of pretended bondage and irresponsibility which Sartre would describe as being-in-itself. Indeed, Bowling's quest to retrieve wholeness of Being is inspired by a desire to demolish this state of inauthentic thinghood into which he has grown. He flies from the alienation of objectivized Being towards the specific mineness of the unique independent individual who is unified with the natural processes of life. Unlike John

Flory and Gordon Comstock, he invents no project of deterministic Being in order to escape the burdens of freedom. He is, rather, like Dorothy Hare, whose flight was precipitated by an existence made deadly by living for others as a dismembered specimen. Both revolt against a false essence. And so it is in these two, Dorothy and Bowling, that we can discern the mode of rebellion to which Winston Smith will also be committed. But Smith is a man apart. In _1984_ the pursuit of an authentic life is of a different order. It is heroic action.

NOTES

1. _Coming Up For Air_ (1939; rpt. Harmondsworth: Penguin Books, 1967), pp. 7-8. Henceforth cited in text by page number to this edition.
2. R.D. Laing, _The Divided Self_, p. 69.
3. Wordsworth, _The Prelude_, _Poetical Works_, p. 495, ll. 21-23.
4. _Being and Nothingness_, p. 614.
5. Edmund Leach, _Lévi-Strauss_, rev. ed. (London: Fontana, 1974), p. 68.
6. Ralph Waldo Emerson, "Blight," _The Penguin Book of American Verse_, ed. Geoffrey Moore (Harmondsworth: Penguin Books, 1977), p. 78.
7. _The Divided Self_, p. 174.
8. Barnes, _The Literature of Possibility_, p. 47.
9. Alexander McKelway, _The Systematic Theology of Paul Tillich_ (London: Lutterworth Press, 1964), p. 145.
10. _Man in the Modern Age_, trans. Eden and Cedar Paul (London: Routledge and Kegan Paul, 1951), pp. 9-10.
11. _Irrational Man_ (1958; rpt. London: Heinemann, 1967), pp. 28-31.
12. _Myths, Dreams and Mysteries_, trans. Philip Mairet (1960; rpt. London: Fontana, 1968), p. 51.
13. "The Waste Land," _Collected Poems_, p. 79, ll. 423-24; p. 74, ll. 301-02.

Chapter Eight

NINETEEN EIGHTY-FOUR

It has been suggested that Orwell is a novelist of situations and that his protagonists derive their distinctiveness from their concrete apprehension of themselves in relation to these situations (see p. 52 above). As a consequence, it is difficult to attribute to each an autonomous vitality. If their situations were to disappear, they would lose their structural supports and fold. One cannot, as it were, reach into the text, subtract them, and bring them to life elsewhere, for they have all been defined by their reactions to specific circumstances. The Orwell protagonists are always seen in reaction. It is as if they have been prodded into existence by external stimuli. Usually there is a feeling of outrage and disgust, and always of estrangement, at being stirred from dormancy into a recognition that the self is threatened. Like sleepers in a cooling room, the point at which they wake is the point where the chill has become intolerable; and this is where the Orwell novel begins. The reader first encounters the protagonist at the time when he has discovered that he is a being in crisis, at the time when he has definitively realized that <u>his life must change</u>. So the reader is immediately confronted with anxiety and choice as characteristic of the Orwellian fictional situation.

The significance of describing Orwell as a novelist of situations is that the situation is fundamental to the definition of existential writing. According to Hazel Barnes, the existential writer 'presents in his imaginative works characters wholly engaged in a specific social situation and confronted with the necessity of making a definite choice, but <u>the conflict is always such that the solution is somehow a commitment as to the nature of the possibilities of man</u>' (My underlining).1 This emphasis represents a decisive shift from the traditional literature of _hexis_ to the literature of _praxis_, and entails a characterological transition from fixity to flux, from being-in-itself to being-for-itself. Significantly, Orwell himself has described this crucial existentialist distinction:

> Why is it that Tolstoy's grasp seems to be so much larger than Dickens's - why is it that he seems able to tell you so much more _about yourself_? It is not that he is more gifted, or even, in the last analysis, more intelligent. It is because he is writing about people who are growing. _His characters are struggling to make their souls, whereas Dickens's are already finished and perfect_.2
> (My underlining)

Formerly, according to Sartre, the situation had no other function than putting these 'finished and perfect' beings into conflict; man was not seen to be _making himself_. The depiction of existential man demands a different perspective:

> No more characters; the heroes are freedoms caught in a trap like all of us. What are the issues? Each character will be nothing more but the choice of an issue and will equal no more than the chosen issue. It is to be hoped that all literature will become moral and problematic like this.... Moral - not moralizing; let it show simply that man is _also_ a value and that the questions he raises are always moral. Above all, let it show the inventor in him. In a sense, each situation is a trap - there are walls everywhere.[3]

This notion of the importance of the situation as a means of provoking self-defining action from the free man is an expression of Sartre's response to the pressures on those in the French Resistance during the German Occupation. In this situation, the coherence and fixity of the self was threatened. Man vividly saw his self as something which could be changed by a sudden decision, reversing the trend of a lifetime. What had previously been seen as man's essential character, now came to be seen as something that he had chosen to be. It was realized that the consistency of self that man had construed as his permanent character was due merely to a long series of similar choices which created a pattern.

Therefore man had been situated in such a way that no crucial choice seemed required of him. No momentous either/or had provoked the realization that he had <u>always</u> been at the crossroads of Being. His authentic possibilities had been disguised by the somnolence of an undisturbed normative life. Under these conditions, the consequences of man's bad faith were of small account, for his ultimate moral worth was not an issue; but under the German Occupation it was:

> A man confronted with probable death or actual torture could not avoid taking full stock of his capabilities as a human being. The situations in which he found himself were such that his choice committed him only to one of two extremes - cowardice or heroism. Moreover, one had a real and present sense of history. One knew that by one's actions one was helping to write the record of the French nation under stress. <u>Even more than that, one was affirming what it meant to be human. It was no longer 'natural' to be a man. Rather it was a question asked and an answer given</u>.4
> (My underlining)

This describes precisely Winston Smith's situation. In Oceania it is 'no longer "natural" to be a man'; it is an actual perversion. Almost all of the common assumptions about the self and the world are in question, and nothing is certain. <u>Nineteen Eighty-Four</u> is a test-case, a kind of laboratory experiment designed to determine the survival factor of those values on which a liberal democracy rests. It measures the stature of man when he faces in solitude the extinction of his individual possibilities. <u>1984</u> is perhaps the most complete example of the limit-situation in English fiction.

Smith's situation is such that no amount of concentrated endeavour can lead to escape. The most radical and daring decision can make no sustained qualitative difference to his life. His is a closed world in which the hostile and indomitable Other is always present. He is locked in with the enemy. And it is this assumption that the Other is never absent and always threatening that is fundamental to Smith's experience of his situation. There is no longer any <u>inside</u>. All places are public places. There is no disguise. The most basic fact about man's being-in-the-world in 1984 is his feeling of constant exposure:

> The telescreen received and transmitted simultaneously. Any sound that Winston made, above the level of a very low whisper, would be picked up by it; moreover, so long as he remained within the field of vision which the metal plaque commanded, he could be seen as well as heard. There was of course no way of knowing whether you were being watched at any given moment. How often, or on what system, the Thought Police plugged in on any individual wire was guesswork. It was even conceivable that they watched everybody all the time. But at any rate they could plug in your wire whenever they wanted to. You had to live - did live, from habit that became instinct - in the assumption that every sound you made was overheard, and, except in darkness, every movement scrutinized.

> The black moustachio'd face gazed down from every commanding corner. There was one on the house-front immediately opposite. BIG BROTHER IS WATCHING YOU, the caption said, while the dark eyes looked deep into Winston's own.... Even from the coin the eyes pursued you. On coins, on stamps, on the covers of books, on banners, on posters, and on the wrappings of a cigarette packet - everywhere. Always the eyes watching you and the voice enveloping you. Asleep or awake, working or eating, indoors or out of doors, in the bath or in bed - no escape. Nothing was your own except the few cubic centimetres inside your skull.[5]

It is to be noted that in the above quote the consequence of being incessantly observed is that the observed loses possession of himself; only the parts of himself which cannot be seen by the Other remain his. All of Smith's visible self, his body, has been dispossessed by the Other; and here we see, in its most extreme development, the ontological perplexity of George Bowling, for whom there were parts of his body which he could no longer reach and claim as his own.

In 1984 the relational dynamics of the self and the Other are decisively of the type revealed by Sartrean analysis, an analysis which explains the nature of Ingsoc's power in terms of the self's unavoidable obligation to effect an ontological change. The domination of the self through the ubiquitous slogan 'BIG BROTHER IS WATCHING YOU' compares with Sartre's notion of the _Look_ as the most basic and prevalent form of tyranny (see p. 47 above). To suddenly be aware that I am being watched by another is to experience the loss of myself and my world, for under the Look of the Other I experience myself as having an _outside_, an objective form which takes its place among the _things_ of the world. As an object, I lose my sense of freedom and subjectivity. No longer an organizing consciousness always at the centre of the world, I become an item in the perceptual field of the Other. My point of view ceases to be the definitive perspective on reality. I merely become part of the Other's world, and as the Other's world is something that I cannot know, I am aware of having a dimension that is not understood by me: 'the profound meaning of my being is outside of me, imprisoned'.[6] As an _un_observed self my understanding of myself is that I _am_ free, unlimited. Under the Look of the Other, I am apprehended as something complete with a circumscribed outside, a totality, an object which has no freedom of becoming. My freedom is suddenly freezed. No longer does it seem that I create myself. I am transformed into a being-for-the-other: 'I have my foundation outside myself. I am for myself only as I am pure reference to the Other'.[7] Sartre graphically describes this possession of the self through the Other's Look: 'it appears that the world has a kind of drain hole in the middle of its being and that it is perpetually flowing off through this hole'.[8] In solitude I am not an object to myself and can thus maintain my freedom; I only become an object to myself through my having consciousness of the Other's consciousness of me, and, as it is not me who makes this object, what I _am_ depends not on myself but on the Other. So being-with-others is a continual conflict. The looked-at, to regain his freedom, attempts to transform the Other into an object, hence abolishing the Other's freedom to objectivize: 'While I attempt to free myself from the hold of the Other, the Other is trying to free himself from mine; while I seek to enslave the Other, the Other seeks to enslave me'.[9]

Being-with-others is, then, always a struggle for power wherein the slave is the one who cannot overcome his objective being-for-others. The slave is encased in his outside by the Other's subjectivity. It is through this observation that we encounter the deeper meaning of the division of Ingsoc society into Inner and Outer Parties. The Inner Party, as the foundation of power, is hidden, purely subjective; no one of the Outer Party can reciprocate the Look of the Inner, so therefore their enslaved objectivity is maintained. Only when Smith can elude visibility in the alcove of his room can he exist as a for-itself and rediscover his freedom, his 'inner' life. Under the Look of Ingsoc he is coerced into having his Being on the 'outside', into being only what he seems. Indeed, the aim to which Ingsoc is committed is the abolition of a personal interior and the elimination of all sense of the mineness of individual existence. The perfect Ingsoc citizen would have no existence, insofar as he would not know that he _is_; he would be a shell stuffed with otherness. During Smith's inquisition, O'Brien says to him: '" You will be hollow. We shall squeeze you empty, and then we shall fill you with ourselves"' (p. 206). Always externally observed and threatened, Smith's situation is, as has been suggested (see p. 15 above), of the kind which typifies paranoic delusion:

> The paranoic has specific persecutors. Someone is against him. There is a plot on foot to steal his brains. A machine is concealed in the wall of his bedroom which emits mind rays to soften his brain, or to send electric shocks through him while he is asleep. The person I am describing _feels_ at this phase _persecuted by reality itself_. The world as it is, and other people as they are, are the dangers.
> .... [A] self is liable to develop which feels it is outside all experience and activity. It becomes a vacuum. Everything is there, outside; nothing is here, inside.[10]

Smith's experience of reality is, then, from the psychiatric point of view, 'insane'; and yet this, under Ingsoc, is sanity, and the one who rejects it is mad. There is, of course, nothing unfamiliar here; we have traced in every Orwell novel perplexing ambiguities and paradoxical transformations, all of which connote existentially. But this time a fresh aspect of some significance is present: the connection between mental disorder and conceptual inversion. Smith's situation is a dramatization of the statement by Orwell that 'we live in a lunatic world in which opposites are constantly changing into one another'.[11] As such, it accords with his notion that 'totalitarianism ... does not so much promise an age of faith as an age of schizophrenia'.[12]

The recognition that Ingsoc has established as 'normal' the experience of the 'mad' immediately predisposes the reader to accept *inversion* as a way of understanding the world of *1984*. Conceptually it is a world upside down, corresponding to its being existentially inside out. Man, outside himself and therefore no longer self-orientating, is adrift and weightless; he is in no condition to determine the logical status of his experience of reality. Consequently he is susceptible to propositions which have no relation to the rational ordering of the world, a susceptibility which is necessary to Ingsoc if it is to maintain its own particular ideology and its absolute power over the individual. These propositions are always in the context of the Look. While the eyes of the Thought Police and Big Brother freeze mankind into the perpetual subjugation of beings-for-others, logically chaotic slogans impress themselves on the captured mind and erode the concept of objective truth: 'WAR IS PEACE', 'FREEDOM IS SLAVERY', 'IGNORANCE IS STRENGTH'. In this way it can be seen that *man's transformation into a being-for-others is vital to his acquiescence to the Other's concept of the nature of reality*. If the truth of one's identity is externally derived as it is for the one who lives as a being-for-others, the world of the Others is seen also as true, and if that world contains logical inversions they too will assume the appearance of truth. *Therefore the notion of objective truth can only be restored by demolishing the for-others and establishing being-for-itself*; only by returning to the 'inside' will the world right itself.

In *1984* the urge for objective truth is symptomatic of, and inseparable from, the urge for authentic life. The discovery of a heterodox truth will signify ontologically, for it will be evidence that the Look has been escaped and some kind of personal life established. Because of the Look under which all those in the Outer Party are confined, we are dealing with a large social stratum whose permanent being-in-the-world is inauthentic; indeed, inauthenticity is definitional of the Outer Party's existence as a class. To lose one's sense of undifferentiated objectness, to lose one's sense of existence as founded in the Other and wholly derived from this source, would mean that individuality is present, a category unrecognized by Ingsoc as having any existence at all. In a world maintained by riddle and paradox, the instant one discovers oneself as a person (self-definitional and autonomous) one becomes an 'unperson'. As soon as one is, one is not. So inevitable and absolute is this procedure that it has the appearance of a causal connection; selfhood seems to be its own negation: 'Thoughtcrime does not entail death: thoughtcrime IS death' (p. 26). Although the bullet may be delayed, the condition for the emergence of selfhood is that the trigger is pulled. In contrast, as a being-for-Ingsoc, one lives for ever. In this dread either/or we see the biblical nature of the choice that is offered to the Outer Party, insofar as trust in oneself is synonymous with certain death, and surrendering oneself to the will of the unseen omnipotent is synonymous with the certainty of eternal life: '"Alone - free - the human being is always defeated.... But if he can make complete utter submission, if he can escape from his identity, if he can merge himself in the Party so that he is the Party, then he is all-powerful and immortal"' (p. 212). Big Brother, like God, offers the ultimate reward for the ultimate sacrifice. Man must either disown himself in order to remain living, or bring about his own extinction in order to claim the selfhood which alone makes the living worth having. In this way the Heideggerian nature of being-in-the-world is revealed, for man, if he is to accept the safety and belonging of the self of the They, has also to accept a 'levelling-down' of all the vital possibilities of life; and if he is to discover his authentic possibilities he has also to accept his being-towards-death. Because Smith's pressing sense of death is inseparable from the claim of individuating himself against the collective, he exemplifies the existential view that when man authenticates himself he conjures his own nothingness:

> People simply disappeared, always during the night. Your name was removed from the registers, every record of everything you had ever done was wiped out, your one-time existence was denied and then forgotten. You were abolished, annihilated: vaporized was the usual word.
>
> For a moment he was seized by a kind of hysteria. (p. 19)

So when Smith, at the beginning of the novel, subversively marks the blank book illicitly bought at Charrington's shop, he does so with the understanding that there is no retraction. The either/or has been decided irrevocably, and the anguish which attends such a choice will oppress him to the end. He has locked himself in on Death Row. Now, as one whose life is dominated by a sense of waiting, he assumes the temporality which Ingsoc denies. By authenticating himself, Smith becomes futurized. With the marking of the page, the clock begins to tick. Bleak though this is, it is essential, for time is a crucial part of the definition of humanness which Smith aims to restore. Man must assert his being-in-time if the tyrannical concept of a perpetual present is to be broken. Only in a world which recognizes the openness of the future can man feel free and project himself forwards and realize his personal possibilities. Effectively, to surrender to being-for-others annihilates the sense of the future, because, as one of the They, the future is not mine but belongs to an abstract mass in which the Who is absent. As a self-for-others, Smith has nothing which he can call his. Being denied ownership of all kinds, he cannot properly generate the feeling of having a personal existence. To possess something would therefore be ontologically meaningful, and this explains Smith's reaction when he discovers the book: he is 'stricken immediately by an overwhelming desire to possess it' (p. 9). By owning, he acquires something of that sense of mineness for which he is fighting, and, through experiencing mineness, he gains the personal strength necessary for further dissent, and this is accomplished in the act of writing. In addition, the book itself represents the idea of temporality, which he makes palpable by using it as a diary. Smith restores the time of the past by appropriating an old book, establishes temporal succession by recording dated events, and, because such acts are punishable by death, he realizes the future in the mode of anticipation. Smith therefore, through an authentic act, has acquired a sense of mineness and recovered the three dimensions of time.

As has been seen with George Bowling, one of the horrors of living outside oneself in the unhistorized present is the ghostly sense of having no roots. Thus for Smith the book would be ontologically affirming because it it is an anachronism. It serves to diminish the *ex nihilo* feeling which arises from the destruction of history. The book has its own past which corroborates his own, and, in using it as a diary, the resumption of authentic time is marked. But at the moment that this resumption is accomplished, Smith's life becomes characterized by a peculiar conflict, for the purpose of his work in the Records Department of Minitrue is the elimination of the means by which the truth of the past may be known. He is a professional liar, and yet he risks his life to tell the truth. So Smith's initial paradox, that of procuring the death of the self through attempting to claim the authentic life of the self, is compounded by the paradoxical fact that while he authenticates himself in the alcove he inauthenticates himself in the cubicle. These contradictions, which are in themselves embedded within a society committed to contradiction, further contribute to the more obvious reasons for believing in the impossibility of _fidelity_ within Ingsoc society. For Smith, the revolt which is a prerequisite of self-authentication, entails an irreconcilable antagonistic split within the self which will affect him with a permanent sense of self-betrayal. From the moment that the 'decisive step' is accomplished, Smith leads a double life (p. 26).

Betrayal, and its necessary correlative, double life, is a consistent feature of the Orwell novel. Prior to _1984_ its presence is most evident in _Burmese Days_, in which its possibility oppressed Flory throughout his long conflict between self-determination and the powers of social orthodoxy. The reason why, in _1984_, betrayal can be so shocking is that the ones who betray have usually been reckoned to be those who are least likely to do so. So the betrayer, to the one betrayed, is seen to have undergone a transformation: he becomes the opposite of what he has been taken for. Friends (O'Brien, Charrington) become enemies. In conformity to this reversal, enemies become friends (Julia, Big Brother). So Smith's experience of what is the case in the world actually corresponds to the kind of world he denies and which he defines himself against. If friends are really foes, and foes really friends, war may be peace, and freedom may be slavery. In these propositions there is, unmistakably, the submerged proposition that to all things there is a dualism composed of an inside and an outside; and it is precisely this dimension which is present in the idea of betrayal, for betrayal can only exist as a derivative of _duplicity_ and _deception_, that is, in man's capacity to exist ambiguously. Because betrayal pervades 1984, and because betrayal can only arise from a binary ontological structure, it may be inferred that a further existential dimension in 1984 is present. That betrayal signifies existentially in a general sense is affirmed by Gabriel Marcel, who seems almost to be speaking as one of the Outer Party:

> It is not enough to say that we live in a world where betrayal is possible at every moment and in every form: betrayal of all and of each by himself. I repeat, this betrayal seems pressed upon us by the very shape of our world. The spectacle of death is a perpetual invitation to deny. The essence of our world is perhaps betrayal.
>
> It may be of my essence to be able not to be what I am; in plain words, to be able to betray myself.
>
> Perhaps on the ontological level it is fidelity which matters most. It is in fact the recognition - not a theoretical or verbal, but an actual recognition - of an ontological permanency; a permanency which implies or demands a history [my underlining], unlike the inert or formal permanency of a pure validity, a law for example.[13]

The validity of interpreting betrayal in 1984 as an existential category gains in substance when it is noted that Smith ultimately becomes not what he is at the moment when his fidelity is broken (he rats on Julia). It is indeed an ontological break. In addition he loses the 'permanency which implies or demands a history', and therefore conforms to the crucial Ingsoc requirement of man as having no sense of the reality of the past on which an authentic identity can be founded. The Thou of the I-Thou has to be destroyed in order for the 'I' to be recaptured and enslaved as an objectivized for-others. In the act of betraying Julia, Smith betrays himself, which illustrates a further point of Marcel's: 'One can betray only oneself'.[14]

Each of the concepts with which we have so far dealt as being fundamental to the meaning of 1984 is an element of the existential crisis as described by Karl Jaspers. Jaspers's interpretation of this crisis also provides a picture of a demoniacal world which resembles in every significant sense the structure of Ingsoc society. In addition he offers the same guide towards individual redemption as the one Smith himself adopts. Thus, for the existentialist, the debt to Orwell is great, for he, perhaps alone since Kafka, has provided a working model of the existential plight. In his dramatization of the threats to authentic selfhood which the existentialists have defined, Orwell gives us access to a world in which it is possible to experience more vividly a perspective which is otherwise only to be found in the relative flatness of non-fictional works.

For Jaspers, as for Smith, there is a basic insecurity over one's relations with the forces of the world:

> He who just now seemed our opponent, has become our ally. What in accordance with the objectivity of our voluntary expectations ought to have been our adversary, joins forces with us; what seems really antagonistic, lays down its arms; what looked like a united front is divided against itself. All this occurs in a medley and amid a turbulent interchange....
>
> The individual does not know where he stands, and no one can know what is obsolete and what is the substance of the future.... There exists no unity, neither that of a past nor that of a future epoch.... A search for the unity of the coming generation cannot help him; but perhaps he can aid himself by the persistent endeavour to unveil from moment to moment the nameless powers which are simultaneously inimical to the life-order and to selfhood. But the nameless powers slip away and metamorphose themselves. If for a moment I seem to grasp them, it is only to find that they are no longer what they are.... They are just as ready to pose as enemies as friends, being equally ambiguous in the one role and in the other.... They do their utmost to render our purposive life futile, and they undermine man's selfhood....
>
> Deprived of his world by the crisis [of today's world] man has to reconstruct it from its beginnings with the materials and presuppositions at his disposal. There opens to him the supreme possibility of freedom, which he has to grasp even in the face of impossibility,

> with the alternative of sinking into nullity .... He must either on his own initiative independently gain possession of the mechanism of his life, or else, himself degraded to become a machine, surrender to the apparatus. He must, through communication, establish the tie between self and self, in full awareness that here everything turns upon loyalty and disloyalty; and in default of this his life will be utterly despiritualized and become a mere function.... The demands made of him are such as to assume him to have the powers of a titan. He must meet these demands, and must see what he is capable of in the way of self-development; for, if he fails to do so, there will remain for him nothing but a life in which he will have the advantages neither of man nor beast....
>
> Man wins destiny only through ties: not through the coercive ties imposed on him as an impotent creature by great forces that lie without; but by ties freely comprehended which he makes his own. Such ties hold his life together, so that it is not frittered away but becomes the actuality of his possible existence. Then remembrance discloses to him its indelible foundations; and the future reveals to him the region wherein he will be held accountable for what he does today. Life grows infinitely vast....
>
> <u>What remains, then, is that I hear the voice of the past which makes me aware of my humanhood, and that, through my own life, I speak that voice into the future</u>.15 (My underlining)

The kind of insecurity which Jaspers describes and from which Smith suffers is important to specify, for we can then proceed to provide a more coherent explanation of the nature of Ingsoc oppression. Smith, as has been seen, experiences the world in a way that resembles the paranoic; he has been emptied within through being persecuted by the structure of external reality. In Smith's case this is objectively true; he <u>is</u> a victim, and he is therefore insecure. If this were all, there would be nothing to distinguish his insecurity from, for example, the condition of a defenceless person alone in a house at night when it is known that there are prowlers around. This kind of insecurity can be defined as fear for one's safety; it would not mean that there was anything wrong with the structure of reality. Everything would still make sense. But there is in Smith's insecurity a radical sense of contingency underlying the basic threat. Unlike the person fearful of prowlers, Smith is scared in an unintelligible world. One does not ask 'Why?' when the prowlers are seen, for the world is understood. But it is Smith's enduring question, the thing that must be answered before sense can be made of the world, and, unlike the question 'Why is the world?' it is a question rooted in the glimpsed understanding that the world has deliberately been made unintelligible by those who watch. For Smith the world is unintelligible because it presents itself as paradoxical and contradictory. What seems obviously true transforms into the false, and what seems obviously false transforms into the true; and then this process may, or may not, revert. As 'anything could be true', anything could be false (p. 223). Everything is always provisional. Thus judgments about the nature of reality, of what is, must be forever suspended. All things must be seen as potentially otherwise. All propositions contain their own negation. By describing Smith's being-in-the-world in such a way, we are in a position to define his kind of insecurity. In that Smith is a man 'utterly lacking in any unquestionable self-validating certainties', he has 'primary ontological insecurity'. In accordance with this definition of Laing's, Smith also lacks 'the experience of his own temporal continuity'.[16]

1984 is a book immensely fertile in insights about the psychology of power, and one which, by any measure, is remarkable, for it compares with a device which was 'discovered' by an inter-disciplinary team in 1956 and which has been described as 'one of the revolutionary ideas of the twentieth century'.[17] By 1948 Orwell was exposing the Oceanic citizen to the same situation which, as a schizogenic structure, has been identified as the 'Double Bind' (see also p. 16 above). As it will be argued that this notion is a basic correlative of Sartrean Bad Faith, the Double Bind structure of Oceanic society may be demonstrated without deviating from the existential.

According to Double Bind theory, schizophrenia results from a person being persistently exposed to commands or propositions which, because they contradict, leave the person in an impossible situation. The person's mother, or any powerful Other, Double Binds by somehow asserting Do-Don't or Yes-No, or, in Ingsoc terminology, 'blackwhite' (p. 169). The Binder, therefore, presides over the Bound in a manner which resembles Ingsoc over the Outer Party: 'This peculiar linking together of opposites . . . is one of the chief distinguishing marks of Oceanic society' (p. 172). Additionally, with no past as evidence for asserting an alternative reality, 'the citizen of Oceania is like a man in interstellar space, who has no way of knowing which direction is up or down' (p. 160). The citizen's situation, then, compares with Laing's description of one of the Bound: 'the fabric of this girl's sense of "reality", of what is the case and what is not the case, was in shreds'.[18] This is the 'primary ontological insecurity' which precipitates schizophrenia. Schizophrenia is seen as a 'strategy' that the Bound adopts in order to escape from a world in which it is impossible to determine what those in positions of power actually intend. He retires from the oppressive constraints on his mind by losing his mind. He becomes unbound, but mad. By responding to the mad logic of the Double Bind, he goes mad himself. But under Ingsoc, the orthodox Outer Party member <u>never</u> goes mad, for the powers which drive him towards it also make provision to ensure that he never arrives, for madness destroys the self-for-others which must be maintained if Ingsoc is to maintain control. Madness is Ingsoc's great enemy and a thing to which it is constitutionally susceptible: 'the prevailing mental conditions must be controlled insanity'. To deal with the implicit schizogenic effects of a Double Bound society, Ingsoc has devised Double Think, 'for it is only by reconciling contradictions that power can be maintained indefinitely' (p. 172). 'Doublethink' is 'reality control':

> His mind slid away into the labyrinthine world of doublethink. To know and not to know, to be conscious of complete truthfulness while telling carefully constructed lies, to hold simultaneously two opinions which cancelled out, knowing them to be contradictory and believing in both of them; to use logic against logic . . . to forget whatever it was necessary to forget, then to draw it back into memory again at the moment when it was needed, and then promptly to forget it again: and above all, to apply the same process to the process itself. (pp. 31-32)

Doublethink is a device created by Ingsoc in order to limit its own tendencies. It establishes a boundary between maximum self-for-others and its complete abolition through the escape into madness. The Double Bind erodes the possibility of deciding the either/or, and doublethink eliminates the vexatious inference that there is something to decide.

Throughout this book an attempt has been made to reveal in particular a coherent correlation between Sartre and Orwell. But it is, perhaps, only when we encounter doublethink, which 'lies at the heart of Ingsoc', that it is possible to demonstrate an unequivocal indenticalness about their fundamental assumptions concerning the structure of the human mind (p. 171). It is on this shared premise that Orwellian totalitarianism and the entire system of Sartrean authenticity rests: 'It is, according to Sartre, a simple fact about human beings that they are able to hold two contradictory beliefs at one and the same time, or to believe and not believe the same thing at the same time'.[19] This position, it must be emphasized, is absolutely fundamental to Sartre's whole enterprise; it is as vital to his philosophy as buoyancy is to a boat. Without it, bad faith cannot exist:

> What unity do we find in these various aspects of bad faith? It is a certain art of forming contradictory concepts which unite in themselves both an idea and the negation of that idea. The basic concept which is thus engendered, utilizes the double property of the human being. (My underlining)
>
> The decision to be in bad faith does not dare to speak its name; it believes itself and does not believe itself in bad faith.[20]

Orwell, of course, did name it: doublethink. The man in bad faith, the inauthentic man, is practising doublethink. He cannot be in bad faith *unless* he practises doublethink.

Never, perhaps, has a society been described which is so deeply coerced into accepting inauthenticity as a way of life. Freezed by the Look into the objectivity of a for-others, and constantly exposed to the Double Bind, the Outer Party citizen suspends himself inertly on the boundary of sanity by the application of doublethink. Only by first eluding the Look can the citizen restore sufficient independence of mind to resist the other constraints and decide the nature of the 'real'. Smith *can* elude the Look because of his alcove, and because he can elude he can possess something and therefore sense his mineness; and because what he possesses is a blank book, he can write in it and restore the 'sharpness' of 'outline' that his life has lost through the absence of 'external records' (p. 29). For the first time since the establishment of Ingsoc, he can recognize his own authentic possibilities. With the it-ness of the self dissolved, he is now prepared for relation, for one can only say 'You' when the 'I' is felt to be.

Appropriately, the first communication between Smith and Julia is 'I love you' (p. 89). Smith, having dominated the it-ness of the self, becomes an 'I', and, having become an 'I', creates the possibility of becoming a You to another. A clear expression of the previous it-relations is given with his estranged wife Katherine, who copulates for the Party. Living for others, her conception of herself is purely instrumental. Her freedom has been captured by the Look, 'frozen for ever by the hypnotic power of the Party' (p. 57). In addition, their sex-for-the-Party is characterized by the Do-Don't of the Double Bind: 'To embrace her was like embracing a jointed wooden image. And what was strange was that even when she was clasping him against her he had the feeling that she was simultaneously pushing him away with all her strength' (p. 57). Katherine, as a Party instrument, uses him also as an instrument (an It as opposed to a You), and, as an instrument of the Party, he is defeating himself. Intercourse is therefore ambivalently conducted, similar, in fact, to his work in the Records Department, a job that is his only real pleasure but which furthers his own subjection. He cannot act for himself without simultaneously acting for others; so during the act in which he is Double Bound he is ensnared in another paradox, which is a logical variant of 'freedom is slavery'. Smith, ambivalent, used as an It by an It which Double Binds, experiences sexuality in terms of contradiction: intimacy is alienation.

So to become an 'I' to a You and a You to an 'I' will not only mean deliverance from the it-world into authentic relation; it will be an act purged of ambiguity: no Double Bind, no doublethink, no bad faith. It will be an existential victory over ideology. In the bleak ossified realm of the It, Smith has been recognized, and the momentousness of this must be grasped. Not since childhood when the family was sundered at the inception of the New

Order has Smith been You'd in a way which refers to him specifically and which implies a reciprocal relation. It is a contact utterly independent of the grand mediator Big Brother, who exists for the Outer Party as Napoleon did for the people. Napoleon was, writes Buber,

> the demonic You for the millions and did not respond; to 'You' he responded by saying: It; he responded fictitiously on the personal level - responding only in his own sphere, that of his cause, and only with his deeds. This is the elementary historical barrier at which the basic word of association loses its reality, the character of reciprocity: the demonic You for whom nobody can become a You.[21]

Only Big Brother can be a You; only Big Brother can be loved; and only through the love of this You can anything termed the 'I' come into Being. Because the object of love is not Big Brother, each word of Julia's message is criminal. Everything must issue from Big Brother. Big Brother is the source, the power by which all things come to be. Heresy is therefore a denial of origins; consequently the heretic is denying that he is. One makes oneself an 'unperson'. And that is the ontological subtlety behind heresy: if one only is through Big Brother, a denial of him cannot but be a denial of oneself. The heretic unpersons himself. Ideologically there are no ontological choices: one lives through Ingsoc and for Ingsoc. This, and only this, is what life is.

The progress of Smith's existential restoration is furthered when he and Julia, like Comstock and Rosemary, leave the it-world for the natural world, thus entering the appropriate environment for the physical affirmation of the I-You. Having been 'recognized' himself, he now recognizes the landscape. Somehow the world is unifying, making sense. Connections are being made. A tangle of memory and dream, he sees the Eden from which he has been estranged for so long, a place of belonging and peace similar to the one George Bowling remembers before the time of division and loss. It is 'the Golden Country', Housman's 'land of lost content' in which Smith believes his true origins lie (p. 28). Here, a genuine selfhood is possible. In the lost paradise everything lived as a for-itself; it merely was without reference to the Other. And it is this crucial contrast between the deadness of living for others and the life of living for oneself which Orwell captures in the lyric thrush: 'Winston watched it with a sort of vague reverence. For whom, for what, was that bird singing? No mate, no rival was watching it. What made it sit at the edge of the lonely wood and pour its music into nothingness? . . . . He stopped thinking and merely felt' (p. 102). And it is immediately after this experience of feeling his new Being that Julia, in a gesture suggestive of both a liberation of the self and its revelation, flings away her clothes. The uniform blue overalls which represent the outer for-others of the it-world are dismissed to reveal the inner for-itself. To Smith it is therefore a gesture 'by which a whole civilization seemed to be annihilated' (p. 103). Sex, hitherto for the Party, becomes sex for oneself and against the Party: 'It was a blow struck against the Party. It was a political act' (p. 104). And sex, being against the Party, is absent of the Double Bound ambivalence which characterized sex with Katherine:

> The next moment, it was hard to say by whose act, she was in his arms. At the beginning he had no feeling except sheer incredulity. The youthful body was strained against his own, the mass of dark hair was against his face, and yes! actually she had turned her face up and he was kissing the wide red mouth. She had clasped her arms about his neck, she was calling him darling, precious one, loved one. (p. 99)

Thus from the time when Smith buys the diary to the time when he leaves the countryside he has, in distinguishable phases, overcome his alienation from the three-fold dimensions essential to authentic being-in-the-world:

> First, there is Umwelt, literally meaning 'world around'; this is the biological world, generally called the environment. There is, second, the Mitwelt, literally the 'with-world', the world of beings of one's own kind, the world of one's fellow men. The third is Eigenwelt, the 'own-world', the mode of relationship to one's self.[22]

The blank book which inspired his progress towards the recovery of these relations is both evidence of there having been a past independent of Ingsoc 'history' and also a symbol of the absence of history during the long interim between the making of the book and the year 1984; and because the reckoned age of the book is approximately the same as Smith's it functions as a symbol of Smith's own unhistorized condition. He discovers an image of himself. Having no history, he is a blank book, a *tabula rasa*. So when Smith decides that the book will be a diary and writes in it, he exemplifies the existential prescription that fiction should present characters who, in an anguished act of choice, are *making themselves out of nothingness*. The act itself is suggestive of the magical, a kind of sacrament which evokes the 'real' time of his origins. In recreating time through starting a diary in a book about the same age as himself, he reconnects himself to his authentic beginnings prior to the establishment of inauthentic self-for-others under Ingsoc. The act *by which* he *re*authenticates himself is also an act which reconnects him to his original for-itself.

The predominant ontological characteristic of man under Ingsoc is thrown being-for-others, and it can be seen that the two aspects of this characterization arise indivisibly from the same cause. In the old world of which the thrush is a symbol man could live for himself with an historical perspective which substantially tranquillized the distress which attends thrown Being. Man could look back to his foundations and trace the developing self up to the present. He had *roots*. He had what Smith describes as the 'human heritage' (p. 26). Always he was in contact with a coherent sense of becoming which provided the substance of his *identity*. Because of this he could feel his life to be *his* life. He owned himself, and, in owning himself, he could live independently as a for-itself. The now, the present, could always be seen as the *result* of an explicable process, a concatenation of acts which were felt to be free because existence was *mine*. The possession of a comprehensible past created the means by which an autonomous selfhood could be gained. Without this past, man's identity for himself loses in substance: 'When there were no external records that you could refer to, even the outline of your own life lost its sharpness' (p. 29). He becomes 'a lonely ghost' (p. 26).

Ingsoc's sociopolitical revolution involves not only a shift from freedom to slavery but to *dependence*; in this lies the distinctiveness of Orwellian totalitarianism. The orthodox Oceanian

<u>needs</u> Ingsoc. He needs Ingsoc because the revolution effected an ontological transformation from being-for-itself to being-for-others. Through the effect of the Look this transformation was made possible; but its efficacy is substantially derived from another condition: the intensification of thrownness due to the erasure of the past. Having no past delivers man over to the thrall of the Look, generating that ontological debility which encourages surrender to the Other, who is represented by Big Brother. It is a weakness which grows with time, as man, while accumulating blankness behind him, becomes increasingly remote from the self which Ingsoc has suppressed. This, of course, corresponds to the Bowling condition, but in <u>1984</u> mankind has sunk to a more desperate level of obscurity. For Bowling the structure of the world was such that he found it impossible to recover personal selfhood; but it was neither made impossible through intent, nor was his failure more than marginally significant for humanity in general. Bowling had no critical choice to make. He was not wrung by the angst of responsibility. His acts made no mould in which the human future was set. Had he been successful in recovering his lost Being, the world would still have run its course to where the brute in the dungeon patiently snuffs all the various lights by which man has guided himself towards the human. What Smith inherits is the global meaning of personal ontology. He must realize his possibility as a missing link and thereby provide for others the possibility of a pre-revolutionary origin. He must transcend the timeless and revitalize the significance of man as a being-in-time. He must assert that man <u>is</u> his past. He must reduce the acute thrownness of Ingsoc man by disclosing his origins in the timed world of the for-itself. He must reveal the past as constitutive of identity and mineness, showing Being to be free. Only then can man, as a being-for-itself, become ontologically equipped for the necessary resistance to the objectifying possessiveness of the Look. Being no longer thrown and floating rootless in the world of the It, he will no longer need the Other in order to <u>be</u>. The ghostliness of life will fade and he will emerge as the foundation of himself. In this lies the existential meaning of the past for existential man. Only by restoring the meaning of individual existence can the 'human heritage' be continued.

The motive behind Smith's quest for the past is to locate what he was prior to the alienating transition to existence-for-others. As with Bowling, man has been wrenched from a stable state of Being and abandoned to the contingent. Being-for-others is, by definition, contingent, as one's Being has been surrendered to arbitrary control. So man, having already transformed from a being-for-itself, lives, as a for-others, in a permanent condition of flux: he will be whatever he is instructed to be. Thus it can be seen that the betrayal which characterizes Oceanic society is symptomatic of an ontological change. Betrayal is an expression of the contingency derived from living for others. It would therefore be expected that the reverse would be true in the pre-revolutionary world; and this is precisely the case. Betrayal springs from living as a being-for-others; fidelity, from living as a being-for-onself:

> Tragedy, he [Winston] perceived, belonged to the ancient time, to a time when there was still privacy, love, and friendship, and when the members of a family stood by one another without needing to know the reason. His mother's memory tore at his heart because she had died loving him, when he was too young and selfish to love her in return, and because somehow, he did not remember how, <u>she had sacrificed herself to a conception of loyalty that was private and unalterable. Such things, he saw, could not happen today</u>.
> (pp. 27-28) (My underlining)

> He did not suppose, from what he could remember of her, that she had been an unusual woman, still less an intelligent one; and yet she had possessed a kind of nobility, a kind of purity, simply because the standards that she obeyed were private ones. <u>Her feelings were her own, and could not be altered from the outside</u>.
> (p. 134) (My underlining)

Fidelity, therefore, was a constituent part of the lost authentic self, and so although Julia and Winston would be prepared to perform the horrible ('"throw sulphuric acid in a child's face"') in order to undermine Ingsoc, they are not prepared to separate and betray one another, for the fall from fidelity instantly restores the contingent self-for-others which rebellion aims to destroy (p. 140). Fidelity transcends the myriad transformations which occur through contingency, and revives the possibility of permanence, of essence.

The quest for essence, then, doomed though it is (and, in other circumstances, possibly inauthentic, in that the aim may be, as it was for Flory and Comstock, to make a thing of the self) is an attempt to achieve the immutability of monistic Being over against the mutable dualistic Being which is a prerequisite for the dissembling act of betrayal. Smith's quest substantially involves therefore a disambiguation of the world, and consequently its demystification. The either/or has to be retrieved, and the Yes-No consciousness implicit to blackwhite sundered, each of the antithetical categories being restored to what Bowling described as their 'appointed places'. In other words, the axiom must exist again. The world must become a thing about which it is possible to make indubitable decisions. The structural contingency of Ingsoc which allows anything to be anything must be destroyed, for on this destruction depends the survival of the concept of authentic existence. Through this reasoning the rather opaque equation 'freedom is the freedom to say that two plus two make four' becomes clear, in that, because axioms function _independently_ of Ingsoc, they signal an escape from the bondage of living in the dependent condition of being-for-others. The axiom can only mean _one_ thing. It cannot be made duplicitous. _So it is therefore a logical correlate of a monistic ontology_.

As a being-for-Ingsoc, the Oceanic citizen's sense of choice is deadened. Decisions no longer felt to be _his_, he becomes distanced from himself. He becomes the spectator of a predetermined process. The overwhelming sensation is that of vicariousness, of someone else doing the living _for_ him and, through Newspeak, someone else doing the speaking. And herein lies the 'ghostliness' of life when mineness is lost. One is possessed by the Other in a way comparable to those who express their sense of unreality by saying they are possessed by spirits. The 'I' is occupied by a self which speaks through the 'I'; the 'I' has become an instrument for conveying the presence of another. This dispossession of the 'I', and its occupation by the They, we first witnessed in Dorothy Hare, who was accustomed to speaking to herself in the _third person_. It is this speaking for the Other which Ingsoc aims to achieve through establishing Newspeak as the only means of discourse. Newspeak is the language of the they-self. Dispossessed already by thrownness, and captured by the Look, the Oceanic citizens' being-for-others will be irreversibly effected by around the year 2050:

> The purpose of Newspeak was not only to provide a medium of expression for the world-view and mental habits proper to the devotees of Ingsoc, but to make all other modes of thought impossible. It was intended that when Newspeak had been adopted once and for all and Oldspeak forgotten, a heretical thought - that is, a thought diverging from the principles of Ingsoc - should be literally unthinkable, at least so far as thought is dependent on words. (p. 241)

> The intention was to make speech, and especially speech on any subject not ideologically neutral, as nearly as possible independent of consciousness. (p. 248)

> 'The revolution will be complete when the language is perfect. Newspeak is Ingsoc and Ingsoc is Newspeak.' (p. 45)

In devising Newspeak, Ingsoc is attempting to transform man's being-in-the world, believing that man's possibilities are modified in accordance with the possibilities of the language. Man is born into the language and his Being is circumscribed by what that language will let him be and do. Newspeak therefore functions in the same way as Heidegger's Idle Talk (see p. 34 above). Idle Talk is the discourse of the They:

> This everyday way in which things have been interpreted is one into which Dasein has grown in the first instance, with never a possibility of extrication. In it, out of it, and against it, all genuine understanding, interpreting, and communicating, all re-discovering and appropriating anew, are performed. In no case is a Dasein, untouched and unseduced by this way in which things have been interpreted, set before the open country of a 'world-in-itself', so that it just beholds what it encounters. The dominance of the public way in which things have been interpreted has already been decisive even for the possibilities of having a mood -

> that is, for the basic way in which Dasein lets the world 'matter' to it. The 'they' prescribes one's state of mind, and determines what and how one 'sees'.23 (My underlining)

Here the familiar goal of language discourse is reversed. Language no longer speaks Being. Instead of revealing the self, it conceals it; and because the self cannot speak for itself, langauge can no longer create meaningful relations. The I-Thou cannot arise from it, and so all possibility of fidelity is stifled.

Both the Idle Talker and the Newspeaker discourse for the authoritarian They. Therefore Heidegger's judgments about the existential significance of Idle Talk apply also to Newspeak: 'Idle talk has been uprooted existentially, and this uprooting is constant. Ontologically this means that when Dasein maintains itself in idle talk, it is - as Being-in-the-world - cut off from its primordially genuine relationships-of-being towards the world, towards Dasein-with, and towards its very Being-in. Such a Dasein keeps floating unattached'.[24] So we find in the discourse of the They the uprooting of the three-fold relations which it was suggested that Smith was in the process of overcoming his alienation from (see p. 194 above). Perhaps, then, of all the threats which Ingsoc impose, none is more existentially undermining than Newspeak in its ultimate form. It attacks the source of the human, man's essence, in that language both constitutes man's humanness and is its revelation. Without language there is nothing to express: this is the view on which Newspeak is founded. Language is the means by which man knows himself. And we can see instantly the significance of this. Ingsoc, through Newspeak, obliterates mineness and sucks the self for ever into the mode of unconscious being-for, that is, into an in-itself helplessly maintaining its own subjugation. In the canteen of Minitrue there is already to be found a prototype of homo Ingsoc. Even now, in the year 1984, man is blending with the it-world:

> His head was thrown back a little, and because of the angle at which he was sitting, his spectacles caught the light and presented to Winston two black discs instead of eyes. What was slightly horrible, was that from the stream of sound that poured out of his mouth it was almost impossible to distinguish a single word

> .... Whatever it was, you could be certain that every word of it was pure orthodoxy, pure Ingsoc. As he watched the eyeless face with the jaw moving rapidly up and down, Winston had a curious feeling that this was not a real human being but some kind of dummy. It was not the man's brain that was speaking, it was his larynx. The stuff that was coming out of him consisted of words, but it was not speech in the true sense; it was a noise uttered in unconsciousness, like the quacking of a duck. (pp. 46-47)

With this image of man we arrive at a point where all the inauthenticating forces in _1984_ cohere to express a perspective which can be defined as the Absurd. Like the Absurd man, the Oceanic citizen has been thrown into a contingent incomprehensible world in which the normal means of communication cannot express the strange unreality of his condition. As with Bowling, the lack of understanding the significance of things creates a sense of not belonging, of homelessness. In a sundered world there are no 'appointed places' to which it is possible to refer in order to discover one's orientation, and 'this divorce', writes Camus, 'between man and his life, the actor and his setting, is properly the feeling of absurdity'.[25] But Bowling had a past; although he was uprooted, he knew the 'country', or _ground_, of his Being; through a remembrance of origins, he had an essence which could be construed as causal. His life was peripherally Absurd; whereas Smith's is centrally so: 'In the absurd vision', writes R.W.B. Lewis, 'the sense of before and after . . . has vanished. There is no real yesterday as distinguished from tomorrow, and events pulsate dimly in a permanent present. Nor is there any discernible causal relation: the concept of cause no longer pushes perceptions into a usable order'.[26] And Camus' image of man in this condition is strikingly similar to the duckspeaker in the canteen of Minitrue: 'Men, too, secrete the inhuman. At certain moments of lucidity, the mechanical aspect of their gestures, their meaningless pantomime make silly everything that surrounds them. A man is talking on the telephone behind a glass partition; you cannot hear him but you can see his incomprehensible dumb-show: you wonder why he is alive'.[27]

Smith is thrown and abandoned, a self-for-others in an absurd world, and in this hopeless condition he commits himself, like Bowling, to reconnecting himself to the lost world of his origins. Through the recovery of coherence he would understand, and through understanding he would learn how to belong to himself and to the world. But no such understanding is accessible. He will never again stand in the ground of his Being. Even the ostensible alternative to Ingsoc, the Brotherhood, may impose a transformation of identity. Whichever way he turns he confronts some sort of personal deformation. He is engulfed by otherness:

> 'Do you understand that even if he survives, it may be as a different person? We may be obliged to give him a new identity. His face, his movements, the shape of his hands, the colour of his hair - even his voice would be different. And you yourself might have become a different person. Our surgeons can alter people beyond recognition.' (p. 141)

Smith stands between nothingness and otherness, unhistorized 'phantom stuff' pursuing for himself the kind of primordial ontological security imaged by his second possession, the anachronistic paperweight:

> He turned over towards the light and lay gazing into the glass paperweight. The inexhaustibly interesting thing was not the fragment of coral but the interior of the glass itself. There was such a depth of it, and yet it was almost as transparent as air. It was as though the surface of the glass had been the arch of the sky, enclosing a tiny world with its atmosphere complete. He had the feeling that he could get inside it, and that in fact he was inside it, along with the mahogany bed and the gateleg table, and the clock and the steel engraving and the paperweight itself. The paperweight was the room he was in, and the coral was Julia's life and his own, fixed in a sort of eternity at the heart of the crystal. (p. 120)

In the microcosm of the paperweight we have the finite, hermetic, self-subsisting harmony of the Aristotelian cosmos which characterized the world of Bowling's childhood, where things only changed in conformity to a comprehensible scheme. If Bowling's world came to be Copernican after the cataclysms of puberty and war, Smith's has advanced to the Einsteinian where the relativity of time and space serves as the ultimate physical expression of existential 'thrown Being'. And it is in these cosmic terms that Orwell conveys the sense of Ingsoc man's position: 'the citizen of Oceania is like a man in interstellar space, who has no way of knowing which direction is up and which is down' (p. 160). Oceanic man can no longer touch the corners of his world; he has been thrown onto the outside and lost.

So while Smith's first possession, the blank book, suggested the vacuity of thrown Being, his second possession, the paperweight, suggests the fulness of fixed Being. The book corresponds to Bowling's frankfurter in the same way as the paperweight does to the statue of Og. Both men have been transformed into the opposite of what they were through being penetrated by the otherness of the outside. Consequently both feel 'ghostly', not themselves, experiencing that 'uncanniness' of Being which Heidegger ascribes to those who live as one of the anonymous They. What they come to be is not the 'real' authentic self. Both have lost that 'inexhaustibly interesting thing', the thick enclosing glass which ensures the survival of the authentic self, dividing the inner from the outer, the me from the They, the subjective from the objective. They are no longer worlds within worlds. The 'whale' so often referred to in Orwell's writings is now extinct; Mother Bowling can no longer pull down the shutters before the invading otherness. With this division breached, cosmos becomes chaos. The distinctive character of things melts. Identities blur. Contrasts and opposites disappear. The inner cannot be asserted against the outer. The collapse of this division is the explanation for the abolition of the axiom and the creation of a new kind of truth: war is peace. Without self, nothing can be self-evident.

When the Thought Police burst in on Smith and Julia's pre-revolutionary enclave above Charrington's shop, it is like the mythic ritual enactment of the inception of the New Order: the Other brutally blunders into the self and takes it over. Mineness ends, so the paperweight shatters: 'The fragment of coral, a tiny crinkle of pink like a sugar rosebud from a cake, rolled across the mat. How small, thought Winston, how small it always was!' (p. 177). The dam-like division between the self and the Other is swept away, and the fragile foetal self, deprived of its world, drops for ever onto the outside where it can no longer be itself.

The self is _thrown_ from its place of origination into the control of the Other. Having lost its essence, the self can now be transformed. It becomes a _thing_ to be manipulated, to be kneaded into the mould of _homo Ingsoc_. No longer 'fixed in a sort of eternity', it is contingent flux. Without the identity of essence, man is a nothingness. He is whatever he is made to be. O'Brien says: 'we create human nature. Men are infinitely malleable' (p. 216).

This image of thrownness, of the coral ejected from its primordial setting, is followed by its literal realization. Smith is wrenched out of his 'pocket of the past where extinct animals could walk' (p. 123) and removed to a place of _no glass_ in which he loses all spatial and temporal orientation:

> He did not know where he was. Presumably he was in the Ministry of Love; but there was no way of making certain.
> .... It might be twenty-four hours since he had eaten, it might be thirty-six. He still did not know, probably never would know, whether it had been morning or evening when they arrested him. (p. 181)

> More often he wondered where he was, and what time of day it was. At one moment he felt certain that it was broad daylight outside, and at the next equally certain that it was pitch darkness.... In the Ministry of Love there were no windows. His cell might be at the heart of the building or against its outer wall; it might be ten floors below ground, or thirty feet above it. He moved himself mentally from place to place, and tried to determine by the feeling of his body whether he was perched high in the air or buried deep underground. (p. 184)

The Ministry of Love is that familiar place where the abased individual plays his last feeble cards against the limitless aces of State power. It is the place of ultimate dread, the place where people lose their way and come out strangers to themselves. In this Ministry are to be found those ''Orrible revelations' about the nature of things which so horrified Bowling in the milk-bar. Here also are the mutant processes of those 'food-factories in Germany where everything's made out of something else. Ersatz, they call it'. But civilization has moved on. Now, it is people who are ersatz'd, and instead of 'making sausages out of fish', love is made out of hate; and the principal agent of this transformation is O'Brien. He is the Dr Moreau of ontology.

O'Brien is truly at home in the it-world, one of those sublimely favoured sadists who are licensed to indulge their hatred of the human professionally. He has time; he can linger over the process of torment in a calm laboratory atmosphere. He can pull levers and observe dials, regulating pain while measuring the queer output of the soul as it squirms in its trap of flesh. From the gross substance of the in-itself he wrings the pure intangible freedom of 'ownlife'. He converts inner mineness into outer theyness. Out of the uniquely existing individual he makes an anyone, and then has it shot. He is the crushing refutation of Julia and Winston's belief that '"they can't get inside you'" (p. 136). He personifies the achievement of the totalitarian ambition described by Hannah Arendt: 'Totalitarianism is never content to rule by external means, namely, through the State and a machinery of violence; thanks to its peculiar ideology and the role assigned to it in this apparatus of coercion, totalitarianism has discovered a means of dominating and terrorizing human beings from within'.[28] In 1984 these 'means' involve the reversal of the process by which existential fulness is achieved. We have seen that Smith, up to the time of his capture, has been progressing towards this fulness, authenticating himself by repossessing the sense of his tripartite existential relations: 'world around', 'with-world', and 'own-world'. But through imprisonment and disorientation in Miniluv, he is instantly deprived of the world around; and it is with his victim in this weakened position that O'Brien painstakingly endeavours to sunder the with-world (the I-Thou) and the own-world (mineness, or ownlife).

Ontologically, Smith, at the time of his capture, could have been described as composite: he was a private for-itself in the public mode of a for-others. He had, like every Orwell protagonist, a double life; but this doubleness was, existentially, of an exceptional kind, for his situation was such that, in order to preserve the idea of authentic existence in the world, he was obliged to exist in the inauthentic mode. This was the uniqueness of Smith's situation. Not knowing that he had been detected by the Thought Police from the beginning, he believed that the only way to defer his extinction and, furthermore, to disseminate among others the possibility of restoring the 'human heritage', was to behave as if he were still a self-for-others. His double life was not therefore maintained in bad faith. Unlike, for example, Flory and Comstock, he had, in a situation of incomparable hostility, both repudiated sociopolitical determinism and anxiously assumed responsibility for himself. Through this act he restored to himself that aspect of man which he believed was once definitional to the meaning of being human: fidelity. For Smith, as for his mother, fidelity signifies a commitment to self-determination irrespective of contrary external forces. And it is now, as he anticipates torture in the cold brightness of Miniluv, that Smith inherits the full burden of his commitment to resist the powers that would have him betray.

All torture whose objective is renunciation relies on betrayal, and the act of betrayal, as a tangible measure of one's commitment, can only signify an erosion of what one _is_. Betrayal subverts authenticity because fidelity to self is definitional of the authentic life. One cannot de-authenticate oneself without some kind of betrayal being present. It is because betrayal signifies in this way that Smith must maintain his fidelity to himself and to Julia; and it is because it is through the body that O'Brien aims to effect Smith's betrayal that the body comes to be symbolic of inauthentic life in _1984_. The body, in fact, is inimical to authentic life in two ways. Firstly, through an involuntary 'facecrime' it can expose 'ownlife' to the Thought Police; and secondly, under the tortures of the Thought Police it can extinguish ownlife for ever. It destroys what it reveals. This subversiveness of the body is noted well before Smith's imprisonment, at the time when he still believed Julia to be an enemy and wanted to kill her with the paperweight:

> He thought with a kind of astonishment of the biological uselessness of pain and fear, _the treachery of the human body which always freezes into inertia at exactly the moment when a special effort is needed_.... _He had lost the power to act_. It struck him that in moments of crisis one is never fighting against an external enemy, but always against one's own body.... And it is the same, he perceived, in

> all seemingly heroic or tragic situations. On the battlefield, in the torture chamber, on a sinking ship, the issues that you are fighting for are always forgotten, because the body swells up until it fills the universe. (p. 85) (My underlining)

This response, based as it is on the misconception that Julia is an enemy, is precisely the response which eventually compels Smith to betray Julia as a lover. Julia passes from enemy to friend, and O'Brien passes from friend to enemy; and O'Brien eventually uses 'the treachery of the human body' to demolish that which it initially preserved (Julia). First through fright, and then through torture, Smith realizes that the body is freedom's prison. From being in normal life the executor of freedom, the body, under stress, becomes freedom's deterministic limit.

Smith's process of deauthentication starts and ends with the body. O'Brien, through pain, attempts to annihilate everything else but the sensation of existing through the flesh. Under his management 'the body swells up until it fills the universe', and Smith becomes 'simply a mouth that uttered, a hand that signed, whatever was demanded of him' (p. 194). This reduction of Smith to the behavioural, to a conditioned response in a closed room of uncertain location, stands in absolute contrast to the self-image of the for-itself thrush singing in the open countryside. From the voluntary spontaneous communication of the free agent, Smith transforms into an enslaved mechanism whose function it is to express only otherness. Body has usurped spirit. What, existentially, happens to Smith, is precisely that transformation which Sartre describes when the victim surrenders to the sadist:

> The spectacle which is offered to the sadist is that of a freedom which struggles against the expanding of the flesh and which finally chooses to be submerged in the flesh. At the moment of the abjuration the result sought is attained: the body is wholly flesh, panting and obscene; it holds the position which the torturers have given to it, not that which it would have assumed by itself; the cords which bind it hold it as an inert thing, and thereby it has ceased to be the object which moves spontaneously. In the abjuration a freedom chooses to be wholly identified with this body;

> this distorted and heaving body is the very image of a broken and enslaved freedom.[29]
> (My underlining)

Sartre, it is to be noted, offers no excuse for man, even under torture: the victim 'freely chooses to be submerged in the flesh'. The victim decides the moment of his surrender to deterministic thinghood: 'he would have been able despite all to wait ten minutes, one minute, one second longer'.[30] And in _1984_ we see the agony of this deferred choosing: 'he said to himself: "I will confess, but not yet. I must hold out till the pain becomes unbearable. Three more kicks, two more kicks, and then I will tell them what they want"' (p. 193). So as in the beginning, when Smith momentously chose to execute the decisive, rebellious, authenticating act of marking the diary, he is freighted with the choice of deciding when the similarly radical act of _de_authentication should occur. Both choices are choices of _Being_, and nowhere in Orwell's novels are the distinctions more obviously and significantly present. As in no other novel of our time, Smith is choosing for all mankind, and the either/or is between the authentic for-itself and the inauthentic in-itself. In a sense far more actual than Sartre ever showed in his own fiction, Smith's choice 'carries the weight' of the 'entire world as a peopled world', for he is the _last_ man, the only one by whom the human heritage can be continued.[31] And it is, existentially, appropriate that it will be the failure to _be_ human which will bring about the end of this heritage: to preserve the _idea_ of authentic existence, authentic _Being_ is necessary. Smith _is_ the heritage. He does not possess it in the ordinary sense of possession, as, for example, a person possesses a library which contains the values of liberal civilization. What he 'has' is something structural to the self which can only be lost through an ontological transformation. The custodian can lose his library and remain as he is because his loss is external, and this is why the custodian can grieve over his loss. The man who has been changed from the inside has nothing whatever to mourn, because he has not been reduced but replaced. He has no sense of being less of a man. This utter conversion of man is Ingsoc's aim, and this is why O'Brien's command is not '"Thou shalt not"' or '"Thou shalt"' but '"_Thou art_"' (p. 205). This explicitly reveals that Ingsoc's aims are ontological: it is not Don't or Do but _Be_. Smith will be replaced by a they-self which is permanently in the mode of a for-others, and during the process which leads to this he is subjected to an intensification of the Look, under which, according to Sartre, 'it appears that the world has a kind of drain hole in the middle of its being and that it is perpetually flowing off through this hole': 'He was in a cell which might have been either dark or light, because he could see nothing except a pair of eyes.... The eyes grew larger and more luminous. Suddenly he floated out of his seat, dived into the eyes, and was swallowed up' (p. 195).

O'Brien's subtlety as a torturer lies in his ability to perplex and undermine the resolve of his victim by applying the Double Bind. After cultivating in Smith the feeling that he is responsible for a sin which _demands_ punishment, he, like the executioner in a 'A Hanging', insidiously arouses in Smith the feeling that it is he who has _caused_ O'Brien to be a torturer. He tacitly expresses Sambo's response to breaking his cane on Orwell's backside in 'Such, Such Were the Joys': '"Look what you've made me do!"' He conveys also the feeling that he is with Smith _against_ the torturer, that he is actually helping Smith to elude persecution: 'He had the feeling that O'Brien was his protector, that the pain was something that came from the outside, from some other source, and that it was O'Brien who would save him from it' (p. 201). The result of this mystifying process is that O'Brien comes to exist for Smith as the personification of blackwhite: 'He was the tormentor, he was the protector, he was the inquisitor, he was the friend' (p. 196). Through the illusion of this friendship, O'Brien is able to generate in Smith guilt about what he is in terms which are both personal and immediate: not only is Smith responsible for his captivity, but his resistance to an easy conversion is distressing a friend.

At the same time, the freedom of will in which Smith is urged to believe is presented in a perspective of slavery. Somehow, even though he is free, it is Smith's inescapable destiny to become another person with no freedom at all. Inevitably he _will_ surrender, but _freely_: '"When finally you surrender to us, it must be of your own free will"' (p. 204). And the man he will be, irrespective of choice, is already planned:

> 'What happens to you here is for ever. Understand that in advance. We shall crush you down

> to the point from which there is no coming back. Things will happen to you from which you could not recover, if you lived a thousand years. Never again will you be capable of ordinary human feeling. Everything will be dead inside you. Never again will you be capable of love, or friendship, or joy of living, or laughter, or curiosity, or courage, or integrity. You will be hollow. We shall squeeze you empty, and then we shall fill you with ourselves.' (p. 206)

So even here, towards the end, Smith is oppressed by the problems of paradox which have dogged him from the beginning. The co-existence of freedom and destiny in himself, and the ambiguity of O'Brien, both confirm the outrage which he is pledged to deny: the Ingsoc logic of Yes and No, of X and not X. Throughout his torture he personifies this logic by experiencing himself as an _enslaved freedom_. The despair of Smith's freedom is that, in the form in which it is offered him, it means only the freedom to surrender freedom, the choice of when to relinquish it and become united with the thinghood of his flesh.

One crucial stage on the route to this destination is when Smith is revealed to himself in the shape that the Other has made of him. The striking aspect about Smith's confronting himself in the three-sided mirror as a physical ruin is that he is suddenly seeing himself as a stranger, _as the Other_, and, as the Other, he apprehends himself as an object, a _thing_. This sudden and profound disclosure signifies in a similar way to the opening scene in _Coming Up For Air_, when Bowling sees himself in the bathroom mirror and proceeds to make an inventory of the body. Both men see themselves as outside themselves, the body estranged from the self and no longer 'mine'. Having already lost the 'world around', the seeing of himself as the Other implies a loss of the 'own-world', the ending of ownlife:

> He had stopped because he was frightened. A bowed, grey-coloured, skeleton-like thing was coming towards him. Its actual appearance was frightening, and not merely the fact that he knew it to be himself. He moved closer to the glass. The creature's face seemed to be protruded because of its bent carriage.... Certainly it was his own face, but it seemed to

> him that it had changed more than he had changed inside. The emotions it registered would be different from the ones he felt.... At a guess he would have said that it was a body of a man of sixty, suffering from some kind of malignant disease. (p. 218).

This is Smith seeing himself as the Other would. It is (and this is crucial) the seeing of a self which has been caused to be by the Other. So Smith is in the nightmare position of seeing himself as an object which is not him. What comes to meet him in the mirror is the ultimate self-for-others, and O'Brien has to make Smith accept this degraded alien as the true image of what he now is. Like Sartre's sadist, he has to coerce his victim's freedom to 'freely identify itself with the tortured flesh'.[32] O'Brien, by describing Smith's body as if it were Smith's actual personality, gets Smith to feel that all that remains of himself is a revolting outside:

> 'Look at the condition you are in!' he said. 'Look at this filthy grime all over your body. Look at the dirt between your toes. Look at that disgusting running sore on your leg. Do you know that you stink like a goat? Probably you have ceased to notice it. Look at your emaciation. Do you see? I can make my thumb and forefinger meet round your bicep. I could snap your neck like a carrot. Do you know that you have lost twenty-five kilograms since you have been in our hands....
>
> 'You are rotting away,' he said; 'you are falling to pieces. What are you? A bag of filth. Now turn round and look into that mirror again. Do you see that thing facing you? That is the last man. If you are human, that is humanity.' . . . .
>
> 'You did it!' sobbed Winston. 'You reduced me to this state.'
>
> 'No, Winston, you reduced yourself to it.' (pp. 218-19)

So Smith surrenders. He identifies with his body, and the for-itself sinks and dies into the in-itself flesh. Effectively, the mineness of the 'own-world' is at an end. Of the three existential relations, only the 'with-world' remains: '"I have not betrayed Julia," he said' (p. 220).

By now, fidelity, based as it is on the existence of ownlife, is almost an abstraction, a residuum of the lost authentic self maintained by the lingering tenacity of memory. Only when this impoverished I-Thou is sundered can Smith's new emptiness have that purity of hollowness necessary for its total occupation by Ingsoc. If Smith is to resist this occupation he must, somehow, keep 'the inner heart inviolate' (p. 225). And what is extraordinary about this attempt to sustain fidelity is that he is obliged to employ doublethink:

> It was not easy to preserve inscrutability when you did not know what your face looked like. In any case, mere control of the features was not enough. For the first time he perceived that if you want to keep a secret you must also hide it from yourself. You must know all the while that it is there, but until it is needed you must never let it emerge into your consciousness in any shape that could be given a name. (pp. 225-26)

This buried love for Julia is the last remaining ingredient of Smith's authentic inside, and O'Brien has to draw this stubborn root so that nothing whatever exists in Smith which could reverse his identification with the body.

What happens in Room 101 decisively vindicates the existential meaning of the body in _1984_. Indeed, without this particular meaning, Smith's mode of betrayal would not achieve that definitive break between the 'I' and the Thou which is described in Room 101. Smith's mode of betrayal achieves this break because, at the moment when the rat-cage approaches his face, he no longer apprehends Julia _as a person_:

> Everything had gone black. For an instant he was insane, a screaming animal. Yet he came out of the blackness clutching an idea. There was one and only one way to save himself. He must interpose another human being, the _body_ of another human being, between himself and the rats....
>
> .... Too late, perhaps too late. But he had suddenly understood that in the whole world there was just _one_ person to whom he could transfer his punishment - _one_ body that he could thrust between himself and the rats. And he was shouting frantically, over and over.
>
> 'Do it to Julia! Do it to Julia! Not me! I don't care what you do to her. Tear her face

> off, strip her to the bones. Not me! Julia! Not me!' (p. 230)

Smith has understood what O'Brien requires: to have Julia become an in-itself, a body only, a thing, an instrument to be used, a mere means, *through Smith's own agency*. *He* converts *her*, and, in converting *her*, he *finally* converts *himself*, because his fidelity was the last element of the old self. In the moment that he sees Julia as an It, the fidelity which depends on his maintaining her as a Thou vanishes irrevocably, and thus all three of Smith's authentic relations have been sundered. He survives Room 101 at the expense of his existential extinction.

Smith, like all those brought to Miniluv, has been subjected to hyper-correction; that is, he has been altered beyond what is actually sufficient for proper Oceanic citizenship. He has not merely been normalized in terms of the current general standards of Being, but has been made into the type of Being which will exist in the year 2050 when Newspeak is perfected. He has been anachronized in precisely the opposite direction from the one towards which he was previously aiming. He has become the future in the present, not the past in the present speaking into the future (see p. 26). Sociopolitically and ontologically therefore, his time in Miniluv corresponds to sixty-six years. Only now, as an exemplary citizen of Oceania Super-State, is he permitted to see Julia again. Enslaved, they are free for one another. And of all the desolations in *1984*, nothing digs deeper than the meeting of those two frozen hearts.

NOTES

1. *The Literature of Possibility*, p. 9.
2. "Charles Dickens," *The Collected Essays, Journalism and Letters*, vol. 1, p. 500.
3. J.-P. Sartre, *What is Literature?*, trans. Bernard Frechtman (London: Methuen, 1967), p. 217.
4. Barnes, *The Literature of Possibility*, p. 11.
5. *1984* (1949; rpt. Harmondsworth: Penguin Books, 1976), pp. 6,25. Henceforth cited in text by page number to this edition.
6. *Being and Nothingness*, p. 363.

7. Ibid., p. 260.
8. Ibid., p. 256.
9. Ibid., p. 364.
10. Laing, The Divided Self, pp. 79-80.
11. From a Review of Lionel Fielden's Beggar My Neighbour, The Collected Essays, Journalism and Letters, vol. 2, p. 358.
12. "The Prevention of Literature," The Collected Essays, Journalism and Letters, vol. 4, p. 89.
13. Being and Having, pp. 105, 116, 130.
14. The Existential Background of Human Dignity, p. 59.
15. The Divided Self, pp. 39,42.
16. Man in the Modern Age, pp. 173-77, 182, 199.
17. C. Sluzki and D.C. Ransom, eds., Double Bind, vii.
18. "Mystification, Confusion, and Conflict," Double Bind, eds. C. Sluzki and D.C. Ransom, p. 213.
19. Mary Warnock, Existentialism (Oxford: Oxford Univ. Press, 1970), p. 110.
20. Being and Nothingness, pp. 56, 68.
21. I and Thou, p. 117.
22. Rollo May, E. Angel and H.F. Ellenberger, eds., Existence (New York: Basic Books, 1958), p. 61.
23. Being and Time, p. 213.
24. Ibid., p. 214.
25. The Myth of Sisyphus, p. 13.
26. The Picaresque Saint (London: Victor Gollancz, 1960), p. 69.
27. The Myth of Sisyphus, pp. 20-21.
28. The Origins of Totalitarianism (London: George Allen and Unwin, 1958), p. 325.
29. Being and Nothingness, p. 404.
30. Ibid., p. 403.
31. Ibid., pp. 553, 555.
32. Ibid., p. 403.

CONCLUSION

The aim of this book has been to introduce a perspective with which it would be possible to identify and analyze an aspect of the Orwell novel which other approaches would not ordinarily distinguish. The engagement of Orwell's novels existentially has led to the conclusion that, in every instance, his primary concern is with the conflict between the authentic and inauthentic modes of existence. This conclusion, however, is not intended to imply a rejection of the centrality of the sociopolitical in the Orwell novel; rather, it suggests what kind of sociopolitcal writer Orwell was.

The kind of existentiality found in the Orwell novel does, in fact, depend on the sociopolitical context, for the specific conflict which we have described as existential arises from the self's response to a situation which is sociopolitically derived. Those sociopolitical contexts in the Orwell novel which define the terms of the individual's conflict between authentic and inauthentic existence represent the powers which encourage man into 'essentially public, non-individual activities'.[1] In each novel the relevant sociopolitical context with which the protagonist is specifically in conflict, and from which the existential action stems, can be identified: _Burmese Days_ (Imperialism), _A Clergyman's Daughter_ (Patriarchal Conservatism), _Keep the Aspidistra Flying_ (Capitalism), _Coming Up For Air_ (Militarism and Fascism), _Nineteen Eighty-Four_ (Ingsoc Totalitarianism).

The patterns of existential action in Orwell's novels are basically flights from and towards authentic and inauthentic life. At the beginning of _Burmese Days_ it is clear that Flory has adopted a way of life governed by a deterministic principle. The novel traces an intermittent progress from this position towards an authentic life, culminating in the act of nominating Dr. Veraswami. But this is the highpoint in Flory's authentic resolve. In killing himself in reaction to shame and disgrace, he accepts as definitive a description of himself identical to the one that had originally inspired his inauthentic self-for-others. In _A Clergyman's Daughter_, Dorothy's flight from an inauthentic life is not motivated by a conscious choice; it is precipitated by external pressure. So, formally, we have a flight from an inauthentic life but not towards an authentic one. In deciding to return to the Rectory, she is refusing the perils of individual existence and resuming on different terms the safety of a dependent life. In _Keep the Aspidistra Flying_, the more obvious interpretation of Comstock's flight from the They is that it is a flight towards authentic life. However, because he has generated a deterministic scapegoat in order to both justify his flight and elude responsibility for himself, his flight is, existentially, a motion without change. And when his scapegoat fails, he adopts another in order to justify his return. Throughout the novel he denies that he has the freedom to direct his life. In _Coming Up For Air_, Bowling's mode of being-in-the-world is one which he has grown into unwittingly. His alienation from his original authentic self is seen as due to the natural process of life and the unavoidable impact of historical change. He, as it were, 'discovers' himself in an inauthentic state which he did not will. Unlike his predecessors, his inauthenticity is not of the kind that he can choose to abandon. Therefore Bowling's flight back to Lower Binfield can only be a flight to recover the sensations of authentic living, not authentic life itself. And since these sensations can issue only from being in the authentic state, they are irrecoverable. In _Nineteen Eighty-Four_, Winston Smith's flight from an inauthentic life is decisively a flight towards an authentic life. Under unprecedented pressure to accept a life determined by others, he celebrates his freedom to choose his own life by an act which will inevitably kill him. An ordinary man, he assumes total responsibility for himself. He exemplifies classic existential action.

NOTES

1. "Why I Write," _The Collected Essays, Journalism and Letters_, vol. 1, p. 28.

BIBLIOGRAPHY

(In addition to the works cited in the text, the bibliography includes those which were of particular use in forming the critical perspective of this book. The translated works of individual authors are listed in the order of their appearance in the original.)

I: Works on and by George Orwell

Alldritt, Keith. The Making of George Orwell. London: Edward Arnold, 1969.

Atkins, John. George Orwell: A Literary Study. London: Calder and Boyars, 1954.

Bracken, Henry. "Descartes-Orwell-Chomsky: Three Philosophers of the Demonic." Human Context, pp. 523-536.

Calder, Jenni. Chronicles of Conscience: A Study of George Orwell and Arthur Koestler. London: Secker and Warburg, 1968.

Cosmān, Max. "George Orwell and the Autonomous Individual." Pacific Spectator, 9 (1955), pp. 74-84.

Deutscher, Isaac. "1984 - The Mysticism of Cruelty." Russia in Transition and Other Essays. New York: Coward-McCann, 1957, pp. 250-65.

Dutsher. Alan. "Orwell and the Crisis of Responsibility." Contemporary Issues, 8 (1956), pp. 308-16.

Fiderer, Gerald. "Masochism as Literary Strategy: Orwell's Psychological Novels." Literature and Psychology, 20, (1970), pp. 3-21.

Gross, Miriam (ed.) The World of George Orwell. London: Weidenfeld and Nicolson, 1971.

Hamilton, Kenneth. "G.K. Chesterton and George Orwell: A Contrast in Prophecy." Dalhousie Review, 31 (1951), pp. 198-205.

Hooning, Theodorus. "George Orwell in His Time." Acta Historiae Neerlandica, 5 (1971), pp. 68-102.

Howe, Irving. "Orwell: History as Nightmare." American Scholar, 25 (1956), pp. 193-207.

Karl, Frederick. "George Orwell: The White Man's Burden." A Reader's guide to the Contemporary English Novel. 1962; rpt. London: Thames and Hudson, 1963, pp. 148-66.

Knapp, John. "Dance to a Creepy Minuet: Orwell's Burmese Days, Precursor of Animal Farm." Modern Fiction Studies, 21 (1975), pp. 11-29.

Kubal, David. Outside the Whale: George Orwell's Art and Politics. Notre Dame, Indiana: University of Notre Dame Press, 1972.

Lee, Robert. Orwell's Fiction. Notre Dame, Indiana: University of Notre Dame Press, 1969.

Lief, Ruth Ann. Homage to Oceania: The Prophetic Vision of George Orwell. Columbus, Ohio: Ohio State University Press, 1969.

Mander, John. "One Step Forward: Two Steps Back." The Writer and Commitment. London: Secker and Warburg, 1961, pp. 71-110.

McCarthy, Mary. "The Writing on the Wall." The Writing on the Wall. 1970; rpt. Harmondsworth: Penguin Books, 1973, pp. 153-171.

Myers, Jeffrey. "Orwell's Painful Childhood." Ariel, 3, (1972), pp. 54-61.

----- A Reader's Guide to George Orwell. London: Thames and Hudson, 1975.

----- (ed.) George Orwell: The Critical Heritage. London: Routledge and Kegan Paul, 1975.

Orwell, George. Down and Out in Paris and London. 1933; rpt. Harmondsworth: Penguin Books, 1966.

----- Burmese Days. 1934; rpt. Harmondsworth: Penguin Books, 1975.

----- A Clergyman's Daughter. 1935; rpt. Harmondsworth: Penguin Books, 1967.

----- Keep the Aspidistra Flying. 1936; rpt. Harmondsworth; Penguin Books, 1966.

----- The Road to Wigan Pier. 1937; rpt. Harmondsworth: Penguin Books, 1966.

----- Homage to Catalonia. 1938; rpt. Harmondsworth: Penguin Books, 1966.

----- Coming Up For Air. 1939; rpt. Harmondsworth: Penguin Books, 1967.

----- Animal Farm: A Fairy Story. 1945; rpt. Harmondsworth: Penguin Books, 1967.

----- Nineteen Eighty-Four. 1949; rpt. Harmondsworth: Penguin Books, 1976.

----- The Collected Essays, Journalism and Letters of George Orwell. Ed. Sonia Orwell and Ian Angus. 4 vols. 1968; rpt. Harmondsworth: Penguin Books, 1971.

Rees, Richard. George Orwell: Fugitive From the Camp of Victory. London: Secker and Warburg, 1961.

Rieff, Philip. "George Orwell and the Post-Liberal Imagination." Kenyon Review, 16 (1954), pp. 49-70.

Sandison, Alan. The Last Man in Europe: An Essay on George Orwell. London: Macmillan, 1974.

Small, Christopher. The Road to Miniluv: George Orwell, the State, and God. London: Victor Gollancz, 1975.

Smith, Marcus. "The Wall of Blackness: A Psychological Approach to 1984." Modern Fiction Studies, 14 (1968-69), pp. 423-33.

Smyer, Richard. Primal Dream and Primal Crime: Orwell's Development as a Psychological Novelist. Columbia: University of Missouri Press, 1979.

Steinhoff, William. George Orwell and the Origins of '1984'. Ann Arbor: University of Michigan, 1975.

Thody, Philip. "The Curiosity of George Orwell." University of Leeds Review, 12 (1975), pp. 57-68.

Trilling, Lionel. "George Orwell and the Politics of Truth." The Opposing Self. London: Secker and Warburg, 1955, pp. 151-72.

Van Dellen, Robert. "George Orwell's Coming Up For Air: The Politics of Powerlessness." Modern Fiction Studies, 21, (1975), pp. 57-68.

Voorhees, Richard. The Paradox of George Orwell. Layfayette, Indiana: Purdue University Studies, 1961.

Wain, John. "Orwell in Perspective." "Here Lies Lower Binfield." Essays on Literature and Ideas. London: Macmillan, 1963, pp. 180-93, 194-213.

West, Anthony. "George Orwell." George Orwell: The Critical Heritage. Ed. Jeffrey Meyers. London: Routledge and Kegan Paul, 1975, pp. 71-79.

Williams, Raymond. Orwell. London: Fontana, 1971.

Woodcock, George. The Crystal Spirit: A Study of George Orwell. 1966; rpt. Harmondsworth: Penguin Books, 1970.

II: Existentialism, Psychology, and other works

Arendt, Hannah. The Origin of totalitarianism. London: George Allen and Unwin, 1958.

Barnes, Hazel E. The Literature of Possibility: A Study in Humanistic Existentialism. Lincoln: University of Nebraska Press, 1959.

Barrett, William. Irrational Man: A Study in Existential Philosophy. 1958; rpt. London: Heinemann, 1967.

----- The Illusion of Technique: A Search for Meaning in a Technological Civilization. New York: Doubleday, 1978.

Becker, Ernest. The Birth and Death of Meaning: An Interdisciplinary Perspective on the Problem of Man. 2nd ed., 1971; rpt. Harmondsworth: Penguin Books, 1972.

Berdyaev, Nicolas. Slavery and Freedom. Trans. R.M. French. London: Geoffrey Bles, 1943.

Bierman, A.K. The Philosophy of Urban Existence. Columbus: Ohio State University Press, 1973.

Binswanger, Ludwig. Being-in-the-World. Trans. Jacob Needleman. London: Basic Books, 1963.

Blackham, H.J. Six Existentialist Thinkers. 1952; rpt. London: Routledge and Kegan Paul, 1961.

Brown, Phil (ed.) Radical Psychology. London: Tavistock Publications, 1973.

Buber, Martin, I and Thou. Trans. Walter Kaufmann. Edinburgh: T. & T. Clark, 1975.

----- Between Man and Man. Trans. Ronald Gregor Smith. London: Kegan Paul, 1947.

----- The Knowledge of Man. Trans. M. Friedman and R.G. Smith. New York: Humanities, 1965.

Camus, Albert. The Outsider. Trans. Stuart Gilbert. 1946; rpt. Harmondsworth: Penguin Books, 1969.

----- The Myth of Sisyphus. Trans. Justin O'Brien. 1955; rpt. Harmondsworth; Penguin Books, 1977.

----- The Rebel. Trans. Anthony Bower. 1953; rpt. Harmondsworth: Penguin Books, 1977.

Eliade, Mircea. Myths, Dreams and Mysteries: The Encounter Between Contemporary Faiths and Archaic Reality. Trans. Philip Mairet. 1960; rpt. London: Fontana, 1968.

Eliot, T.S. Collected Poems 1909-1962. London: Faber and Faber, 1974.

Esslin, Martin. The Theatre of the Absurd. London: Eyre and Spottiswoode, 1962.

Bibliography

Friedenberg, Edgar. Laing. London: Fontana, 1973.

Friedman, Maurice. Problematic Rebel. 1963; rev. Chicago: University of Chicago Press, 1970.

----- To Deny Our Nothingness: Contemporary Images of Man. London: Victor Gollancz, 1967.

Fromm, Erich. Escape From Freedom. New York: Holt, Rinehart and Winston, 1941.

----- Man For Himself: An Enquiry Into the Psychology of Ethics. London: Routledge and Kegan Paul, 1949.

----- The Sane Society. 1955; rpt. London: Routledge and Kegan Paul, 1963.

Goffman, Erving. The Presentation of Self in Everyday Life. 1959; rpt. Harmondsworth: Pelican Books, 1978.

----- Stigma: Notes on the Management of Spoiled Identity. 1963; rpt. Harmondsworth: Pelican Books, 1968.

Grene, Marjorie. "Authenticity: An Existential Virtue." Ethics, 62 (1952), pp. 266-273.

----- Heidegger. London: Bowes and Bowes, 1957.

Heidegger, Martin. Being and Time. Trans. from the 7th ed. by John Macquarrie and Edward Robinson. Oxford: Basil Blackwell, 1978.

----- The Question of Being. Trans. William Kluback and Jean T. Wilde. London: Vision Press, 1958.

----- Existence and Being. Trans. Alan Crick, R.F.C. Hull and Douglas Scott. London: Vision Press, 1968.

----- The Question Concerning Technology and Other Essays. Trans. William Lovitt. New York: Harper and Row, 1977.

Heinemann, F.H. Existentialism and the Modern Predicament. 1953; rpt. London: Adam and Charles Black, 1958.

Bibliography

Hoffman, F.J. The Mortal No: Death and the Modern Imagination. Princeton: Princeton University Press, 1964.

Jaspers, Karl. Man in the Modern Age. Trans. Eden and Cedar Paul. London: Routledge and Kegan Paul, 1951.

----- Philosophy of Existence. Trans. Richard F. Graball. Oxford: Basil Blackwell, 1971.

----- The Origin and Goal of History. Trans. Michael Bullock. London: Routledge and Kegan Paul, 1953.

Kaufmann, Walter (ed.) Existentialism from Dostoevsky to Sartre. New York: Meridian, 1956.

Kierkegaard, Soren. Either/Or: A Fragment of Life. 2 vols. Trans. D.F. and L.M. Swenson, and W. Lowrie. Princeton: Princeton University Press, 1944.

----- Fear and Trembling and The Sickness Unto Death. Trans. Walter Lowrie. Princeton: Princeton University Press, 1974.

----- Philosophical Fragments, or A Fragment of Philosophy. Trans. D.F. Swenson. Princeton: Princeton University Press, 1974.

----- Concluding Unscientific Postscript. Trans. Walter Lowrie. Princeton: Princeton University Press, 1941.

Krieger, Murray. The Tragic Vision. 1960; rpt. Baltimore: John Hopkins University Press, 1973.

Krutch, Joseph Wood. The Modern Temper. New York: Harcourt, Brace and World, 1956.

Laing, R.D. The Divided Self: An Existential Study in Sanity and Madness. 1959; rpt. Harmondsworth: Pelican Books, 1967.

----- The Self and Others. 1961; rpt. Harmondsworth: Pelican Books, 1971.

----- and Cooper, D. Reason and Violence: A Decade of Sartre's Philosophy 1950-1960. London: Tavistock Publications, 1964.

Leach, Edmund. Lévi-Strauss. Rev. ed. London: Fontana, 1974.

Lewis, R.W.B. The Picaresque Saint. London: Victor Gollancz, 1960.

Lukacs, Georg. The Meaning of Contemporary Realism. Trans. J. and N. Mander. London: Merlin Press, 1962.

Macquarrie, John. Existentialism. 1972; rpt. Harmondsworth: Pelican Books, 1973.

Marcel, Gabriel. Homo Viator: Introduction to a Metaphysic of Hope. Trans. Emma Crauford. London: Victor Gollancz, 1951.

----- Being and Having. Trans. Katherine Farrer. 1949: rpt. London: Fontana, 1965.

----- The Mystery of Being. 2 vols. Trans. G.S. Fraser. London: The Harvill Press, 1950.

----- The Existential Background of Human Dignity. Cambridge, Massachusetts: Harvard University Press, 1963.

Marcuse, Herbert. One-Dimensional Man: Studies in the Ideology of Advanced Industrial Societies. 1964; rpt. London: Routledge and Kegan Paul, 1968.

May, Rollo. The Meaning of Anxiety. New York: Ronald Press, 1950.

----- and Angel, E., Ellenberger, H.F. (eds.) Existence: A New Dimension in Psychiatry and Psychology. New York: Basic Books, 1958.

----- Power and Innocence: A Search for the Sources of Violence. 1972; rpt. London: Souvenir Press, 1974.

McElroy, Davis Dunbar. Existentialism and Modern Literature: An Essay in Existential Criticism. New York: Greenwood Press, 1968.

McKelway, Alexander. The Systematic Theology of Paul Tillich: A Review and Analysis. London: Lutterworth Press, 1964.

Morano, Donald V. Existential Guilt: A Phenomenological Study. Assen: Gorcum and Company B.V., 1973.

Natanson, Maurice. Literature, Philosophy and the Social Sciences: Essays in Existentialism and Phenomenology. 1962; rpt. The Hague: Martinus Nijhoff, 1968.

Nietzsche, Friedrich. The Will to Power. Trans. Walter Kaufmann and R.J. Hollindale. New York: Vintage Books, 1968.

Ollman, Bertell. Alienation: Marx's Conception of Man in Capitalist Society. Cambridge: Cambridge University Press, 1971.

Ortega y Gasset, J. Man and People. Trans. Willard R. Trask. London: George Allen and Unwin, 1957.

----- Man in Crisis. Trans. M. Adams. New York: Norton, Norton, 1959.

Popper, K.R. The Open Society and Its Enemies. 2 vols. 5th ed. London: Routledge and Kegan Paul, 1966.

Ricoeur, Paul. Fallible Man: Philosphy of the Will. Trans. Charles Kelbley. Chicago: Henry Regnery, 1965.

----- The Symbolism of Evil. Trans. Emerson Buchanan. New York: Harper and Row, 1967.

Ross, S.D. Literature and Philosophy: An Analysis of the Philosophical Novel. New York: Scribner's, 1969.

Ruotolo, Lucio P. Six Existential Heroes. Cambridge, Massachusetts: Harvard University Press, 1973.

Rycroft, Charles. A Critical Dictionary of Psychoanalysis. 1968; rpt. Harmondsworth: Penguin Books, 1972.

Sartre, Jean-Paul. Being and Nothingness: An Essay in Phenomenological Ontology. Trans. Hazel E. Barnes. London: Methuen, 1969.

----- Existentialism and Humanism. Trans. Philip Mairet. London: Eyre Methuen, 1973.

----- Portrait of the Anti-Semite. Trans. Eric de Mauny. London: Secker and Warburg, 1948.

----- What is Literature? Trans. Bernard Frechtman. London: Methuen, 1967.

----- Baudelaire. Trans. Martin Turnell. London: Horizon, 1949.

----- Saint Genet: Actor and Martyr. Trans. Bernard Frechtman. London: W.H. Allen, 1964.

Sluzki, Carlos, and Ransom, Donald C. (eds.) Double Bind: The Foundation of the Communicational Approach to the Family. New York: Grune and Stratton, 1976.

Steiner, George. Language and Silence: Essays 1958-1966. London: Faber and Faber, 1968.

----- Heidegger. London: Fontana, 1978.

Sypher, Wylie. Loss of Self in Modern Literature and Art. New York: Vintage Books, 1962.

Thompson, Kenneth, and Tunstall, Jeremy (eds.) Sociological Perspectives: Selected Readings. Harmondsworth: Penguin Books, 1971.

Tillich, Paul. The Courage to Be. 1952; rpt. London: Fontana, 1962.

Trilling, Lionel. Sincerity and Authenticity. Oxford: Oxford University Press, 1972.

Unamuno, Miguel de. Tragic Sense of Life. Trans. J.E. Crawford Flitch. New York: Dover Publications, 1954.

Warnock, Mary. The Philosophy of Sartre. London: Hutchinson, 1965.

----- Existentialism. Oxford: Oxford University Press, 1970.

Wilson, Colin. The Outsider. 1956; rpt. London: Pan Books, 1963.

Wordsworth, William. Poetical Works. Ed. Thomas Hutchinson. New ed. rev. by Ernest de Selincourt. 1936; rpt. London: Oxford University Press, 1969.

INDEX

Index

For Product Safety Concerns and Information please contact our EU representative GPSR@taylorandfrancis.com
Taylor & Francis Verlag GmbH, Kaufingerstraße 24, 80331 München, Germany

www.ingramcontent.com/pod-product-compliance
Lightning Source LLC
Chambersburg PA
CBHW070527100726
47907CB00004B/1010
* 9 7 8 1 0 3 2 9 0 0 4 1 4 *